SUSANNA DE VRIES is an art historian and a retired academic who now teaches weekend courses at the Community Education Department of the University of Queensland. Born in London, she studied art history, literature and history at the Sorbonne in Paris and the University of Madrid.

An Australian citizen since 1975, Susanna has been the recipient of a Churchill Fellowship to study Renaissance art in Italy and has written extensively on European and Australian art and history and on the history of women. She was made a Member of the Order of Australia in 1996 'for services to art and literature'. In 2001 she was awarded a Tyrone Guthrie Fellowship to write in Ireland by the Literature Board of the Australia Council.

Susanna is the author of the following books, several of which have won awards: *Historic Brisbane*; *Historic Sydney: The Founding of Australia*; *Pioneer Women, Pioneer Land*; *The Impressionists Revealed*; *Conrad Martens on the 'Beagle' and in Australia*; *Ethel Carrick Fox: Travels and Triumphs of a Post-Impressionist*; *Strength of Spirit: Australian Women 1788–1888*; *Strength of Purpose: Australian Women of Achievement 1888–1950*; (co-author) *Raising Girls and Parenting Girls*; *Blue Ribbons, Bitter Bread: The Life of Joice NanKivell Loch, Australia's Most Decorated Woman*; *The Complete Book of Great Australian Women*; and *Heroic Australian Women in War*, and co-authored with her husband, Jake de Vries, *To Hell and Back: The Banned Account of Gallipoli by Sydney Loch*. For further details see www.susannadevries.com

DESERT QUEEN

DESERT QUEEN

THE MANY LIVES
AND LOVES OF
DAISY BATES

SUSANNA DE VRIES

HarperCollins*Publishers*

HarperCollins*Publishers*

First published in 2008
by HarperCollins*Publishers* Australia Pty Limited
ABN 36 009 913 517
www.harpercollins.com.au

Copyright © Susanna de Vries 2008

HarperCollins*Publishers*
25 Ryde Road, Pymble, Sydney, NSW 2073, Australia
31 View Road, Glenfield, Auckland 10, New Zealand
1–A, Hamilton House, Connaught Place, New Delhi – 110 001, India
77–85 Fulham Palace Road, London W6 8JB, United Kingdom
2 Bloor Street East, 20th Floor, Toronto M4W 1A8, Canada
10 East 53rd Street, New York, NY 10022, USA

National Library of Australia Cataloguing-in-Publication data:

De Vries, Susanna.
 Desert queen: the many lives and loves of Daisy Bates
 ISBN 978 07322 8243 1 (pbk.).
 1. Bates, Daisy, 1859–1951. 2. Women anthropologists –
 Australia – Biography. 3. Aboriginal Australians – Social
 Life and customs. 4. Aboriginal Australians – Social Conditions. I. Title.
301.092

Cover photograph of Daisy Bates in 1901; other images courtesy of Shutterstock
Cover design by Darren Holt, HarperCollins Design Studio
Author picture © Jake de Vries
Typeset in 12/15.5pt Bembo by Helen Beard, ECJ Australia Pty Ltd
Printed and bound in Australia by Griffin Press
79gsm Bulky Paperback used by HarperCollins*Publishers* is a natural, recyclable product made from
wood grown in a combination of sustainable plantation and regrowth forests. It also contains up to
a 20% portion of recycled fibre. The manufacturing processes conform to the environmental
regulations in Tasmania, the place of manufacture.

6 5 4 3 2 1   08 09 10 11

This book is dedicated to Jim McJannett of Thursday Island, Queensland, whose collection of Daisy Bates papers and photographs, along with his encyclopaedic knowledge and research skills, has been invaluable.

ACKNOWLEDGEMENTS

I am grateful to fellow author Ted Robl, who has edited one book about Breaker Morant — *Breaker Morant:The Collected Verses of Harry 'Breaker' Morant* — and is compiling another with Jim McJannett. Both have generously shared with me the details contained in birth, marriage and death certificates, so important in piecing together Daisy's story. Credit is due to scriptwriter Eleanor Witcombe as the first person to suspect that Daisy did not grow up at Ashberry House, and to research her Irish childhood. I also acknowledge help received from Joe West, in England, who put me in touch with the Archives of the Order of the Sacred Heart in Dublin; from Col and Brendan Carmody of the Roscrea Heritage Centre; and from Brian Redmond, talented architectural photographer, who provided photographs both old and modern and took me to visit the Convent of the Sacred Heart. Thanks also to George Cunningham, local historian at Roscrea, who provided a copy of an eighteenth-century map on which Ashberry House is marked; to the North Tipperary Historical Society; and to Eineclann, the genealogical research arm of Trinity College, Dublin, for help with my inquiries.

I am most grateful to the Literature Board of the Australia Council, which in 2001 granted me a resident Fellowship at the Tyrone Guthrie Arts Centre at Annaghmakerrig. Being an Irish child adopted at birth, the opportunity that gave me to also conduct research into my Irish biological parents was inestimable.

Thanks are due also to Myles Sinnamon of the Family History Department of John Oxley Library.

Many, many thanks to Barbara Ker Wilson for editing my manuscript and making the process so enjoyable. I am very grateful, too, to my much loved husband of twenty years, architect Jake de Vries, for setting out endnotes, drawing maps and scanning photographs.

Thanks to Dr Lilian Cameron for advice on psychiatric syndromes and her retrospective diagnosis that Daisy Bates was suffering not from Alzheimer's disease but from the much slower onset of vascular dementia. I also acknowledge my former husband of sixteen years, Larry Evans, Professor of Psychiatry at the University of Queensland. Without the benefit of knowledge I gained from him I would not have attempted a subject as complex as Daisy Bates.

Susanna de Vries

CONTENTS

❧ ❧ ❧

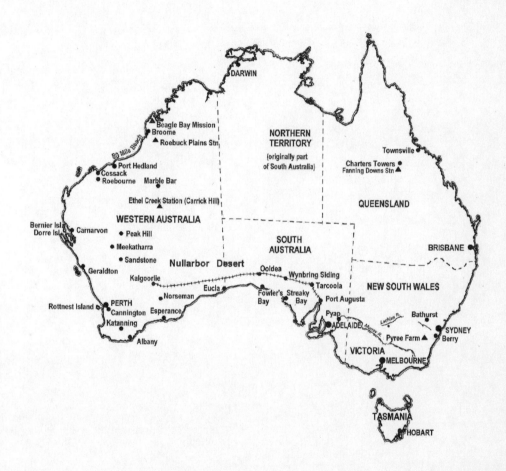

Map showing the places Daisy visited, including the railway that passed through Ooldea

PROLOGUE

꙳ ꙳ ꙳

At one time in our not so distant past, the story of Daisy Bates was taught in every school in Australia. Arriving in Australia in 1883 with no money, family or friends — but with extraordinary pretensions — this remarkable Irish orphan somehow managed to marry three times, bear a child, live in Victorian formality in a tent in the outback and become a pioneer ethnographer and documenter of Aboriginal customs. Her initial research into West Australian tribal ceremonies, customs, languages and kinship systems, carried out at a time when the subjects of ethnology and anthropology were struggling to establish themselves as university disciplines, was extremely valuable. Her important work *The Native Tribes of Western Australia* was not published until 1985 (edited by anthropologist Isobel White), but her observations have underpinned much understanding of Aboriginal society and helped Aboriginal people regain their land.

Daisy Bates was an extraordinary and eccentric woman by any measure. In 2005 she was nominated as one of the world's great female travel writers on the basis of her daring trek from the north-east of Australia 'three thousand miles in a side saddle', escorting a mob of cattle south.[1] Yet before this, she had of course travelled on her own the thousands of miles from Ireland by ship to an unknown continent on the other side of the world.

Marrying the first of her three husbands (none of whom she bothered to divorce), the Boer War soldier Breaker Morant, the pair would go on separately to make themselves legends. Spinning fanciful tales about their pasts they nevertheless lived more astonishing real lives, Morant ending up before a firing squad, and Daisy eventually taking herself, her tent and her young son to the bleak Nullabor Desert, all the while maintaining strict Victorian dress if not morals.

For sixteen years she lived alongside Australian Aborigines, befriending and studying them at the expense of her own health. Her restricted diet in a drought-ridden desert, without fresh vegetables, led to her lack of essential vitamins and minerals and the breakdown in her health. But her many references to Aboriginal cannibalism and her support for removing children from what she viewed as abusive conditions, especially once alcohol took its hold within Aboriginal societies, and her support for a widely held belief in the ultimate extinction of the Aborigines in Australia meant her reputation suffered.

ॐ ॐ ॐ

One of the earliest authors to document Daisy Bates's life was the journalist Ernestine Hill, who collaborated with Daisy Bates from 1932 to write the story of this fascinating woman. During this time Daisy Bates also opened some of her own history in 'My Natives and I', a series of articles published in the Adelaide *Advertiser* between 1936 and 1940.[2] In both the accounts she gave Ernestine Hill — whose *Kabbarli: A Personal Memoir of Daisy Bates,* was published in 1973 — and in 'My Natives and I', Daisy Bates described how she arrived in Australia in 1883 as an orphan from Ireland, where she had grown up under the protection of an adoring father. According to Daisy, some time after her gentleman father died, she was cared for by the Outram family in Dorset, England, where she was attended on by servants, educated by a governess and taken on visits to Balmoral Castle.

Since 'My Natives and I', much of the writing about Daisy Bates's childhood in Ireland has been based on her youthful fantasies and often repeats or embroiders the misinformation of previous biographies.

In 1971 Elizabeth Salter produced a biography of Daisy, *Daisy Bates: The Great White Queen of the Never Never*, yet she never visited Bates's homeland of Ireland. Two decades later, Julia Blackburn, an English writer, published *Daisy Bates in the Desert* (1994), written in the narrative style known as 'faction': part-fact, part-fiction. She tried to discover the secrets of Daisy Bates's mysterious past, but concentrated her research solely in Australia. So when I embarked on this new work, I realised I had to look for more documentary evidence about Daisy Bates, both in Ireland and Australia.

In the summer of 2005, I journeyed to Ireland to investigate what I could of Daisy's past. I found Ireland in the midst of its sustained 'Celtic tiger' economic boom, and Irish people proud of what they had accomplished. Records previously unavailable had now been computerised and much new information had emerged about Daisy, her family background and her formative years as a charity child at the Free Convent School in Roscrea. All of this casts new light on the extraordinary story of this remarkable woman.

Originally I intended to include a brief version of Daisy's life in my collection of short biographies *Great Pioneer Women of the Outback*, but she simply didn't fit in with the wives who obediently accompanied their husbands to the outback. Daisy was different. She was indomitable, her own woman. She travelled thousands of kilometres on her own initiative, abandoned two husbands, while another disappeared in mysterious circumstances, and spent years of her life in arduous conditions studying Australia's first inhabitants. She deserves an entire book to herself.

Daisy O'Dwyer

CHAPTER 1

IRISH ORPHANS

He remained in her memory as the beloved companion of her adolescence.

ELIZABETH SALTER, *DAISY BATES*, REFERRING TO
JAMES EDWARD DWYER, DAISY'S DECEASED FATHER

On the deck of the SS *Almora* an attractive young woman in a well-cut black dress stood out from a group of girls in shapeless garments of buff-coloured calico. These shivering young women wrapped black woollen shawls around their shoulders in a futile attempt to ward off the harsh November wind. Each orphan girl had been given the standard issue of two cheap calico dresses, two petticoats, two pairs of black woollen stockings and a pair of work boots. Clearly, the dark-haired girl in the black dress had no intention of wearing such an unflattering uniform which proclaimed that the wearer was a 'charity child' travelling on an assisted passage. Many were orphans, recruited from Irish workhouses and orphanages. They hoped to escape poverty by migrating to Queensland, where unskilled labour was in demand.[1]

Miss O'Dwyer's passage had also been subsidised but unlike the younger girls who were indentured to various employers as domestic servants, she was classified as a 'free migrant'. She intended to find her own job once she landed, confident that her training by the nuns of the French-speaking Order of the Sacred Heart as a governess would impress a future employer.

Daisy O'Dwyer had paid only one single pound to share a row of bunks in steerage class for which the full rate was forty pounds.[2] Saloon-class passengers paid far more money for the privacy of their own cabins with proper washing facilities, a dining room with better meals and fresh milk from the three cows on board. Steerage passengers, however, were herded like animals into the hottest part of the ship en route from Plymouth, via the Suez Canal and Batavia to Queensland.

Reduced or concessional fares were reserved for Catholic girls of 'good character' aged between fifteen and twenty-one. About to celebrate her twenty-fourth birthday, Miss O'Dwyer knew she did not qualify for a concession but aware that no one could find out the truth without looking in the birth register of St Cronan's Church, Roscrea, Daisy O'Dwyer could lop four years off her age and gain thirty-nine pounds (of the total forty-pound fare), which she would need until she found suitable work as a governess. So Daisy had smiled at the shipping clerk and claimed she was twenty with no birth certificate. He had asked no awkward questions, written 'twenty' in the column marked 'Age', and only charged her one pound for a government-assisted passage. Like the other girls, Daisy was made to sign a bond promising to remain in Queensland for five years, with the proviso that should she break the bond she would repay the balance of her fare — thirty-nine pounds — to the Queensland government.

Accompanied by elderly Matron Chase, the first group of Irish orphans had boarded the *Almora* at Queenstown (now renamed Covh), in southern Ireland, bound for Plymouth. There on Wednesday, 22 November 1882, the orphans had joined a much larger group of largely uneducated English and Welsh girls, all intending to work as skivvies or domestic servants. By law the shipping company had to employ a matron to supervise all the single girls on board and they had engaged one who had a reputation for severity with her charges.[3] Matron Chase assembled all the girls, bonded and free, on deck and called the roll, her stern voice raised against the whistling of the wind. Working her way methodically through the alphabet she reached the names Margaret O'Donoghue, Mary O'Donovan, Margaret O'Donovan, Mary O'Driscoll. On hearing her name, each girl shyly mumbled the word 'Present'.

When Matron Chase called out 'Daisy O'Dwyer', the slim girl in the black dress answered in a clear voice. The matron adjusted her spectacles to inspect this striking-looking young woman. The majority of her charges could neither read nor write so had placed a cross beside their names on the shipping list given to the matron. Their former occupations ranged from milkmaids, housemaids, barmaids, seamstresses and washerwomen. The attractive, dark-haired Miss O'Dwyer had signed her name on the register and was classified as a free migrant, meaning she was at liberty to find her own work on arrival in Queensland.

As the matron looked her over, Miss O'Dwyer tossed her pretty head defiantly. The young governess's chestnut-brown curls framed a heart-shaped face. The determined set of her head marked her out as a young woman who would refuse to be cowed by anything or anybody. A provocative girl such as this could cause trouble among the all-male crew and Matron Chase had promised Captain Hay that there would be no 'hanky-panky' on her ship. The older woman made a mental note to keep a watchful eye on that bold Miss O'Dwyer.

For the first couple of weeks the sea was very rough, the ship rolled badly and most of the girls were seasick and afflicted by coughs and colds. The food provided by the shipping company was truly terrible — salt beef, rapidly deteriorating mutton, and ship's biscuits so hard they could break your teeth unless dampened first in a mug of black tea.

The assisted passengers or 'charity girls', as Matron called them disparagingly, slept in the bowels of the ship where, as the ship travelled southwards, it became stiflingly hot (these were the days before such things as electric fans were available). Washing, toilet and laundry facilities were rudimentary.

As the ship sailed on, it became so hot the piano was moved out of the saloon onto the top deck for the entertainment of the first-class passengers. But Matron Chase continued to treat her girls like cattle, allowing them on deck for only one hour each day before herding them below again and forbidding them to mix with the first-class passengers and even forbidding them to attend Sunday services with the fee-paying passengers.[4]

Matron Chase realised she had been right in singling out Miss O'Dwyer as a troublemaker. Daisy was one of the few girls who remained unaffected by seasickness. Fearless and highly intelligent, she became the spokesperson on behalf of the young orphans and the other girls bullied by Matron Chase, who looked for opportunities to punish the bold Miss O'Dwyer. Some time after the ship crossed the equator, she got her chance. Miss O'Dwyer had by now charmed one of the ship's officers, who encouraged her to emerge from steerage in the hold, come up on deck and join in a concert party on top. Bold as brass, Daisy had borrowed an evening gown from a female passenger named Mrs Diggins and obliged.[5] Matron Chase was outraged at the idea of one of her charges, a Catholic orphan, daring to mingle with people of quality. She reported this breach of the rules to Captain Hay. Miss O'Dwyer received a stern rebuke.

Growing up poor and Catholic in County Tipperary and working as a governess in London, Daisy would have been familiar with anti-Catholic prejudice. She must have hoped that Australia would be different from England and from the equally class-ridden Ireland, where Anglo-Irish Protestants had the money, the best land and the power. She would soon learn that anti-Catholic and anti-Irish prejudice was rife in North Queensland. The Irish were banned from many hotels and lodging houses for their allegedly rowdy ways. Miss O'Dwyer would appreciate how much easier it was to claim a background of the Anglo-Irish aristocracy and be treated with respect.

Daisy was proud of her Irish ancestry. She belonged to the O'Dwyers of Roscrea in County Tipperary, whom she liked to invest with remote aristocratic connections. She proudly re-adopted the 'O' prefix to her name after its use had faded with the decline of the Irish language. The O'Dwyers, or Dwyers, had been Catholics for centuries; her eldest sister, Marian, had become a nun. Yet the remarks Daisy had heard bandied about ship reinforced the lessons from her older sister Kathleen. Daisy and Kathleen, fourteen months apart, had been very close. Like Daisy, Kathleen had been trained as a governess at the Convent of the Sacred Heart in Roscrea. Kathleen had told her younger sister that in a prejudiced, snobbish world you had to assert yourself and claim to belong to the Protestant ruling class of Ireland. Otherwise, employers would take advantage of you.

Kathleen had been employed as a resident governess by a Scottish family, and while she was with them she had met Captain Robert Henry Brownrigg, son of a wealthy Protestant Dublin lawyer.[6] Robert Brownrigg fell in love with Kathleen O'Dwyer, captivated by her good looks and intelligence. Believing that, like himself, she belonged to the Anglo-Protestant gentry, he proposed marriage and she was delighted to accept him. Kathleen successfully upheld her fictitious pedigree and happily fitted into the upper-class lifestyle as the wife of a British Army officer among the Anglo-Irish Protestant gentry.

Daisy's elder sister was no doubt aware that if she revealed the truth about her less fortunate background, her marriage might be in jeopardy. So she invented a wealthier and more stable background for herself, based on childhood fantasies that she and Daisy, as unhappy little orphans, had made up to comfort each other.

One of their fantasies was that they were the loved, indulged daughters of a gentleman farmer, living in a large stone house. They imagined it to be like Ashberry House, which stood in 143 acres (57 hectares) of farmland on the outskirts of Roscrea, and was occupied by a prominent local entity, gentleman farmer Timothy Bridge, his wife and their nine children.[7] The two girls' inventive minds tacked onto this house embellishments from a much grander early eighteenth-century mansion in Castle Street called Damer House, which they often passed by.

Kathleen became word-perfect in repeating this fiction — that her father was James Dwyer Esq, of Ashberry House, Tipperary, a gentleman farmer — and this invention appeared on Kathleen O'Dwyer's marriage certificate. When Daisy arrived in Australia she too would repeat the same story, confident that 10,000 miles (17,000 kilometres) away from Ireland no one would discover the truth.

Kathleen worried that one or other of her family members might betray her humble origins. Consequently, she did not invite any of them to her smart London wedding. If Daisy was hurt, she no doubt understood her sister's reasons. Indeed, Daisy was determined to follow Kate's example: re-invent her background, move in upper-class circles and make a good marriage. In the 1880s an advantageous marriage was the only course open to a young woman ambitious for wealth and the security of becoming a member of 'respectable society'. In Queensland, perhaps, she would find a wealthy grazier who owned a vast cattle station. Then she could marry and return to Roscrea with her head held high and show everyone how the despised orphan and charity child had come up in the world!

With this aim in mind, she became Miss Daisy O'Dwyer, daughter of a leading landowning family of North Tipperary, who, after the death of her father, James Edward Dwyer, went to stay with Sir Francis and Lady Outram at Hallans Hall, their Dorset manor house. It was a story she committed to paper in her series of articles 'My Natives and I' and which was repeated unquestioningly by successive biographers.

器 器 器

Were any of Daisy O'Dwyer's tall tales of an aristocratic upbringing really true? In the summer of 2005 I travelled to Ireland determined to find out the truth about Daisy's family and childhood, why she left Ireland for Australia and what had contributed to her brilliant yet complex personality.

The town of Roscrea which Daisy left behind is one of the most historic in Ireland. It was originally founded in the seventh century as the site of a monastery by St Cronan, to whom its two main churches, one Catholic, the other Protestant, are both dedicated. Later a Norman castle was built there, and over the centuries Roscrea became a busy market town, surrounded by fertile fields.

For generations, ever since Oliver Cromwell's soldiers invaded Ireland in the seventeenth century and re-imposed British rule upon the country, Roscrea was owned by Protestant landlords. One of Cromwell's officers was the infamous William Dawson who, after ordering the killing of large numbers of the Irish population, saw an opportunity to enrich himself and remained in Ireland. According to some accounts he was a collector of taxes. His descendants, the Damer-Dawsons, eventually became so rich that in 1722 one of them was able to buy the entire town of Roscrea and its surrounding agricultural lands. Another was created the first Earl of Portarlington in 1785. The earl's agents let the houses, farms and land to Protestant Irish tenants or English middlemen. Catholics such as the Dwyers were forbidden to own land and had to rent homes and business premises from middlemen who refused to allow them the security of long leases.

By the late 1850s, when Daisy was born, one earl of Portarlington who was addicted to gambling had run into financial trouble. To recoup his losses he sold blocks of land and entire streets in Roscrea to investors. In the same way as before, the new investors rented out houses and farmland to tenants — including the Dwyers. In her book *Roscrea, My Heart's Home*, Kathleen Moloughney stated that Daisy's parents, James and Bridget Dwyer, lived in modest circumstances above the family bootery in Main Street, Roscrea.[8] This was very different from the tales of grand living that Daisy told people once she arrived in Australia.

Many Irish birth, marriage and death certificates and census records were destroyed when the Public Record Office went up in flames during the Easter Rising in 1916, so I consulted the land records for Roscrea and district, held at the Valuation Office in

Dublin's Ely Place, and the Griffith's Valuations, essential when researching Irish family trees. The Griffith's Valuations are a uniquely Irish form of house-to-house survey, carried out under the orders of Richard Griffith from the mid-nineteenth century onwards. The valuers lists the name of each householder (but not who else lived in the house) and from whom they rented. They also gave the value of each house and described it briefly. The valuations were carried out to impose a tax on each householder to support the poor of each parish in the grim years following the Great Famine.

Entries in the various Griffith's Valuations provide evidence that James Dwyer (Daisy's father and/or grandfather) held the lease of what would later be known as No. 2 Main Street, a 'four-room tenement: house, office and yard' with a net annual value of three pounds sterling.[9]

According to trade directories of Roscrea, James Dwyer and his father, James senior, together with Daisy's uncle William Dwyer were boot- and shoemakers who also made horses' harnesses and carried out leather repairs. The younger James, born in 1828, left the public National School for Boys in Roscrea aged fourteen. In his boyhood James would have witnessed terrible sights, as famished families came into Roscrea from the surrounding countryside, often to perish of starvation in the streets. Children whose parents had starved to death were sent to Roscrea orphanage. The Dwyers, being skilled tradesmen, were able to continue with their business during the ravages of the Great Famine.

Although James, his father and his brother William were respected tradesmen, Uncle Joe Dwyer, the cattle dealer who rented Lot 23, Main Street, was the most prosperous member of the family. James Dwyer senior and his son James also bought and sold cattle on the side, but by no means on the scale of Uncle Joe, who exported Irish cattle to Scotland and imported pedigree Charollais cattle from France.

In January 1856, when James, Daisy's father, was twenty-eight, he married twenty-year-old Bridget Hunt, daughter of Catherine and Michael Hunt of Ballychrine, a rural area close to Roscrea. After their marriage she helped in the bootery, serving in the shop. Their first child, Marian (Mary Ann in the baptismal register), was baptised on 25 November 1856. Their second child, Kathleen, was baptised on 3 August 1858. According to custom, babies were normally baptised a few days after birth.

Daisy and her twin brother were born on 16 October 1859, only fourteen months after Kathleen.[10] Baptismal records show that Daisy was baptised Margaret — presumably after her godmother, Bridget's sister Margaret Maher — in St Cronan's Catholic Church, along with her twin brother Francis. Francis (whom Daisy never mentioned) would die less than two weeks after his birth.[11]

Eighteen months later, Bridget gave birth to another son, named James after his father, always known as Jim. Bridget's last confinement, when she was desperately ill with tuberculosis, produced a second set of twins, Joseph (Joe) and Anne. Joe was a sickly child and died relatively young.[12]

Whatever the reason — the horror of the Great Famine, a home

St Cronan's, Roscrea

with too many crying children, a wife who would succumb to tuberculosis — James took to drink. He was said to spend a good deal of his time at the Portarlington Arms or Corcoran's pub-cum-grocery store on Main Street, staggering home late at night, possibly to claim his marital rights from his ailing wife.

During Bridget's illness, her married sisters, Margaret, Eliza and Anne, did their best to help, but they each had six or seven children of their own to care for. Marian, the responsible eldest daughter, presumably helped to prepare the frugal evening meal. Most Irish working people at this time lived on boiled potatoes, scallions (spring onions) and gravy, with the occasional piece of bacon in the pot.

On 20 February 1864 Daisy's mother died from her tuberculosis 'of two years' duration', according to the registry of St Cronan's Catholic Church,[13] leaving her husband with six children under the age of ten: Marian (seven), Kathleen (five), Daisy (four), Jim (two), and the twins Anne and Joe (aged one). For a four-year-old, watching her mother waste away and die must have been traumatic.

Daisy's widowed father hired young Mary Dillon to look after

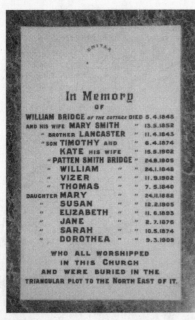 

Left: Bridge family memorial, St Cronan's church.
Right: Headstone of Bridget Dwyer, Daisy's mother.

the motherless brood. Mary was the semi-literate daughter of Edward Dillon, a Derrymore farmer. Seven months later Mary Dillon and James Dwyer became man and wife. From the beginning Mary seems to have taken a dislike to spirited little Daisy. For her part, Daisy hated the young woman who replaced her mother, and it is reasonable to assume she retaliated against her.

Shortly after the wedding, James and Mary Dwyer decided to emigrate to America, leaving the children with various family members. The reason seems to have been the lure of a parcel of land in Virginia that Mary wrongly believed she might inherit. Apparently James expressed some intention of sending for the children later on; however, he died soon after they reached America, and was buried in a pauper's grave in Virginia.[14]

Illiterate or not, Mary Dillon Dwyer somehow found enough money to return to Roscrea shortly after her husband's death.[15] The Griffith's Valuations reveal that Mary Dwyer took over as householder of No. 2 in 1865, having inherited the lease of Lot 17 (which covered two blocks — the present Nos 2 and 3 Main Street). It seems that James Dwyer the elder lived with Mary, his daughter-in-law, until his death.[16]

After James and Mary Dillon Dwyer departed for America, Marian went to live with Uncle William Dwyer and his wife, Mary, who also lived in Main Street, while the other children were passed around between various relatives. Daisy and young Jim and the twins stayed on with their widowed maternal grandmother, Catherine Hunt, at Ballychrine.[17] Catherine Hunt was a caring, dependable grandmother, with a reputation in the district as a 'wise woman' and a healer. At this time, most people were too poor to consult a doctor, relying on bone-setters and herbal remedies when they suffered accidents or fell ill. According to Daisy in her unreliable memoirs written decades later, her grandmother was of a kind and charitable nature, poor but *nouveau*. In 'My Natives and I', Daisy related: 'when the potato crop failed the granaries were empty, so my grandmother fed, clothed and doctored the peasantry for fifty miles around.' Possibly Granny Hunt was the inspiration for the Kabbarli legend — the grandmotherly person feeding and doctoring ailing Aborigines — that Daisy worked so hard to establish for herself in later life.

Daisy's grandmother had been Catherine Cantwell of Camblin before she married Michael Hunt, whose family contained both Catholic and Church of Ireland members. (This could explain Daisy's familiarity with Church of Ireland ritual and her later apparently painless change of faith from Catholic to Protestant.)

The Hunts had a property at Ballychrine, which Daisy stated had been in her mother's family 'for many generations', leased by this Catholic family rather than owned outright. Their farm at Ballychrine was a fair size by Irish standards and it seems that Michael Hunt, who owned an acre of land, would have been reasonably affluent. He also leased over 70 acres (28 hectares) in the townlands (small divisions of arable land) at Ballychrine and Glenbeha. Griffith's Valuations shows that he also owned a share of 24 acres (10 hectares) of peat bog at Shanballynahagh.[18] The peat, known as 'turf', was cut out and carted away to provide household heat in winter. The Hunts also derived income by renting 3 acres (1.2 hectares) of their leased farmland to another Catholic farmer.

But in 1862 Granny Hunt's husband and son both died, and suddenly she could not pay for her leased land and her standard of living plunged. She had to earn a living from spinning and weaving and was forced to move from her pleasant farmhouse to a tumbledown stone cottage on land that had belonged to her husband, now leased by her son-in-law Martin Moylan, husband of her daughter Elizabeth. Granny Hunt's cottage was so dilapidated that no rates were payable on it.[19]

Farm cottages typically had only two bedrooms with tiny windows beneath a thatched roof, and a kitchen-cum-living room, where a kettle and blackened iron cooking pots hung over an open fire. In keeping with the times, Granny Hunt's cottage at Ballychrine would have lacked piped water and interior sanitation. There was probably an outhouse fitted with a board seat with a hole in it over a bucket to act as a privy. Only the ultra-rich Anglo-Irish in large houses had china water closets with flushing systems.

In spite of her reduced circumstances, Granny Hunt still

maintained a higher social standing than the Dwyers. With her Church of Ireland connections and former large land leases, she would have had reason to feel socially superior to the Dwyers and it is reasonable to believe she would have encouraged the children to use the surname O'Dwyer, to distinguish themselves from their Dwyer cousins.

Calamity struck the orphaned Dwyers again when Granny Hunt died in 1868. For Daisy, her grandmother's death meant the loss of the most stable figure in her life. Once Granny Hunt and Grandfather James Dywer were dead Mary Dillon Dwyer became the legal guardian of her stepchildren. Daisy and the twins returned to a house of sad memories, where her mother had fallen ill and died. Daisy alleged her stepmother taunted her with the fact that she too would catch consumption and die young. Clearly, relations between Daisy and her stepmother were difficult.[20]

Younger brother Jim was taken in by his Uncle Joe at his house further along Main Street. Here the young curly-haired boy would be taught his uncle's trade. Marian, the eldest daughter, stayed on in Main Street in the house of her Uncle William and Aunt Mary and decided early in life to enter the Order of the Sacred Heart.

At the age of nine, shortly after returning to No. 2 Main Street, Daisy was enrolled at the Free National School for Catholic Girls. Records in Dublin showed that the Free National School, run by the Order of the Sacred Heart at Roscrea, had Daisy and Kathleen Dwyer of Main Street on its register until Kathleen turned twenty and Daisy nineteen, possibly working as pupil-teachers in return for extra tuition, since the normal school-leaving age was fourteen.

Whatever their experiences with their stepmother, it seems that both Kathleen and Daisy wished to blot out that period of childhood and adolescence and replace it with comforting fantasies.

James Edward Dwyer's pitiable life history and his death from alcoholism in 1865 in Virginia belies the romantic fantasy of the handsome gentleman farmer constructed by the two orphaned sisters. Rather than being 'the beloved companion', as Daisy describes him, her father might better be defined as 'the black sheep' of the Dwyer family.

The sisters based their idea of an ideal man on Timothy Bridge, a gentleman farmer and lawyer, a charitable, kindly man, living in Ashberry House and greatly respected in Roscrea. Daisy wanted to create a father who loved her and valued her. This imaginary father read to Daisy from bound copies of Dickens in his library, laughed with her over jokes in *Punch* magazine, and taught her to dance Irish reels and ride to hounds, all things she had read about in her favourite novels. He was, wrote Daisy, 'the loveliest father in Christendom'.

In this imaginary world, instead of leaky shoes and second-hand clothes, Daisy had a carriage to ride in, servants to tend warm fires in winter and lovely clothes.[21] Although Daisy conspired with Kathleen, neither Kathleen nor any of Daisy's other siblings figured in the stories Daisy told her biographer Ernestine Hill — only little Jim receives a mention.

Rural Ireland was a rigidly snobbish society as portrayed in the novels of Sommerville and Ross, but in a small town like Roscrea the Dwyer girls would at least have known Kate and Timothy Bridge and their children by sight. Land records show that Timothy Bridge rented arable land near Granny Hunt's cottage, which he sublet to Catholic farmers and he must have visited the area on occasions to check on his tenants.

To the orphaned Dwyer sisters the Bridge children, with their nice clothes, their ponies and their large house and garden, would have seemed enviable.

A marble memorial tablet on the wall of the interior of St Cronan's Church of Ireland on Church Street describes Timothy Bridge as dying in 1874 when Daisy was only fifteen. Soon after, his widow, Kate Bridge, and his unmarried children moved away from Ashberry House and wealthy John Sidney Smythe replaced him.

It was not the English-born Smythe, however, who featured in Daisy's further embellished stories, but Sir Francis Outram and his wife Lady Jane, who lived at Hallans Hall near Swanage in Dorset, which she claimed as her new home after the death of her father.

Sir Francis had been injured in India as a young man and was confined to a wheelchair. Daisy claimed to have been entrusted to Sir Francis and his wife by her father before he died. No doubt she had learned about the Outrams from *Bourke's Landed Gentry* and from newspapers. Indeed, Sir Francis's mother came from Emel Castle, Moneygalley near Roscrea, which may be the main reason why Daisy selected Sir Francis as her 'surrogate father' and guardian.

Daisy imagined herself living with Sir Francis and Lady Jane and the Outrams' three boys and three girls, the youngest of whom was Daisy's age. Perhaps she based her fictitious image of Hallans Hall on handsome Damer House in Roscrea's Castle Street, the only grand mansion she was likely to have seen during her childhood. Instead of attending the 'poor school' at Roscrea and doing her lessons writing on a slate in a chilly classroom, she claimed to be wearing lovely clothes and sitting in a heated schoolroom, learning to speak French and German from a German governess who spoke both languages fluently.

> I became one of the family of Sir Francis and Lady Outram
> and with them spent happy years in Europe on travel and
> education . . . There were thirteen of us all told, including
> the six Outram children and I . . . Fraulein Reischauer was
> to supervise our collective studies. We left London for Paris,
> the gay and dainty Paris of the 1870s, bound for
> Switzerland. My memories are somewhat misty [a good
> excuse for any inaccuracies!] . . . I remember a merry party
> of us snowed up in a railway train at Pontarlier on the Swiss
> frontier making a meal of boiled rice, which Fraulein had
> thoughtfully brought along for our sustenance. I shuddered
> at the dungeons of the Chateau de Chillon and the *oubliettes*
> from the bodies were thrown into the lake [Daisy had
> possibly read about this chateau in a life of Lord Byron,
> who visited it]. I ran with terror from hooded monks in the
> streets of Rome, a smelly city . . . From Rome we retraced
> our leisurely way to England through Berlin, Brussels,
> Antwerp and Ostend . . .

> From the continent we returned to Stranorchlar in
> Scotland, near Balmoral Castle. Her Majesty [Queen
> Victoria] was in residence. The Dowager Lady Outram had
> taught me how to curtsey and one day I wandered into the
> castle grounds. Queen Victoria herself was at the moment
> in the Rose Walk and suddenly appeared. I immediately
> remembered my manners and dropped the regulation three
> devout curtseys.[22]

Daisy always claimed 'aristocratic' Anglo-Irish heritage for herself. According to Elizabeth Salter,[23] the Dwyer family tree dated back to a William O'Dwyer who lived in the fourteenth century and was created Baron of Kilnamanagh by King Edward III. However, 'Dwyer' is one of Tipperary's most common names.

Was it possible that the National Library of Ireland held a family tree linking William O'Dwyer of Kilmananagh, who bore a coat of arms, to the Dwyers of Main Street, Roscrea? Daisy herself asserts such a connection, but in the Family Research Section of the Irish National Library I could find no evidence to link the two families.

'Impossible to tell if there was a link,' I was informed by a staff member in the National Library's Genealogical and Family History section. 'Irish records don't go back that far, at least not continuously. William O'Dwyer was definitely *not* created a baron by Edward III. In Ireland, a "barony" is a unit of land measurement, like an English shire. It has *nothing* to do with the English title of baron.' The genealogist reminded me that Dwyer is a very usual name in Tipperary, where hundreds of Dwyer families are distantly related to one another.

The nearest I came to any sort of aristocratic connection in the distant past was when I examined the records of Daisy's maternal family and discovered that the Hunts were very distantly connected to the de Vere Hunts of Cashel, Tipperary, who were in turn related to the Earl of Oxford through the female line.

The Irish scholar Richard Hayes[24] recorded that centuries before Daisy's birth, Dwyers or O'Dwyers of southern Tipperary had been major landowners. Their fierce resistance to Oliver Cromwell's invading forces meant that several of the O'Dwyers were forced to flee to Europe with a price on their heads. They refused to renounce their Catholicism and their lands were confiscated and given to English Protestants.

The O'Dwyers were caught up in the tragic story of Irish dispossession and the subsequent Irish diaspora. The English invaders ensured that most Catholics lost their lands as well as the right to receive a university education or enter a profession; Catholics had no possibility of regaining their lands unless they converted to the Protestant Church of Ireland. Some of the Hunts who had been relatively large landowners did convert. Those who remained Catholic lost their lands so were forced to rent them back from the Portarlington Estate — a very Irish way of surviving during the days of Daisy's poverty-stricken childhood. It was a situation that would only be remedied by the passing of the Irish Land Acts, decades later. The Act ensured that many large estates were split up and either reallocated to or bought by Catholics. William Dwyer's descendants, for their part, would be able to buy the freeholds of three houses in Roscrea's Main Street in the mid-1890s.[25]

Years later, in Australia, Daisy's memory of the Irish people's loss of their lands would arouse her sympathy for the plight of Aboriginal people left to starve during drought years by an Australian government that cared more about stock losses than about the dispossessed. Her childhood among the dispossessed — or 'hovel' Irish — at Ballychrine later roused her to help Aboriginal people who had lost *their* land and this passion would shape her future.

Main Street, Roscrea. The central arch was later removed for motor traffic.

*No. 2 Main Street, leased by Daisy's father and after his death by Daisy's stepmother.
Inset: A slate roof has replaced the thatch of Daisy's time.*

CHAPTER 2

IN SEARCH OF DAISY DWYER

*My earliest recollections are of the green, green hills of Carrick
and Slieve Na Mon . . . where Jim and I would play in the
ruins and fairy forts . . . coming back at nightfall with sodden
shoes to listen to tales by the Ballychrine fireside.*

DAISY BATES, *MY NATIVES AND I*

Roscrea is a delightful town to visit, with its attractive
shopfronts painted in colours of Venetian red, forest green
and royal blue. In early summer, red geraniums and blue lobelia spill
from window boxes and planters along the streets. In Daisy's
childhood, however, it was a very different place. Daisy grew up
among unpaved, muddy streets, surrounded by grey and white stone
houses with whitewashed façades and thatched roofs, which were
later replaced with tiles or slates. Early photographs show a large
Italian-style fountain at the end of Main Street — later removed to
Rosemary Street.

Wednesday was traditionally Roscrea's market day, when
ducks, geese and chickens roamed the streets, along with the

Peasant women brought goods to sell in the market on Main Street.

cattle offered for sale by men in tweed jackets and bowler hats, who clustered around the Market House and weighbridge.[1] Farmers' wives in black shawls brought cream and butter and joints of pork for sale, trundling their handcarts along Main Street.

For decades after she left for Australia no one in Roscrea knew or cared very much about the fate of orphaned Daisy Dwyer — or Daisy Bates. Then, in Australia's Bicentennial year of 1988, as a result of efforts made by the Heritage Committee and the Tidy Towns Committee, a memorial address about Daisy was given by historian Kathleen Moloughney and a plaque was placed in Green Street, near the Public Library, unveiled by the Australian Ambassador.[2] The plaque, however, fails to inform the passer-by about the most significant aspect of Daisy Bates's life: that she was destined to become a pioneer ethnologist, in the days when the science of anthropology was in its infancy. Daisy Bates's passionate interest in the Australian Aborigines was in fact the most notable and enduring component of her long life.

※ ※ ※

My quest to discover the secrets of Daisy's childhood now led me to Ballychrine, and the small stone cottage belonging to her grandmother Catherine Hunt. Accompanied by photographer Brian Redmond, a member of the Roscrea Heritage Committee, I saw for myself the beauty of this area. The land was green and lush with that particular brilliance of Irish fields in summertime, and on either side of the narrow lanes the hedges were filled with sweet-smelling may and elder flowers. Descendants of Daisy's aunt Eliza Hunt Moylan still farmed the former Hunt land at Ballychrine and we hoped to find out more about Daisy. They knew little about her but we saw the area where Daisy spent part of her childhood.

In the 1860s, Ballychrine was part of the farmlands that lay on the outskirts of Roscrea; today it is part of the town's rapidly growing urban development. Following Ireland's new affluence as a member of the Common Market, the old cottages that Daisy knew have been replaced with neat bungalows fitted with every modern convenience, each set in a small neat garden. It has all totally changed from the Ballychrine Daisy recalled in her memoirs, where she described wretched, poverty-stricken villagers, beggars sleeping under the hedgerows and a blind fiddler who called at Granny Hunt's cottage to entertain them.

Her grandmother's ancient cottage has long since crumbled away. But there, in the long twilights, Daisy and her siblings would sit by the peat fire, listening to tales of leprechauns, of ghostly lights leading children into bogs, and the mischievous *pookah*, or fairy, of Gaelic myths who would come after naughty children. Granny Hunt related the old, old tales of the heroes of Ireland such as Brian Borhu and the Kings of Tara.

The Daisy Bates Memorial Garden in Roscrea is surrounded by Australian native trees.

In her later years, when Daisy dictated her childhood memories to the Australian writer Ernestine Hill,[3] she described the dirt-poor Irish peasantry as being 'benighted by superstition' — but she herself was clearly fascinated by these stories as well as the arcane beliefs passed on by Allie, the wife of a Hunt cousin, who kindly helped to look after the orphaned Dwyers. Allie warned the children not to go near the 'fairy rings' of darker green grass that the horses and cattle avoided when they grazed. She said that 'the Little People' danced inside the ring at night, and stole away young girls who tried to join them there.[4] The superstitious Allie never passed a fairy ring without murmuring 'God be with us'. She also told tales of peatcutters who had found bodies of people who had fallen into the peat bogs or been killed in ancient pagan rituals.

The people Daisy referred to as 'hovel Irish' left out saucers of milk at night to placate the Little People, who, it was feared, could be malicious if they were not treated with due respect. At Halloween, the eve of the Day of the Dead, they were supposed to dance with the unquiet spirits of the dead on their tombstones; children like Daisy were warned to beware of churchyards on Halloween, in case the Little People tried to capture them.

With Daisy growing up among these legends it is easy to see how, much later, in Australia, she would respect Aboriginal legends and the belief that the spirits of the dead did not rest and must not be named by the living. She would become as fascinated by the myths of the Aboriginal people as she had been by Celtic folktales. In Aboriginal Dreamtime legends, as in ancient Irish myths and legends, birds, animals and trees possessed their own 'spirit of place', and physical forces such as the wind and rain were endowed with miraculous powers.

Granny Hunt wanted her grandchildren to develop a sense of responsibility by helping with everyday tasks. They were kept busy drawing buckets of water from the well, fetching kindling for the fire, feeding the hens and milking the cows. (In her memoirs, Daisy claimed that she learned to milk a cow during a strike by farmhands in Queensland, but this was one of her 'cover-up' stories: as the alleged daughter of 'James Dwyer Esq of Ashberry

House', she would never have learned how to milk cows.) The pig that inhabited the backyard at Granny Hunt's cottage was known as 'the gentleman who pays the rent', a common expression among the rural Irish; feeding him with scraps was another daily task. Once he was fat enough, the poor beast was slaughtered and sold at the Market House in Roscrea to those who could afford to eat meat, leaving the ears, head and trotters, known as *crubbeens*, for the family.

Wash days in that era were always a marathon effort. Water had to be drawn from the well and tipped into a big copper to be boiled, with soap shavings added to the water. The dirty clothes and linen were prodded with a big stick, then lifted on the stick into the rinsing tubs. Once everything was dry, the iron was heated on the fire in order to press the clean garments.

After the daily tasks were done, Daisy, together with sister Kathleen and brother Jim (little Anne was too young to join them), would roam the countryside round about, discovering the stone dolmens, portal graves and burial cairns on the hillsides, and would 'play in the ruins and fairy forts'.[5] During the warmer months the children ran about freely, but in the freezing winters their legs were always covered in pink blotches that Allie referred to as 'warbles'.

Cooking and breadmaking were Allie's tasks. The main meal of the day usually consisted of boiled potatoes, cabbage and other home-grown vegetables, with an occasional rabbit or piece of bacon to add flavour, accompanied by a slice of soda bread made with buttermilk. Because of the soot that collected in the chimney, lids were kept on the cooking pots so that it would not contaminate the food. In winter the room was often thick with smoke. The table was too small for all of them to gather around, and they took turns to sit on the big wooden settle with their plates on their knees.

Allie showed the girls how to dip rushes into tallow and use metal candle moulds to provide light for the cottage when darkness fell. When it was time to sleep, Granny Hunt would climb the stairs to the bedroom above, which she shared with Kathleen, and the settle would provide a communal bed for the younger children, curled up close like puppies.

Birr Castle was the seat of the 'Astronomer Earl', and Daisy claimed her grandmother took her there on a visit when she was six

Besides the everyday chores, Granny Hunt taught Daisy the art of exquisitely fine darning and how to knit. Their clothes were patched; nothing was ever wasted. Granny's example of frugal living was stored away in Daisy's memory; decades later it would enable her to survive in her small tent in the Nullarbor Plain.

There were no family allowances, no government assistance of any sort in the mid-nineteenth century to help families in crisis. Life cannot have been easy for Granny Hunt. She worked long hours spinning wool and weaving cloth which she sent to the market in Roscrea to be sold. Watching her grandmother toiling at her spinning wheel meant that Daisy came to hate poverty, but during these years she learned to get by on very little and gained the skills she would need to survive. Throughout her long life, she would never be afraid of hard work.

O'Brien, the blind fiddler who visited her grandmother from time to time, taught the Dwyer children Irish step-dancing. They danced on an old stable door placed flat on the ground, and Daisy thoroughly enjoyed herself learning the traditional steps of Irish jigs, keeping her body stiff as she danced. Sometimes Granny Hunt would come to watch. In the series of newspaper articles collected together and published posthumously as *My Natives and I*, Daisy described how, in the midst of his music-making, O'Brien would hear her soft footfall and pause for a courtly bow to 'Herself'.[6]

Treats for the Dwyer children were few and far apart. One was the annual Fair Day, when they would be lucky to be given a penny each to spend at the sideshows. However, Daisy did describe another highlight of her childhood. At the age of six she was taken on an outing in a jaunting car (a light dray or open cart) to Birr Castle, over the border in County Offaly. The pleasant town of Birr was known in Daisy's day as Parsonstown, after the family whose successive heads carried the title of Earl of Rosse. Birr Castle, set in magnificent grounds surrounded by tall hedges of hornbeam, was also famous for The Leviathan of Parsonstown — the name of the world's then largest telescope, the wonder of its era. The gigantic telescope had been constructed in the 1840s by the third Earl of Rosse, known as the astronomer earl, to enable him to see farther into space than any other nineteenth-century astronomer.

Daisy never forgot her visit to Birr Castle. For some trifling misdemeanour, she claimed, she had been shut inside the gigantic metal tube of the Leviathan by the astronomer earl himself and left there for an hour. She may have thought she saw the earl, but when I went to the castle to check this story the manager of the Visitors' Centre of Birr Castle furnished the information that by the mid-1860s the earl had become an invalid and was living in Dublin. It was more likely to have been one of his adult sons, or a steward, who shut Daisy in the telescope — a trick that was often played on children.

Stubborn, defiant, six-year-old Daisy refused to cry out and crouched in the dark for over an hour. When finally she emerged she claimed to have enjoyed an experience that would have scared many children out of their wits.[7]

Roscrea's Convent of the Order of the Sacred Heart, where Daisy attended the Free School

CHAPTER 3

THE GETTING OF WISDOM

Wisdom is the principal thing; therefore get wisdom, and with all thy getting, get understanding.

BOOK OF PROVERBS, 4: 7

Ever since St Cronan founded his monastic church in the seventh century, Roscrea was known as a centre of learning. In the 1860s the town had a number of schools, both Catholic and Protestant, private and government-funded.[1] The Ladies' Hibernian School for Protestants situated on Gaol Road and the Ladies' Intermediate School were probably attended by young ladies like the three Bridge girls of Ashberry House whose affluent parents were happy to pay school fees.

The Dwyer sisters' vast granite convent with its lichen–covered walls still towers above Gaol Road. It was established in 1842 by French nuns from the Order of the Sacred Heart, founded in Paris *circa* 1800 by Madeleine Barat. The Roscrea Convent of the Sacred Heart contained not only the Free National School for Catholic Girls but also a boarding school for fee-paying pupils. It was at the

Free National School that Daisy and her sisters received their education.[2]

Free Catholic and Protestant National Schools for working-class children were established across Ireland by the British government in the 1840s. Formerly, Irish Catholic children too poor to pay school fees received virtually no education at all apart from what they could pick up in 'hedgerow schools' conducted clandestinely, usually by priests. At the Roscrea convent, the nuns of the Sacred Heart served as teachers and school organisers as part of their commitment to help poor and needy children of the parish, who attended school up to the age of fourteen (though some pupils left earlier). The nuns also provided an excellent fee-based education at the convent boarding school for the daughters of the wealthy. The two schools were situated in different premises, across a dividing courtyard. To the snobbish fee-paying pupils the Free National School was known as 'the poor school'.

At 'the poor school', clever girls like Daisy and Kathleen Dwyer considered capable of becoming pupil-teachers, or monitors, could stay on beyond the age of fourteen and receive additional tuition. In return they carried out duties such as sweeping floors, filling inkwells, cleaning brass and performing other household tasks around the convent. In this way these talented but disadvantaged girls were rescued from a life of drudgery after they left school. Apart from an early marriage, they had two options: to take their vows and become nuns, as Daisy's sister Marian did; or find employment as poorly paid governesses, which is what both Daisy and Kathleen decided to do.

Nuns of the Sacred Heart prided themselves on the quality of their tuition and gave their star pupils an excellent grounding in Latin, Greek, French, German, history, geography, needlework and literature. All three eldest Dwyer girls, Marian, Kate and Daisy, were lucky to be selected as pupil-monitors, whereby they received a tiny wage and additional tuition from the nuns until they turned nineteen.

From the nuns' tuition as well as years of observing the ladylike demeanour of the nuns and the fee-paying pupils across the yard the

Dwyer sisters acquired many of the attributes of young ladies, such as good deportment (Daisy's back was always ramrod straight, even in old age), and Daisy learned to speak and write excellent French and German, ladylike attributes which aided her tales of an aristocratic upbringing.

At the poor school, classes were suspended for two weeks in October each year so that the farm children, who made up a large proportion of the pupils, could help their parents with the harvest. Many parents were too poor to buy shoes or steel-nibbed pens for their children. During the nineteenth century most pupils used chalk and slates for their lessons. The nuns did not insist on the 'charity' pupils wearing shoes, but they did insist on well-brushed hair, and faces that were washed every morning. In 1872, when Daisy was thirteen, one nun described her class as being 'mostly in ragged clothing, faces wan with malnutrition'. She added that 'listening with eager attention, they never complained'. The nuns always emphasised the importance of good manners, something Daisy would insist on for the rest of her life. One can imagine the Mother Superior exhorting the little girl: 'Daisy Dwyer, sit up straight; use your handkerchief, not your sleeve; put this book on your head and learn to walk like a lady. If you do so, perhaps you can become a governess.'[3]

Since the courtyard that separated the charity school from the fee-paying boarders was used by both groups for recreation (though never at the same time), each group must have had some idea of how the other half worked and played. It's likely that Daisy and Kathleen soon began to notice how the private pupils dressed and spoke. Later on, as pupil-monitors, the two sisters may have performed duties in the boarding-school house. Did they find themselves kneeling on the stairs as they polished the brass stair-rods or entering the girls' rooms to sweep the floors and dust the furniture? Did they overhear the privileged girls talking about the concerts, parties and private balls they had attended, and grand social events such as the Dublin Horse Show? They would definitely have observed the graceful posture and refined behaviour of their favourite nuns, some of whom came from wealthy homes in France.

Unlike the private schoolgirls across the courtyard in their smart clothes, the free pupils came to school each day dressed in a motley collection of ragged or hand-me-down garments. Often these had been doled out by the nuns, whose rules decreed that they should provide clothing and free lunches for needy children. Some of the garments were donated by the fee-paying girls, and Kathleen and Daisy may well have worn these, knowing that their previous owners might recognise them. Certainly for the rest of her life Daisy felt a strong aversion towards charity. In Australia, she would insist that 'her Aborigines' be given brand-new clothes rather than charitable hand-outs, which Daisy argued might pass on disease.

A publication produced for the centenary of the Sacred Heart Convent reveals how different were the lives of the fee-paying pupils across the courtyard.[4] The wealthy boarders were given lists of clothes and other items to bring with them when the boarders entered the convent; besides silk frocks, blouses and school dresses, they brought sets of bed linen and cutlery, including a silver spoon — which inevitably brings to mind the phrase 'born with a silver spoon in her mouth'. Some private pupils arrived with a lady's maid to help them unpack and iron their clothes, as ladies did not perform menial tasks.

The fee-paying pupils had appetising meals. The National School children ate basic lunches of porridge or potatoes from tin or enamel basins using wooden or pewter spoons — washed down by cups of tea. Their classes were held in the smaller house that appears in the front of the nineteenth-century photograph of the convent, and as more and more pupils arrived, additional school benches and desks were set up in the next house. At that time the emphasis in National Schools all over Ireland was on 'the three Rs': reading, writing, arithmetic. There was a good deal of learning by rote — multiplication tables, historical dates and geographical place names were dinned into the children in this way. Needlework was a compulsory subject. An 1858 edition of a teachers' manual for the 'National Female Schools of Ireland' emphasised that needlework training was vital for working-class girls in order to prepare them for a life of domestic service, followed by even more hard work as the wives of working men and the mothers of large families:

> The practical knowledge of needlework with its appendages of cutting out and repairing [whether applied to domestic purposes, or as a mode of procuring remunerative employment] must be regarded as useful to all females, but particularly to those of humbler classes.

Some 300 girls were enrolled at Roscrea's free National School in Daisy's time. According to the register, Margaret Dwyer of No. 2 Main Street started at the school when she was nine. The name Margaret Dwyer also appears on a roll call of pupils conducted by a school inspector in 1870, when she was eleven. That day some fifty children were absent. Many may have stayed away to help with farm chores or look after younger brothers and sisters, while others would have been ill. Tuberculosis was the most prevalent disease, often brought about by living and sleeping in overcrowded conditions. Both the children and their parents, many of whom had been denied an education before the National Schools were established, regarded education as a privilege and were grateful to receive it. Few children were in the habit of 'wagging' school — education was a privilege.

Several sources note that French was the language spoken by private pupils at the convent during the 1880s and 1890s. Former pupils recalled having to speak French to the nuns at mealtimes, and being served breakfasts of milky coffee in large bowls into which they dunked their bread in the French manner.

The boarders and the Free School pupils observed each other but rarely mingled. One exception was the Reverend Mother's Feast Day, when they were all provided with a delicious tea by the convent. A former National School pupil, Betty Delaney (later Donegan), remembered that 'on Reverend Mother's Feast Day we stood in front of the nuns and had to file up and shake hands with Reverend Mother and as a treat receive an apple, an orange or a sugar stick'. She also recalled that 'Latin plain-chant was taught and we could all read

Latin. We also learned Irish dancing. We wrote on rough slates with chalk — some of the slates had wooden frames around them and everyone wanted those. In winter we were always cold.'[5]

Another occasion in which both fee-paying and charity pupils took part was the bishop's celebration of the girls' first communion. The special day of Daisy's first communion would have vividly demonstrated the vast gulf between the rich and poor girls. The rich girls were attired like brides. Small wreaths of white flowers held their veils in place as they entered the chapel two by two to the sound of the organ, clasping their mother-of-pearl rosaries and leather- or ivory-cased prayer books. They knelt at the altar, in front of tall stools covered with white muslin and flowers, with a tall candle burning before each girl. In contrast, Daisy and the other girls from the 'poor school' knelt in front of smaller stools without flowers or candles. Their white cotton hand-me-down frocks, although freshly laundered, must have looked shabby in comparison with the exquisitely embroidered frocks of the fee-paying pupils.

ॐ ॐ ॐ

National School registers in the archives of the Order of the Sacred Heart show Margaret Dwyer, orphan, missed a year of schooling when she was fourteen. She missed another year when she was seventeen and was probably placed 'in service' in the north of England with Mrs Goode, widow of the Bishop of Ripon, who later gave Daisy a Bible, inscribing it as a gift on the flyleaf. Daisy described herself as moody and difficult, and claimed in an ABC radio interview in February 1941 that she had refused to learn and was badly behaved. Quite possibly this was a consequence of conflict at home with her stepmother, and this may have been when she went to stay with Mrs Goode.[6]

Aged eighteen and nineteen, Margaret Dwyer's name reappears on the school register as a monitor, or pupil-teacher, but by the time she turned twenty her name had disappeared altogether.

In 1874 Griffith's Valuations records show Daisy's stepmother gave up the tenancy of No. 2 Main Street. After returning from her 'missing' year Daisy may have continued to live with her at a new address or possibly with one of her maternal aunts in Roscrea, resuming her schooling at the National School.[7]

Like Kathleen, Daisy owed a great deal to the nuns of the Sacred Heart. Apart from teaching her to speak French and German fluently — she had a flair for languages — they gave her a good knowledge of literature and history. She also appears to have received some tuition in science, an unusual subject for a girl of her time.

But in the Ireland of the 1870s there were no opportunities for young women to receive tertiary education, however talented they might be.

By the time the two Dwyer sisters left the convent to become governesses they had, besides acquiring ladylike manners, learned to soften their broad Irish brogues and to express themselves in a more English way. They must have pored over copies of *Debrett's Peerage* and *Burke's Landed Gentry* to discover who owned many of Ireland's and England's most handsome old houses — knowledge that Daisy would use to good effect when she went to Australia. In short, both sisters successfully remodelled themselves as plausible members of the Anglo-Irish Protestant ascendancy, Kathleen as the elder and more successful sister, being the ringleader. Their Uncle Joe, the prosperous cattle dealer whose business often took him to Scotland, helped the more pliable Kathleen to find employment with a highly respectable Protestant family there, where she met Robert Browrigg whom she would marry and — by telling tall tales of an aristocratic background and a cultivated father — was accepted as a suitable daughter-in-law by the Brownriggs.

Most young women who worked as resident governesses in the Victorian era did so only because they lacked money and were not so lucky as Kathleen Dwyer. The writers Charlotte Brontë and her sister Anne are clear examples of this, and they both used their experiences as governesses in their novels. A governess occupied an ambivalent social position, midway between the family and the servants. In Charlotte Brontë's novel *Jane Eyre*, her eponymous heroine — like Daisy, a poor orphan — is humiliated by the snobbish Lady Ingram, who declares in Jane's hearing: 'All governesses are detestable and . . . ridiculous. I have just one word to say about the whole tribe. They are a nuisance.' Only at the end of the novel does penniless Jane manage to break through the social barriers and marry the widowed Mr Rochester, after he has been blinded in a fire.

Similarly, orphaned Becky Sharp, the young governess in William Makepeace Thackeray's novel *Vanity Fair*, is humiliated because she is thought of as being 'not quite a lady' — as George Osborne declares when he realises that his brother-in-law, the wealthy widower Jos Sedley, might propose marriage to Miss Sharp. George adds: 'A pretty governess is all very well [as a mistress], but I'd rather have a *lady* for a sister-in-law.'

For an ambitious young woman like Daisy O'Dwyer, there were lessons to be learned from the humiliations of Jane Eyre and Becky Sharp. As an avid reader, Daisy must have read Brontë and Thackeray, but her memoirs confirm that it was Dickens who became her favourite author. Daisy claimed that she 'learned what good there was in the world from the novels of Charles Dickens', who described the lives of sad, abandoned children such as Nicholas Nickleby, David Copperfield and Little Nell (whose story made Daisy cry). Orphaned Pip in *Great Expectations* and orphaned Oliver Twist were other characters with whom she evidently identified and empathised. She always kept a set of Charles Dickens's novels in the tent she lived in on the Nullarbor Desert, and was able to quote long passages from them.

❧ ❧ ❧

Daisy decided to leave Ireland and seek her fortune in London. She was determined to succeed and better her life, as Kathleen had done. In London she must have realised just how much the English despised and reviled the Catholic Irish, who were regarded as a drunken, feckless lot; Irish girls were only fit to be servants, Irish boys to become labourers. Irish poverty was often seen as the fault of the Irish themselves or of the Catholic Church.

We know next to nothing of her time in London except that Daisy suffered a humiliation when she was rejected out of hand as a potential bride for Ernest Baglehole, the son and heir of wealthy Methodist businessman William Baglehole, a ship and factory owner whose own humble origins were in the dockyard area but who had high ambitions for his only son and heir, Ernest.[8] It appears that Ernest already had an 'understanding' with Miss Jessie Rose, daughter of a Scottish engineer and descendant of the Rose clan of Nairnshire, and his parents were anxious for him to go through with that marriage. No doubt they considered Jessie a superior match for their son, but they were also afraid that if Ernest did not honour this 'understanding' he might be sued for breach of promise. It seems Daisy was eventually dismissed from her London position and thus the menace of Miss Dwyer was removed. Ernest Baglehole is recorded as having married Jessie Rose at Lewisham in January 1881 but it seems Ernest could not forget Daisy.

This humiliating and hurtful experience seems to have spurred Daisy to apply for an orphan's assisted passage to Australia, a country where no one would know the truth about her origins. In addition, it is possible that breathing the smoke and fog of London renewed her fear that she might have a spot on her lung like her mother and could also become a victim of tuberculosis. Decades later, in an article in 'My Natives and I', Daisy would claim that 'the discovery of a lung spot, an inheritance from my dead young mother, brought Australia on my life's map'. Queensland's warm climate may well have been another reason contributing to her decision.

Ernest Baglehole in his wedding photograph from the Lewisham Chronicle, *January 1881*

Daisy Dwyer never quite overcame the impact of being orphaned and unprotected in a harsh and snobbish world that rated women in terms of status, money and dowries. She would take her fantasies to Australia with her, and insist for the rest of her life that she came from the Anglo-Irish Protestant landowning classes and blue blood.

Shipping records show that in November 1882 Miss Margaret O'Dwyer, spinster, embarked at Plymouth on the SS *Almora*, owned by British India Associated Steamers, en route to Townsville in northern Queensland.

It was a strange coincidence that Ernest Baglehole would later be employed by the British India Steam Navigation Company, which later also took ownership of the *Almora*. He and Daisy had not seen the last of each other.

CHAPTER 4

MEETING AND PARTING

I arrived in Queensland in the early eighties on the SS Almora, just at the time when the Krakatoa earthquake played havoc with the charts of the Malay Archipelago, and left the South Seas a legacy of magnificent Turner sunsets.

DAISY BATES, 'MY NATIVES AND I', 1936[1]

'I like to fall in love, just meet and then part. Life was fun that way.'

DAISY BATES, SPEAKING TO A LONDON JOURNALIST[2]

After a long and miserable journey for the girls in steerage, the SS *Almora* arrived at the Queensland coast and anchored off Townsville on 14 January 1883. The following morning it entered harbour. Townsville, the nearest port to the booming gold-rush town of Charters Towers, was a bustling, busy town. Saloon-class passengers and their servants disembarked first. While another matron came on board to take charge of the girls who were

Engraved view of Townsville harbour in the 1880s, at the time when Daisy O'Dwyer arrived there aboard the Almora *with a group of Irish orphans*

travelling to ports further down the coast, it was left to Matron Chase to usher the disembarking group, bedraggled in their travel-stained and crumpled calico dresses, down the gangplank.

Some of the older girls — domestic staff like Augusta Blist, Ellen Cartwright, Fanny Jennings, the Shepherd sisters and Salome Llewllyn — were claimed at the docks by the employers to whom they were indentured.[3]

As her moral guardian, Matron Chase may have insisted Daisy accompany the younger girls to the Immigration Barracks.[4] Ashamed as she might feel to be herded along with a band of penniless orphans, this was a new beginning. For Daisy, Australia was the passport to a new life and the shedding of her old one.

Daisy always claimed that she paid her own fare to Australia in a first-class cabin, concealing the fact that she had travelled steerage on the *Almora* under a widely advertised assisted passage scheme. She also advanced the date of her arrival by a year, claiming to have arrived just months after the eruption of Mount Krakatoa in Indonesia in August 1883, presumably thereby either investing her arrival with some natural significance or distancing herself from the party of orphan servants that landed in January.

Somehow or other, Daisy escaped from Matron Chase and managed to call on the Bishop of Townsville, George Henry Stanton, possibly telling him, quite truthfully, that her elder sister Kathleen had married Captain Robert Brownrigg, a cousin of his ecclesiastical colleague Canon Marcus Brownrigg of Hobart, Tasmania.

One can imagine petite Daisy, demure in a white high-necked blouse and ankle-length skirt, smiling up at the bespectacled bachelor bishop, claiming she was a member of the Church of Ireland, daughter of the late James O'Dwyer, Esquire of Ashberry House. She might have added that she had come to Queensland on medical advice, as her mother had died of consumption in Ireland.

Daisy may have received a character reference from the bishop, which could have seen her invited to stay at homesteads, but her statement in old age to Ernestine Hill that she stayed at the bishop's residence is likely to be another of Daisy's fantasies. In later years she would also put forward the unlikely claim that she became 'the ward' of Bishop Stanton and that he was 'an old friend of my father'.

In 1883, when Daisy arrived in North Queensland, the economy was booming. Not only was there a huge demand for servants, there were also large numbers of unmarried young men in search of wives: small farmers, wood choppers, gold diggers, stockmen, jackaroos and cane cutters. But Miss O'Dwyer, with her good education and her appreciation of the better things in life, wanted someone superior as a husband. Her sister Kathleen had married into the upper classes and now moved among educated people. Daisy was also ambitious and intelligent and enjoyed being with people who talked about books and ideas and never had to worry about money.

There was no way the feisty Daisy could improve her precarious financial situation other than by an advantageous marriage. In those days, females were barred from tertiary education and independent careers. She realised that her best chance of success was to let it be known that she had (mythical) money of her own and hope to meet and marry a wealthy grazier or cattle baron. Yet if she had really possessed a private income, the marriage stakes might have proved dangerous. Husbands were accustomed to claiming their wife's assets as their own. The *Married Women's Property Act*, which would allow wives to keep their own assets, was still under discussion.

The immediate difficulty Daisy faced was that she was bonded to the Queensland government for three years to work as a governess or a domestic. If she failed to do this, she was legally obliged to pay back to the government the full cost of her sea passage — the large sum of thirty-nine pounds. Another danger was that the story she had told Bishop George Stanton, of being the independently wealthy Miss O'Dwyer, daughter of the late James O'Dwyer Esquire of Ashberry House, might be exposed as untrue once her fellow passengers started leaving the Immigration Barracks, where they'd been housed. Some of them might even work as maids for parishioners of Bishop Stanton or even at the bishop's residence. Daisy knew very well how servants gossiped among themselves.

It may have been this sense of urgency that persuaded her to accept a position on the isolated Hann cattle station, Maryvale, west of Townsville on the Burdekin River. Daisy claimed later that she was a guest at Maryvale, but it is likely that she was employed as a general factotum or possibly as a domestic. She later also told Ernestine Hill that she learned how to slaughter and skin a beast and milk a cow while at the Hanns, unusual accomplishments in a girl of the upper classes or even in a governess, suggesting she did quite menial tasks.

The Hanns were explorers as well as owners of cattle and sheep stations, but they had struggled with hostile Aboriginal people, spear grass, drought and falling wool prices. Shortage of funds meant they had to surrender two of their grazing leases and devote themselves to beef cattle, which they sold to the goldminers of Charters Towers. They were still living in primitive log cabins on the property when Daisy joined them. This may explain Daisy's statement in later life about Queensland in the 1880s, 'I saw many a little log hut that was the beginning of a fine pastoral home.'[5]

How long Daisy stayed with the Hanns is unclear. Daisy herself claims that she sailed to Tasmania in 1884 'with a sheaf of introductions'[6] to stay at the homesteads of wealthy Tasmanian pastoralists. Presumably, if she did make this journey, she had used her connection, through Kathleen, to Canon Marcus Brownrigg to obtain such introductions. It's possible that the mere mention of her relationship to the Brownrigg family in Ireland may have provided Daisy's passport into this exclusive Anglo-Protestant group. The fact that Canon Brownrigg was only a distant relative of her sister's husband, Captain Robert Brownrigg, would not have worried Daisy overmuch. All she needed were social contacts whose names she could drop. Perhaps she explained to Tasmanians she met that her father, James O'Dwyer Esquire, had become acquainted with relatives

Daisy O'Dwyer

of the New South Wales and Tasmanian grazing families through his membership of Dublin's exclusive Kildare Street Club, where 'old money' gathered — a club that would only have admitted a bootmaker through the tradesmen's entrance. Daisy's former study of the lists of Ireland's aristocracy and landed gentry and her retentive memory would have come in useful in all this.

According to stories Daisy told the writer Ernestine Hill in her later years, she spent several months in Tasmania, intent on enjoying herself, riding, partying and attending grand balls in the homes of leading members of Tasmanian society. This was the era when Tasmania, at the height of its prosperity, rode on the sheep's back. The pastoralists owned handsome stone-built houses such as Woolmers, Quamby, Clarendon and Malahide, the latter with its links to Ireland. (The Talbots, the titled Irish family that lived at Malahide, also owned Malahide Castle on the coast near Dublin.) These large Tasmanian houses formed the hub of colonial social life on the island.

If she did indeed travel to Tasmania, the question arises: how did Daisy support herself in Tasmania? Daisy claimed she lived off a bequest from her father, which was another fantasy. It is possible that she found herself a wealthy lover to support her, possibly a married man. Decades later at Ooldea Daisy showed Ernestine Hill a trunk filled with expensive ball gowns and satin dancing shoes, claiming she had worn them at squatters' balls in Tasmania.

A Tasmanian interlude in which wealthy graziers entertained her would certainly have suited Daisy. Perhaps the countryside, with its soft green fields surrounded by hedges and apple orchards reminded her of Ireland. She claimed to have 'ridden to hounds with Antipodean hunt clubs' and walked through fields of wildflowers accompanied by young men who expressed their admiration for her; she spoke of pretty stone bridges and water wheels, and told how she had danced the nights away at balls held in the grand houses. Letters from Daisy describing a visit to grazier Donald MacKinnon at Dalness, a Tasmanian sheep property, give credence to the claim that she did in fact spend time in Tasmania.[7]

Pretty, amusing Miss O'Dwyer regaled the Tasmanian graziers' wives she met with fictitious anecdotes. She named the wealthy former military officer, Sir Francis Outram, as her guardian and made out that the wife of this 'friend' of her father's had organised a glittering coming out for Daisy. Had any of the graziers' wives checked her stories of hunting and attending grand balls in Ireland, as well as her imaginary London debutante season, Daisy would have been finished socially. But letters took almost three months to reach Britain or Ireland by sea and the responses took another three months to return. Fortunately for Daisy, no Tasmanian squatters seemed to know of Timothy Bridge or Ashberry House, and Sir Francis Outram, wheelchair-bound since being wounded in India in active service, was a recluse, otherwise her cover story would have been blown.

But we must not forget Daisy's fondness of fantasy. The Tasmanian squattocracy formed a snobbish clique and may not have admitted her to their inner circles at all. And while she apparently spent her time in the southern colony flirting with the eligible men, dancing the waltz and the polka with young squatters 'while the home-grown beauties were ranged like hollyhocks along the wall',[8] somehow or other Miss Daisy O'Dwyer did not succeed in finding a husband in Tasmania.[9]

❀ ❀ ❀

After her stay in Tasmania, Daisy returned to Queensland, to Charters Towers, the prosperous gold-mining town inland from Townsville whose population was soaring. It may have seemed the ideal place to find a wealthy husband who had struck it rich — but it was at Charters Towers that Daisy's cover story, which she had repeated so often, could well backfire on her. Would the alleged wealth of Miss Daisy O'Dwyer of Ashberry House attract the wrong type of man?

The gold-rush boom acted like a magnet for upper-class remittance men from Britain, whose families supplied them with regular sums of money to keep them as far away as possible from home, especially if they drank heavily or gambled. Some acquired an opium habit after they arrived — a habit they may have picked up from members of the Chinese community at Charters Towers, who fossicked for gold in the creeks, tended market gardens or worked as laundry men. Nicknamed 'The World' because it drew people from so many different countries, Charters Towers was also full of free-spending gold miners who were always delighted to meet a pretty, single girl.

The outskirts of the town were bleak, a wilderness of mullock (mining waste) heaps and mining machinery. In the centre of town, things were very different. There were restaurants, dance saloons, brothels, shops, even a stock exchange. Chinese opium dens lurked in the dark back lanes. The principal streets, built wide enough to accommodate bullock carts, were unpaved. In the residential area stood houses with shady verandas, their posts entwined with climbing mauve wisteria and crimson bougainvillea.

From Daisy's viewpoint there was only one problem. The majority of these gold miners were rough men, totally preoccupied in making money and uninterested in books and culture. Not exactly Miss O'Dwyer's image of the ideal husband.

As an attractive single girl, she was very popular. She was invited to parties on those wide, shady verandas where French champagne was served. Soon Miss O'Dwyer acquired more elegant clothes, possibly paid for by new admirers. One of them, a young American journalist cum accountant who worked for the *Northern Miner*, fell completely under Daisy's spell. His name was Arnold Knight Colquhoun. Initially Daisy may have encouraged his attentions: Arnold seemed well travelled and well educated. But there were signs that he had acquired a drug habit from visiting the opium dens in the back lanes. He told her that his parents had emigrated from Scotland to America, where they had made their fortune, and that he had left America to work his way around the world.[10] Arnold's air of a cosmopolitan traveller would have appealed to Daisy — until she realised how unstable he was. (Inquest reports into Arnold's death would reveal that he was being treated with mercury for syphilis.) It wasn't long before Daisy became desperate to untangle herself from Arnold's attentions.

The *Northern Miner* newspaper was owned by an effervescent Irish editor, Thaddeus O'Kane, known to his friends as Thaddy. He received numerous writs for defamation: his pen sometimes

Arnold Colquhoun

appeared to be loaded with vitriol. In fact, Arnold's employer Thaddy O'Kane had a good deal to hide. In London he had been accused of trying to obtain money under false pretences from Lord Palmerston, the British Prime Minister. O'Kane had been living with an actress called Martha, whom he claimed was his wife. At the same time she was enjoying the sexual attentions of Lord Palmerston. When O'Kane tried to sue for divorce, with the object of ruining Lord Palmerston financially and socially, Palmerston's lawyers produced evidence that O'Kane was not in fact married to his paramour. Publicly disgraced and the subject of far too much unwelcome attention from rival editors, O'Kane fled from Britain to Australia, changing his name from Timothy to Thaddeus, and in Australia, with its love of short names, he became Thaddy.

In Charters Towers, Thaddy and Arnold belonged to a circle of influential people. Their stimulating conversation must have come as a relief to Daisy after endless contact with men who talked about nothing but mining. Her brief connection with Thaddy O'Kane and his son John, who was Arnold's friend, may have prompted her to think about taking up journalism herself, although it would be another decade before she did so.

Did Daisy attempt to cool Arnold's ardour by telling him of some other relationship — that she was having an affair with another young man? In any event, two things now hit Arnold hard: he was rejected by Daisy, and he fell into debt after being laid off by O'Kane, who no doubt realised Arnold was addicted to opium and had become an erratic employee.

After being dismissed by O'Kane, Arnold went to Townsville, where he took up uncongenial clerical work in the store of Messrs Allen. The *Northern Miner* of 1 November 1883 recorded that Arnold returned from Townsville to Charters Towers by train one night in late October 1883. The next day he had an interview with Thaddy O'Kane, no doubt pleading for another chance to work for him.

After his unsuccessful interview with Thaddy, Arnold may have visited Daisy and implored her in vain to return to him. Perhaps she had been advised Arnold was receiving treatment for syphilis, which was a virtual death warrant in those days. Receiving yet another rejection may well have caused Arnold to see suicide as the way out, as implied in the statement of Thaddeus O'Kane to the Police Magistrate on 10 November 1883.[11]

That fateful day, Dr David Graham Browne gave Arnold a prescription for a quantity of mercury, the only known treatment for syphilis in that era.[12] But after his unsatisfactory meeting with

O'Kane and/or Daisy, Arnold did not swallow the mercury. Instead, he went to the chemist and bought a large dose of morphia (an opium derivative available at the time without a doctor's prescription). In a highly excitable state he returned to his room in Chick's Hotel and wrote two farewell messages, one to John O'Kane and the other to Daisy. He placed the note to John O'Kane in a large envelope and enclosed the letter for Daisy in a smaller sealed envelope inside the larger one. In a separate note to John he asked him not to open the smaller envelope but instead to deliver it by hand to Daisy. Then Arnold took a lethal overdose of morphia combined with alcohol. The next day Arnold's corpse was found in his room by Mary Chick, wife of the hotel owner.

Arnold's final request was not carried out — his farewell note to John O'Kane and his letter to Daisy were handed over to the coroner.

On 1 November 1883, the *Northern Miner* announced Arnold's demise.

> We regret to record the death of Mr Arnold Colquhoun by his own hand. He bought four grams of morphia at Mr Lewis the chemist and then went to Chick's Hotel, where he was found dead this morning. He was a good accountant and well-educated, professing to understand Latin, Greek, French and Italian. His manner was occasionally wild and his conduct strange. Drink excited him in an extraordinary manner . . . and he suffered from pecuniary embarrassment but conducted himself on this paper with scrupulous honesty.

According to Thaddeus O'Kane's evidence at the inquest, Arnold 'spoke rationally on certain subjects', but O'Kane did not reveal the fact he had fired Arnold for drug addiction. He also told the coroner about Arnold's 'pecuniary embarrassment', and Daisy's name was never mentioned.

Arnold's final note to John O'Kane was read out in court:

I am foolish but I have considered this thing over and am
willing to take the consequences. Think well of me if you
can and pardon me for the course that I have chosen. My
warmest regards and honest respects to Mr O'Kane . . .
I suppose he will think me contemptible.

   Yours resignedly, Arnold.[13]

At the inquest, the coroner's verdict was that Arnold Colquhoun's
death was due to a drug overdose, but did not carry out any further
inquiry into the reason why Arnold had chosen to end his life.
Fortunately for Daisy, he did not read out Arnold's sealed note.
Possibly it indicated whether the American had committed suicide
because Daisy had told him there was someone else in her life.

   If in fact there *was* another man, he didn't last long.

The pen drawing that accompanied the announcement in the
Northern Miner *of the wedding of Edwin Henry Murrant and Daisy May O'Dwyer;*
photographs of Harry 'Breaker' Morant.

MARRIAGE.

MURRANT—O'DWYER.—On March 13th, at
Charters Towers by the Rev. C. G. Bar-
low, Edwin Henry Murrant, of Wemhdon,
Somersetshire, England, to Daisy May
O'Dwyer, of Glenacurra, Tipperary,
Ireland.

CHAPTER 5

A MARRIAGE OF SORTS

O what a tangled web we weave,
When first we practise to deceive!

Sir Walter Scott, *Marmion*, 1808

Daisy had failed to find a wealthy husband in Charters Towers. It was now impossible for her to remain in the gold-mining town, where idle gossip pointed her out as the woman for whom Arnold Colquhoun had killed himself. But she was still determined to prove that she could succeed in the marriage market and find a wealthy cattle king or a young man with prospects. In the meantime, she wanted nothing more than to quit Charters Towers and its gossip.

At this point her thoughts must have returned to her training as a governess. According to Daisy, Bishop Stanton had written her a glowing character reference to help her find employment. Plenty of outback families needed a governess, especially one from a good family with a character reference from a bishop. In the early 1880s cattle properties were booming as a result of the gold rush — 'cattle kings' were making fortunes from 'squatting' on land with good water and stocking it with cattle; they sold their beef at top prices to the newly affluent gold miners in Charters Towers and other mining towns that were springing up along the Palmer River.

So Miss O'Dwyer applied for the post of governess at Fanning Downs Station, forty kilometres outside Charters Towers. Fanning Downs was owned by a grazier called Frederick Hamilton. An Englishman in his late forties, he had made money on the Victorian goldfields. Instead of returning to England he moved to the frontier colony of Queensland, where he took up land and began to breed cattle. His wife was something of a pioneer: before Hamilton acquired the lease of Fanning Downs, she had accompanied him to isolated Hinchinbrook Station in Queensland.

The Hamiltons had six boys and four girls.[1] They were delighted to appoint Miss O'Dwyer as their governess.

When Daisy arrived at Fanning Downs, she maintained her fantasy of an Ashberry House upbringing, a private income and her position as a member of the Protestant ascendancy. She may have told them that she was only working to fill in time and to experience something of the Australian way of life.

Fanning Downs cattle station near Charters Towers, c. 1880.
Inset: Owner, Frederick Hamilton.

In the 1880s, as Daisy had realised, to be Irish and Catholic in colonial Australia was a social liability. Even in the Parliament of New South Wales, derogatory remarks were made about Irish immigrants and their lack of education. Premier Sir Henry Parkes went as far as to call the Irish 'jabbering baboons', an insult that was widely repeated. Daisy may have been told that Hamilton, who had also built and run the Burdekin Hotel for a while, did not like Irish Catholics any more than Parkes.

Apart from this, the restricted life of a governess, cooped up all day with fretful children and snubbed by her employers, offered a less than satisfactory lifestyle to an educated, ambitious young woman. An affair with a son of the family or even the head of the household promised excitement and expensive presents and on occasion could lead to marriage. Yet for every fictional Jane Eyre, hundreds of real-life governesses were entangled with some male member of the household who regarded them as nothing more than a sexual convenience. Governesses could face instant dismissal should the affair come to light, and be denied a reference to enable them to find another position.

Daisy had already suffered slights and snubs. She was determined that no one was going to despise her again. A resident governess had three options at meals: she could take high tea with the children, eat with the cook and domestic staff, or dine in style with the family and their guests. At Fanning Downs, Daisy selected this last option as her due.

On special occasions, the young jackaroos working on the property, some of whom came from wealthy families, changed into evening dress to dine with the station owner, his family and any guests. Daisy, with her clever turns of phrase, may well have enlivened the gatherings with tales of her imaginary life at Ashberry House, and with Sir Francis and Lady Outram at their homes in London and Dorset.

One young jackaroo and horse breaker sitting at the polished table hung on her words, fascinated by the petite governess, who seemed exceptionally well travelled for a woman of her era. He was attracted by her amusing manner of talking and by her chiselled profile and dark brows over eyes as blue as the Queensland sky. Here was a girl of quality who any man would be proud to have as a wife.

It was either at Fanning Downs or at Charters Towers that Daisy first met this well-spoken, handsome young migrant from England. Edwin 'Henry' Murrant of Bridgewater, Somerset,[2] had arrived aboard SS *Waroonga* at Cooktown in Queensland on 5 June 1883.

Like Daisy, Eddie Murrant had obtained an assisted passage and like Daisy he was living a life based on fantasy.

He had grown up in Somerset, where his father, Edwin Murrant, and Irish-born mother, Catherine, now both dead, had been employed as the Bridgewater workhouse keeper and matron respectively. As a boy he had won a scholarship to Silesia College, an exclusive English private school where, again like Daisy, he had continued his studies as a pupil-teacher. At college he was taught to behave like a gentleman by an avuncular figure named George Whyte-Melville, who acted as his mentor and friend. After the death of the young man's parents, Whyte-Melville invited him out fox hunting, turned him into an excellent horseman and taught him that gentlemen rarely pay their bills on time — a lesson the young man would take to heart. Some time later, possibly encouraged by Daisy, he began to call himself Harry Morant. He apparently

The grim workhouse at Bridgewater, in the west of England, where Breaker Morant spent his early years as the son of the workhouse keeper.

believed that his mother, Catherine Murrant (née O'Reilly or Reily), had conducted a clandestine affair with a young naval officer named Digby Morant, who was now a famous admiral (Digby Morant vigorously disputed this). The young man would refer to Admiral Morant as his 'Guv'nor', the way upper-class young men spoke of their fathers, and implied that he had considerable expectations from him.[3]

When the penniless Eddie Murrant first arrived in Queensland, he was employed as a rough rider in a circus. He had all the airs and graces of an English gentleman, but did not admit to the fact that he had no money to back up this plausible façade.

At Fanning Downs, Eddie Murrant was popular with the jackaroos, among whom he was nicknamed the 'Breaker' because of his outstanding skill with horses, although officially employed as 'horse-boy'.

The 'Breaker' and Daisy both had charm and shared a love of literature and horses. Each believed the other had 'great expectations'; each sought to escape a past that held them back. Smitten by Daisy's charms, Eddie invited her to go riding. Since Daisy loved horses (and doubtless improved her horsemanship under Eddie's expert tuition) the pair of them went out riding whenever their free time coincided. Their romance flourished: Eddie, with his good looks and outstanding physique, was just the type of man Daisy admired. He could quote reams of poetry, enjoyed writing romantic little verses, and was well read and witty. Plus he could make Daisy laugh, a sure way to a woman's heart.

Daisy's habit of larding her conversation with French and German phrases, her fastidious cleanliness, her ladylike manners and elegant clothes convinced Eddie that Miss O'Dwyer belonged to the landed gentry. The fact that she was living at Fanning Downs without a chaperone and had no parents seemed to him ideal for acquiring a wealthy wife without facing a barrage of awkward questions about his finances from prospective in-laws or guardians.

These attractive young people had a lot to conceal. Did either know the other's actual age? It is unlikely Daisy told her future husband that she had lowered her age by three years in order to qualify for her assisted passage to Australia. For his part, Eddie had raised his age by two years, giving it as twenty-one instead of nineteen. Eddie was a handsome young daredevil with a great deal of charisma: Daisy may have had no idea that he was almost five years younger than she was. This apparently minor detail had some serious implications. Under Queensland law, a man had to be twenty-one in order to get married (a woman had to be at least eighteen).

Their relationship became what is known as a *folie à deux*, with each leading the other on with tales of an imaginary past.

჻ ჻ ჻

Soon enough, Daisy had made a match. She accepted Eddie's proposal and slipped his engagement ring on her finger, having no idea it had been purchased with a worthless cheque. (Passing cheques that bounced had already landed Murrant into trouble in England.) He may have been only too happy to buy Daisy an expensive ring, convinced that, once they were married, his wealthy wife would be footing the bills.

It was a hasty wedding. Some researchers have speculated that Daisy may have been pregnant, and there have been suggestions of a son named William.[4] Both Daisy's long-term friend Beatrice Raine and her landlady much later at Streaky Bay, South Australia, Mrs Matthews, recorded that in old age Daisy cried for a son named William, but this is scarcely conclusive. If she was indeed pregnant, she would not have wanted to delay too long. A photograph taken on 13 March 1884, her wedding day, shows Daisy wearing a dark dress with a big lace collar reaching down to her waist in a V shape. Did she hope it would hide her growing 'baby bump' or had good food at Fanning Downs been responsible for her plumpness? Subsequent photographs show Daisy as ultra-slim. The groom refused to be photographed; instead, a line drawing was substituted in the *Northern Miner*'s account of the ceremony.

Eddie Murrant had arranged for his friend and witness James Veal and his wife to hold the wedding in their home at Plant

Street, Charters Towers. The Veals had been friends of the late Arnold Colquhoun as well as Eddie, and seem to have encouraged Eddie's romance with Daisy. Daisy and Eddie's wedding certificate makes interesting reading. Daisy cited her place of residence as Fanning Downs Station, and her birthplace as Glencunna in North Tipperary, Ireland. Glencunna was a small division of agricultural land called a 'townland' (something like a shire), near Ballychrine, home of Granny Hunt. Her next marriage certificate would give her birthplace as Glenbeha, also near Ballychrine. Her parents were recorded as James O'Dwyer and Marguerite (rather than Bridget) O'Dwyer, née Hunt. Daisy also claimed to be twenty-one (in 1884) when her real age was twenty-four. Eddie likewise claimed to be twenty-one when in fact he was nineteen. His birth certificate records his birth date as 9 December 1864.[5] It was an Anglican ceremony and Eddie asked the Reverend Barlow to officiate.[6] On the wedding day, the groom's lack of money was revealed when he was unable to pay the Reverend Barlow his modest fee for officiating. Perhaps Eddie laughed this off, saying that he was expecting funds to arrive from England any day. At the time he was only receiving fifteen shillings a week as a horse-boy.

After the wedding the newlyweds returned to the small cottage that had been made available for them at Fanning Downs. Since Daisy and Eddie both had a quick temper and strong will, the newlyweds managed to live together at Fanning Downs for only a short time. Things came to a head when the cheque

Wedding photograph of Daisy, in the Northern Miner

Eddie had paid the jeweller for Daisy's engagement ring bounced. Then, to make things worse, the Reverend Barlow appeared at the door of their little cottage demanding his fee for officiating at the ceremony. And to make matters worse still, Eddie was then accused by a lady of his acquaintance of having stolen several pigs and a saddle.

It seems likely that once Daisy discovered her husband had no money and slim prospects of inheriting any, sparks flew. He, for his part, must have realised that Daisy's private income was a myth and there was no way she could pay his debts. Their mutual deception must have exploded in joint recriminations in direct contrast to their earlier wooing — it's easy to imagine an angry duet fit for a comic opera. To avoid the consequences of his latest deeds, as well, perhaps, as Daisy's fiery temper, police evidence at his trial records that Eddie fled Fanning Downs on a horse saddled with one of the property's saddles.[7]

Police Constable Quinn rode after him in hot pursuit. He caught up with Harry on the Cloncurry road, twenty-five kilometres from Charters Towers, arrested and handcuffed him, and brought him back to the Charters Towers lockup.[8] Daisy was mortified to find herself once again the subject of scandal and innuendo throughout the district.

Doubtless the Hamiltons were considerably annoyed by the scandal that now enveloped two of their employees. To add to Daisy's fury, when the truth of her husband's age came out she found herself being described as a 'cradle snatcher'.[9] The fact that her husband was in jail must have humiliated Daisy, who came from a small Irish town where reputation was everything. People would have whispered that the Hamiltons' former governess, that aristocratic Irish girl with all the fancy airs and graces, had married a jailbird.

Daisy's marriage had turned into a farce. She who specialised in telling tall tales was now the victim of her husband's fantasies and deceptions. Young Murrant had no 'great expectations'. Even worse, he was a thief. She had dreamed of a marriage that would bring respect and money; she now envisaged a degrading future as the spouse of a common conman. She decided she never wanted to see her husband again.

In the Charters Towers courtroom Eddie claimed he'd been given a saddle, like the one he was accused of stealing, as a gift from a Mrs Brooks, in whose house he had once stayed. Mistakenly, he had taken a more valuable saddle than the one given to him. And the business of the missing pigs had been misunderstood. As for the cheque he had given the jeweller, Eddie, remembering his mentor Whyte-Melville, claimed that gentlemen were often short of cash but always paid their debts in the end.

The magistrate, a racing man who had seen Eddie win a steeplechase, was sympathetic. He dismissed the case, saying there was insufficient evidence to convict. Eddie was released and headed off to Longreach where records show he found a job on Manooroo Station.

Daisy's lack of money was an overwhelming obstacle to obtaining a divorce. In the Victorian and Edwardian eras, divorce cost a great deal of money so, effectively, was reserved for very wealthy people. Moreover, the divorce laws were weighted in favour of men, and only granted on the grounds of adultery or extreme cruelty. Wives were usually deemed to be at fault even if the husband had been unfaithful.[10] The Queensland *Divorce Act* of 1865 gave the grounds for divorce as incest, rape, sodomy, bestiality, bigamy or two years' desertion of a wife by her husband. It too was biased against women, for it demanded only one year's desertion of the husband by the wife. And were she divorced, she would lose the right to see her children or receive any income from her husband. Divorce was considered an 'unnatural' procedure for a woman to institute. Rarely were judges sympathetic to wives, even if desertion could be proved. It was believed the fault must be due to the unwomanly behaviour by the wife.

We do not know if Daisy was pregnant; no stories were passed down. If she did quietly give her baby away, suffered a miscarriage or had an illegal abortion, the secret went with her to the grave.

Eddie Murrant went on his merry way, working through Queensland and rural New South Wales, apparently now using the name Harry Morant. Like Daisy, he was creating a new persona for himself, and shedding his identity as a man charged with theft. But old habits die hard, and on an admission form when he went to Mullaburra Hospital he gave the name 'Horsebreaker' Morant as well as his correct birth date and the Christian names of Eddie Murrant's parents, Edwin and Catherine. He continued to live on his wits, writing bush ballads, and able to grace any grazier's table with his conversation — or else brawling in the bush pubs where he drank to excess and often paid his bar bills with more cheques that bounced.

After years of buckjumping, droving and drinking, accumulating debts and winning admiration for his skill with horses, Breaker Morant would enlist in the Imperial army when the Second Boer War broke out in South Africa in 1899. On leave from the army, 'Breaker' Morant visited England with his friend Captain Percy Hunt, and became engaged to the sister of Captain Hunt's fiancée, by which time Daisy was travelling through the Murchison Ranges of Western Australia.

By mid-1884 Daisy did not know her husband's whereabouts and cared only that he never crossed her path again. Perhaps they had some kind of pact never to mention their misguided marriage and each other and to start afresh.

Towards the end of the year Daisy left North Queensland and went to New South Wales, intent on forgetting the past and starting a new chapter in her life. Claiming to be a single girl, she removed her wedding band (no one would have employed a runaway wife) and took a job as governess on a small property near Nowra, about 150 kilometres south of Sydney, owned by Mrs Catherine Bates, an Irish-born Catholic widow with six children.

Mrs Bates was struggling to keep the rundown farm on the Berry estate going. Her eldest son John (known as Jack) had left home to work as a drover, leaving his younger brother Charlie to help his mother. Like Daisy, Catherine Bates believed strongly in the importance of education, and engaged her to teach her four lively young daughters as well as to keep the house clean and tidy. Daisy, who had been an unpaid skivvy during her childhood in the homes of her aunts and stepmother, loathed washing, ironing and all other forms of domesticity. Nevertheless, always neat and clean herself, she did her share of the cleaning up and tidying away. The primitive bush kitchen with its slab walls, Coolgardie safe and iron range was not exactly what she had hoped for when she migrated to Australia.

But something more lay in store.

Jack Bates

CHAPTER 6

DAISY, THE DROVER'S WIFE

'Men loved Daisy too much.'

DAISY'S FUTURE SISTER-IN-LAW, MRS CHARLIE BATES

The sad story of Daisy the drover's wife who wanted her husband to turn himself into a wealthy pastoralist started on Christmas Eve 1884. The Bates family were looking forward to Jack's homecoming. He was bringing back with him a mob of brumbies, wild horses for the local rough-riding show. His young sisters, excited by the imminent arrival of their brother, chattered away excitedly, telling Daisy what a brilliant horseman Jack was, how handsome and how kind.

Later that evening when Jack finally arrived, Daisy noted approvingly that he had inherited his mother's good looks. But instead of being fair-haired, Jack had a thatch of black hair, a luxuriant black moustache and piercing blue eyes in a tanned face.

With his long legs, lean muscular body in the bushman's rig of tight-fitting moleskin trousers and check shirt, Jack Bates was the sort of man Daisy found attractive. She set much store by appearance and noted approvingly that Jack had polished his riding boots until you could see your face in them. Everyone said that good drovers earned a great deal of money and became very knowledgeable about cattle: from drover to station owner was an achievable step and some had made it.

Jack Bates excited Daisy but she was dismayed to find that his table manners were rather rough and ready and that, unlike the Breaker, who was the life and soul of any party, Jack was very quiet. The pair spent most of the evening together and Jack could not take his eyes off her. According to hearsay, he impressed Daisy by showing her the silver cups he had won, allegedly when he played for the Geebung Polo Club (which club is the subject and title of a poem by A.B. 'Banjo' Paterson).

Daisy, who loved nothing more than talking about books, had to overlook the fact that Jack never talked about them. Instead, having dropped out of school, he declared that he despised 'book learning'; in his opinion, what he called 'the school of hard knocks' was what taught a man all he needed to know.

After he had run away from school at fourteen he had found a job rounding up brumbies for 'Hungry' Jim Tyson, then Australia's richest cattleman. Already a brilliant horseman, Jack Bates proved himself an honest and hard worker and had been promoted to head stockman on Tyson's huge Tinnenburra Station on the Warrego. This cattle station was so large it turned off 10,000 to 15,000 bullocks each year. The job of head stockman on Tinnenburra was one of considerable responsibility and prestige in the cattle industry.

But Jack Bates's well-paid job ended after he lost his temper with an Aboriginal stockman who had disobeyed an order. An argument ensued. Jack had a vile temper and he knocked the man senseless with a branding iron. Tyson, who valued his Aboriginal stockmen highly for their skills with horses and cattle, promptly dismissed his head stockman and made sure that no one else would employ him either. So Jack Bates had become a self-employed drover. He made good money, but it was scarcely the occupation of a gentleman.

In the late nineteenth century, when vast herds of cattle had to be moved overland, drovers did very well indeed, even though many of them were illiterate or semi-literate. One English-born drover, who spent four years working in Queensland and New South Wales, wrote:

> Large mobs of mixed cattle are continually being moved
> about from one station to another . . . In consequence
> droving becomes a profession and numbers of men make a
> very good living from it. The work is not easy. To take
> 1,000 fat bullocks over all sorts of country and bring them
> to market in prime condition involves a great deal of skill
> and responsibility. A drover's reputation depends on the
> good order in which his cattle end their journey. The
> drover averages between four and five miles [about seven
> kilometres] a day and is always on horseback. He never gets
> more than four hours sleep at a stretch . . .[1]

While droving held a certain charm for men like Jack, who enjoyed an open-air life and the sense of freedom and mateship it engendered on the road, for those women unfortunate enough to marry a drover, life was often lonely and bleak. 'Matrimony does not come easily to a drover and their wives spend a great deal of time alone': this was a theme repeated in tales by Henry Lawson such as 'The Drover's Wife' and 'Water Them Geraniums'.

Daisy, who up to now had only met station owners and their wives, had no idea when she agreed to Jack's whirlwind proposal of marriage that a drover's wife led a rough life with few creature comforts. If she had, it seems unlikely she would have accepted Jack Bates as a husband.

The mismatched affair began that fateful Christmas Eve, presumably after the family had drunk a bowl or two of punch, and everyone in the Bates family kissed each other under the mistletoe. Jack invited Daisy to accompany him to the Boxing Day rodeo, or rough-riders show, for which he had free tickets. He told her he did not intend to ride in it himself. Meanwhile, Christmas Day was a happy family occasion. She and Jack spent time amusing the children; she liked the way he responded to them.

On Boxing Day, Daisy put on her best dress and a fetching sun-bonnet and Jack drove her in the pony trap to the event. By Daisy's account, she was surrounded by squatters' wives. '[Everyone was] dressed up to the nines in Dolly Vardens [bonnets] and bustles and bombazines, a fashion parade, you know. They'd made lashings of cakes and pies and sandwiches for luncheon under the trees . . . great fun for man, woman and child.'[2]

Daisy and Jack, who was on the rodeo committee, were given ringside seats. She was impressed. Years later she told her biographer Ernestine Hill about Jack's riding feat that day. One big roan brumby seemed to know all the tricks to throw his riders off, tossing them onto the rails. Big prize money awaited any rider who could stay on for a minute or more. Since Jack had brought in this stallion from the bush, he felt responsible when several riders were thrown off and injured. Suddenly he rose from his seat and strode down the steps into the ring. There he vaulted onto the back of the bucking roan stallion. With consummate skill he managed to stay on the beast although the roan did its best to throw him, rearing, bucking and twisting beneath its rider. Jack dominated that roan stallion and rode him to a standstill, then vaulted off the horse and with easy grace threw the reins to one of the other men.

Daisy must have felt a thrill of excitement and watched fascinated as Jack raised his hand for silence, then made an announcement through the loud hailer. 'I was one of the jokers who brought this brumby in, and if I wasn't game to get on him myself I wouldn't be asking any of them to.'[3] He said he would divide the prize with the men who'd tried to ride the horse.

So Daisy found herself the sweetheart of the hero of the hour; the pretty girl in the ringside seat. She told the writer Ernestine Hill that she'd said to a friend: 'I'll marry that man!'[4]

Jack Bates was passionate about sport and horses, with little time for anything else. For years he had resisted his mother's attempts to marry him off to one or other of the local Catholic girls. Religion played no part in his philosophy. Droving was thirsty work, constantly out in the heat and dust of the outback, and after the day's work was over, the drovers and stockmen would gather in the

Pyree Farm, near Berry, owned by the widowed Catherine Bates,
the mother of handsome drover Jack Bates

only place available to them — a hotel bar or pub saloon — where they drank, gambled, then drank some more. In this way the money they earned through their hard work easily slipped through their fingers.

It seems that Jack was so intoxicated by Daisy's allure that, to ensure no one else could have her, he proposed marriage a few days after he met her. Unfortunately no diaries or letters remain to explain why Daisy agreed to marry a man with very little education and no money in the bank. After they spent a whole day kissing and cuddling in a boat on the Shoalhaven River the couple returned to the Bates property, Pyree, in Mrs Bates's pony trap. At dinner that night Jack announced that he and Daisy were to be married before he left home again.

Catherine Bates, ignorant of Daisy's previous marriage to Eddie Murant/Harry Morant and lulled into believing she was a practising Catholic, must have hoped that Jack's marriage to the hardworking governess who did not approve of alcohol would settle him down. At last he would stop drinking and carousing with his mates, work hard, and save money to buy a cattle run of his own and build a homestead. These, it seems, were exactly what he had promised Daisy when he proposed — promises that must have seemed very attractive to an orphan who had never had a home of her own. Her brief, dubious marriage to Breaker Morant may have been solely to give an unborn child a name. It had proved a disaster, but now here was a handsome man who was prepared to work hard for her and wanted her to marry him before he left Pyree to go on his next droving trip.

She knew that Jack's new contract would take him away from her for many months, and that he would receive a handsome bonus if he delivered his herd of cattle safely from North Queensland to Melbourne. He told her he loved her and she agreed to become his wife, unaware that he had never shown a scrap of evidence that he was capable of saving money and building up any capital. Mistakenly, she believed marriage to Jack meant that she would have a home of her own at last on a cattle property that he would provide. In old age, Daisy would show Ernestine Hill Jack's photograph and say with a rueful smile that their hasty courtship proved the truth of the old adage, 'Marry in haste, repent at leisure' — 'I never could run in double harness,' she added. She said that Jack had taken her out riding one morning then rushed her off to the Nowra church, having obtained a special licence without informing her, so that they could be married before he went away. She had no time to obtain a wedding dress and was married in her long-skirted riding habit, worn with a small bowler hat with a fly veil.

Their marriage certificate, dated 17 February 1885, records that Daisy O'Dwyer, spinster, daughter of James O'Dwyer, 'gentleman farmer of Ballychrine', had married Jack Bates, bachelor, of Pyree, in an Anglican ceremony at the Church School at nearby Nowra.[5] Once again Daisy gave her age as twenty-one, rather than twenty-five. Fearing discovery of her earlier marriage at Charters Towers, she gave her normal place of residence as Townsville. Perhaps she was convinced her marriage to Breaker Morant did not count in the eyes of God or the law: not only had it taken place in an

Anglican church but Eddie Murrant/Harry Morant had been under the legal age for marriage in Queensland.[6] Yet now Daisy in her role as a socially acceptable Anglican (the religion of the governing classes) again insisted on a Protestant ceremony. Although Jack himself was a lapsed Catholic, this upset her mother-in-law; from that point the relationship between Daisy and Catherine Bates deteriorated. Jack's droving contract meant that there was no time for a proper honeymoon, and he left for the north almost immediately.

❧ ❧ ❧

Three days after her marriage to Jack Bates, Daisy received a message sent by someone else from her chequered past. Ernest Baglehole, whose family in London had quickly banished Daisy once he had declared his love for her, was in Sydney and determined to see Daisy. He had made the passage to Australia as fourth mate aboard the merchant ship *Zealandia*, owned by the Shaw Savill & Albion line. The ship's home port was Glasgow.

Piecing together the few facts known about Ernest, who remains a shadowy figure (Daisy would later burn his letters, together with her diaries and wedding photographs), it seems that he had finally had enough of his wealthy, domineering father, who had forbidden him to marry Daisy and insisted he should marry the well-bred Scottish Protestant Jessie Rose instead. That marriage had taken place in 1881 at the Anglican church of Lewisham in London.[7] A Rose descendant claimed Ernest had subsequently refused to work either in his father's London shipping office or in his chemical and fertiliser factory on the Thames estuary.

Instead, in an impulsive bid to escape both his autocratic father and enforced marriage, Ernest joined the merchant navy. In those days ships took clerks on board to list cargoes and write pay slips for the crew. Ernest began his seagoing career ranked as an able seaman and was rapidly promoted to fourth mate. No doubt he hoped to obtain his master's ticket and eventually become a captain.

Left behind on the struggling farm at Pyree with Catherine Bates, the younger son Charlie and the little girls after Jack's departure, and carrying out her share of household chores as well as teaching the children, Daisy found to her dismay that she was working just as hard as she had before her marriage to Jack. Only now, as one of the family, she did it on an unpaid basis.

At this point she may have thought despairingly that all the privation she had endured on board the SS *Almora*, in order to reach Australia, had been in vain. She was right back to the situation she had known in her adolescence — as a household drudge living with relatives, washing, ironing and cleaning. Was there no way out? So far her experience of being a governess had let her down badly, but she was not trained to do anything else. She must have felt trapped.

Or did she? Ernest Baglehole's message more or less coincided with Jack's departure. This really seems like a plotline from one of the romantic novels Daisy enjoyed. And why had Ernest come to Australia? Confused thoughts must have rushed through Daisy's mind. Perhaps by now she had forgiven Ernest for marrying Jessie in order to please his father. Did she still feel that it was Ernest she should have married? Did he regret that he had not gone ahead and married her in defiance of his father? Had he now left Jessie? Daisy may have been thrilled by the notion of Ernest coming halfway round the world to find her. Impetuously, she decided to go to Sydney to see him.

Of course, Daisy could not tell her mother-in-law the truth, so she invented an excuse to get away from Pyree. Telling Catherine she needed to go to Sydney to buy household goods for the home she and Jack planned to set up together, Daisy escaped from Pyree for her reunion with the man who had let her down.

The question remains, how did Ernest Baglehole manage to trace Daisy's whereabouts in Australia? Presumably she received his message at Pyree, and since there was no telephone communication at that time, it probably arrived in the form of a letter. Daisy had kept up her correspondence with a few members of her family, including her sister Kathleen — who had been in London when Daisy was employed there as a governess — and it is quite possible that Daisy introduced Ernest to Kathleen at that time.

Kathleen meanwhile had suffered her own tragedy, with the

death of her husband Robert Brownrigg of consumption in April 1884 at Didsbury, Lancashire, leaving her with two tiny girls to raise. In an all too familiar coincidence he had died from the disease Daisy and Kathleen feared, the tuberculosis which had killed their mother, Bridget Dwyer.[8]

Perhaps Ernest Baglehole contacted sister Kate to find out how he could get a message to Daisy in Australia. But this is all speculation. Ernest may have begun to trace Daisy's whereabouts only after he arrived in Sydney.

One thing is certain: Daisy's flight to Sydney certainly took place and a single piece of direct evidence proves it: her certificate of marriage to Ernest Clark Baglehole, dated 10 June 1885 — not four months after she had married Jack Bates — her third wedding in two years, with no mention of filing for divorce.[9]

THE MYSTERY OF THE THIRD HUSBAND

Australian history is almost always picturesque . . . It does not read like history, but like the most beautiful lies; and all of a fresh new sort, no mouldy old stale ones. It is full of surprises, and adventures, the incongruities, and contradictions and incredibilities; but they are all true, they all happened.

MARK TWAIN, *FOLLOWING THE EQUATOR*, 1865

It is possible that Ernest planned the wedding ceremony simply so that Daisy would spend time with him while he was in Sydney, having signed off from the *Zealandia*. A 'honeymoon' in Sydney would mean that Daisy could enjoy restaurants of good hotels, indulge in shopping sprees and go to the theatre. Perhaps she visited the brand-new Art Gallery of New South Wales, which had opened earlier in the year. And doubtless she received a handsome wedding present from her new 'husband'. But what were Daisy's true feelings about becoming 'Mrs Baglehole' (as well as 'Mrs Bates')? Did she discover that she still loved Ernest? What were his true feelings towards her? We shall never know.

On their wedding certificate Ernest falsely claimed to be a bachelor, describing himself as a seaman, aged twenty-nine. But he was not a bachelor: he was still married to Jessie, just as Daisy was married to Jack. This strange, long-hidden bigamous marriage ceremony, only discovered in these days of computerised records, took place at St Stephen's Anglican church, Newtown.[1] Both parties gave their religion as Church of England. Ernest, who did have Irish relatives in his background, falsely claimed on this new wedding certificate that he was Irish. Perhaps he thought this might make Daisy keener to fall in with his 'marriage' plan.

There are grounds for claiming Daisy's marriage to Jack Bates had been legal rather than bigamous, since, according to Queensland law, Breaker Morant was under age when she married him. But this, Daisy's third marriage and Ernest's second, was definitely bigamous for both of them. Both bride and groom were economical with the truth on their marriage certificate. Ernest claimed he was born in Dublin, although his birth certificate reveals that he was born at Deptford, a dock area in south-west London, in the days before his father had made money. Like Daisy, he gave his Australian residence as Stanmore, a Sydney suburb, and stated (correctly) that his parents were William Baglehole, shipowner, and Sarah Wilkinson Baglehole. A check through the 1881 British census records reveals that Ernest's parents, then in their sixties, owned a large free-standing house at Lee Green, near Blackheath, where they employed a resident maid and a cook.[2] Jessie Rose lived in a house in Lewisham bequeathed to her by her late father, William Edward Rose, and this may have been the house where Ernest and she lived after their marriage.

For her third trip to the altar, Daisy lopped a few years off her age once more and claimed to be a spinster of twenty-one, born in Ireland — vague enough to make her hard to trace. She cited her late father as James E. O'Dwyer and left blank the spaces for her occupation and her mother's name. The witnesses to the marriage were Thomas and Julia Clarke, presumably no relation to Ernest Clark Baglehole, whose middle name was spelled without an 'e'.

Sydney Harbour, c. 1880s. It was in Sydney that Ernest Baglehole and Daisy met again, in 1885, barely four months after her marriage to Jack Bates.

To prevent anyone finding out the details of her third marriage, decades later Daisy carefully winnowed the personal papers she gifted to the National Library of Australia. They contain no love letters and do not mention Ernest Baglehole. But neither did she mention the name of her first husband, Breaker Morant. There are no letters between Daisy and Jack Bates or between her and her son.

What was the motivation for this latest, bizarre marriage ceremony? Did either Ernest or Daisy take it seriously? Did they believe that their former love had been rekindled? Or did the newly wed Mr and Mrs Baglehole simply enjoy sex together in a rented house while Jack Bates was away on his long droving trip?

Whatever the truth of the matter, the relationship didn't last.[3] Ernest left Sydney presumably by ship, though neither British, American nor European shipping records list him as a crew member.

Ernest never returned to England: his death remains as mysterious as his marriage. British 1891 census figures reveal that Jessie, describing herself as a widow, was living with a married brother and his wife. By now she had cast off the name Baglehole, no doubt angry at being deserted by Ernest, and reverted to her maiden name of Rose, the Rose family being a very honoured one in Nairnshire. Jessie had also no doubt infuriated her Methodist father-in-law, the now widowed William Baglehole, by converting from the Protestant to the Catholic faith.

Perhaps Jessie's conversion explains why, also in the year 1891, William Baglehole, having lost two sons — Ernest and his baby brother, William — made a new will and omitted any mention of a bequest to Ernest's widow in it. Intensive searches have failed to produce Ernest's death certificate. Of course, the movements of seamen often went unrecorded. He may have drowned at sea on some subsequent voyage or died of fever in a foreign port. Since crewmen were considered less important than passengers or officers, such information may never have been registered in Britain. Jessie must have had some proof Ernest was dead to have declared herself a widow in the 1891 census.[4]

What Daisy's matrimonial career shows is that in Australia it was relatively easy to commit bigamy, given the paucity of centralised marriage records. And what made it easier for Daisy to avoid detection was the lack of ready communication between Sydney and Pyree, as well as Jack's isolation in the outback.

※ ※ ※

Whatever the reason, Daisy eventually returned to Pyree, probably in time to meet up with Jack on his return from his six-months droving expedition. Jack would have stayed at the family home for only a relatively short time before going back to work and moving another mob of cattle across the outback.

In May 1886, Daisy was still (or again) in Pyree, when she told her mother-in-law that she was feeling tired and ill, but she did not reveal that she was expecting a baby. But by that time she was four months pregnant and must have suspected as much.

Catherine Bates sent Daisy to her local doctor, who confirmed that Daisy was indeed expecting a child. Daisy blurted out to the astonished doctor that she was horrified at the idea of being a mother, a sentiment shocking for a young wife in the reign of Queen Victoria.[5]

The big question is: who was the father? The baby boy was born on 26 August 1886, so was conceived around November 1885. Jack would have returned to Pyree from his six-months' droving expedition in August 1885, but it seems unlikely that he would have stayed home until November.

Catherine Bates was an intelligent woman. She would soon have guessed that Daisy had not gone to Sydney to shop, but possibly to meet someone. If Jack had not been home at the time of the conception of Daisy's child, Catherine would have known that her son could hardly have been the father of the unborn child.

In view of Jack's likely absence from home by November 1885, the other possibility is that Daisy had returned to Sydney by that time, or had stayed there for at least five months after she had married Ernest.

Whatever harsh feelings Catherine may have harboured against Daisy, she was after all her daughter-in-law. Catherine would not have wanted to harm her family's reputation and as a Catholic did not believe in divorce. Perhaps Catherine and her daughter-in-law arrived at a truce, whereby Daisy agreed to stay at Pyree and wait for Jack's return from his latest journey. Whatever happened, this bizarre situation must surely have been one of the worst Daisy was forced to confront in what was becoming an increasingly strange life.

❀ ❀ ❀

Jack had arranged to meet Daisy at Bathurst when one of his journeys brought him there. Bathurst, across the Blue Mountains, could be reached by coach from Sydney and by that time Daisy's pregnancy was near its term. Whether by design or by accident, Daisy gave birth to a son on 26 August 1886, in the hotel where she and Jack were staying. While Daisy was in a long and painful labour upstairs, Jack sat laughing and drinking in the bar below her bedroom with his mates.

Did Jack realise that he may not have been the father of Daisy's son? If Jack had been certain that the baby was his, following the custom of the times he may have wanted his dead father's name of 'Hugh' included among the baby's names. But it seems the naming of the child was left to Daisy. She named her baby son Arnold Hamilton Bates, in a twofold gesture of expiation and gratitude.

Arnold Colquhoun was the man who had become obsessed with Daisy, then taken his own life at Charters Towers while Frederick Hamilton, her former employer at Fanning Downs, had provided a matrimonial cottage for Daisy and Breaker Morant after their marriage.

Not surprisingly, the birth of a child did not draw Mr and Mrs Bates closer. The more time they spent together, in between Jack's droving trips, meeting at intervals at one small country town or another, the more they fought. Daisy detested sitting around waiting for Jack to return from his trips; she pined for a more exciting life. She did not return to the Bates farm at Pyree; instead, she and Arnold stayed with people who paid her to teach their children. So far as she and Jack were concerned, their sex life seemed to be over. Possibly she used her unfortunate experience of childbirth as an excuse to deny her husband his marital rights. Years later, she told Ernestine Hill how Jack understood that after her terrible experience of giving birth, she could not risk getting pregnant again. On the other hand, it may have been Jack who broke off their physical relationship. He did at least assume responsibility for Arnold by giving him the Bates name, and thereby upheld Daisy's reputation as well as that of his own family. He continued to lead the free and easy life of a drover, drinking and gambling away a large part of the money he earned. To Daisy's despair he seemed incapable of saving money to buy a 'selection' or block of land to run his own cattle and build a homestead. One thing was clear: he was not going to be another Jim Tyson, a drover turned wealthy cattle king.

Arnold grew into an active toddler, then reached the stage where Daisy taught him to read — but to her disappointment he showed no real interest in learning. Together they travelled by Cobb and Co coach to the homesteads of wealthy graziers, where Mrs Bates the genteel governess taught the children to read and write in return for free board and lodging for herself and Arnold.

In 1893, when Arnold was six, Daisy actually did visit Tasmania. A photograph taken at this time shows Arnold with long fair hair — it was the fashion for little boys to wear their hair long. Daisy claimed to have been invited to various Tasmanian homesteads: mother and son are recorded as staying with the MacKinnons of Dalness, when Daisy accompanied widowed Donald MacKinnon to Ben Nevis in search of the elusive Tasmanian tiger. She also stayed with the aristocratic Irish-born Talbots at Malahide. Daisy bubbled with energy and high spirits and men still found her attractive, but Arnold's cousin on his father's side, Charles Carney, remembered him as withdrawn and unforthcoming at this age.

Daisy arrived back in Sydney to find the banks in crisis and the economy crumbling following an extended property and land boom. The recession years of the 1890s had arrived. Naturally she was resentful that Jack had not bought a property earlier, as he had promised. Their relationship went from bad to worse. Arnold doubtless witnessed many rows — Daisy could be very fierce when she was angry.

ॐ ॐ ॐ

Some time in 1893–94, Daisy conceived the idea of returning to Ireland. She told Jack that her mother's youngest sister had died of consumption, and she needed to return to Ireland to see her family again. Sister Kate's husband had also died, so perhaps she was hoping for some money from her widowed sister. But Jack had no money to give her for such a trip. Daisy racked her brains to think how else she could return home.

Arnold Hamilton Bates, aged six

The Macquarie, *the three-masted barque on which Daisy sailed back to England*

Finally she managed to secure a free passage by approaching a shipping company and volunteering to act as a stewardess on a sailing ship returning to England via Cape Horn.[6]

Before her departure she found a place for Arnold in a Catholic boarding school at Campbelltown, and it was agreed he would spend school holidays with his grandmother at Pyree. Much later, Daisy told Ernestine Hill that she left Jack Bates and sailed home because he did not buy a cattle property where she could make a home and a future for her son. She felt cheated because throughout her marriage she'd had to live in other people's houses, just as she had done in her childhood after her father had deserted them. She complained that Jack was a drifter who poured down his throat the money he earned droving, instead of saving it as he'd promised.

The barquentine *Macquarie*, a wool clipper, set sail for London on 9 February 1894. Daisy, now in her mid-thirties, was still a very attractive, vivacious woman eager for new experiences. Once again she had escaped from an existence she felt unable to endure: in this instance a loveless marriage and sole parenthood of a very active boy who resisted her attempts to interest him in 'book learning', and who resembled Jack and seemed to care only for sport. Sadly, her relationship with her son was now fraught with conflict and would end in tears.

It must have been with relief she handed Arnold over to his grandmother at Pyree, from where she departed by coach for Sydney's Circular Quay. There she boarded the *Macquarie* bound for London and yet another life change.

CHAPTER 8

A VISIT TO IRELAND AND A TRAINING JOB
IN LONDON

'But you have a library and an office. I'll dust one and scrub out the other . . .'

DAISY BATES, SEEKING WORK WITH THE CELEBRATED NEWSPAPER
TYCOON WILLIAM THOMAS STEAD

It would be three months before the *Macquarie* reached England with her passengers. The voyage was often extremely rough and dangerous, and Mrs Bates as stewardess would have been kept busy by all those who took to their berths with seasickness. Luckily she herself was immune to it. Indomitable, she appeared unafraid when a particularly fierce storm seemed likely to sink the vessel and comforted other passengers. Wind howled through the rigging, huge cliffs of ice towered above them and giant icebergs floated past as they sailed around the dreaded Cape Horn, known as the sailors' graveyard. Many of the passengers were terrified, but Daisy gave the impression that she enjoyed the sensation of life-threatening danger.

Years later when queried as to why Daisy had no family photographs of her Irish childhood she would blame the voyage and explain how a huge wave swamped her cabin, washing her photographs onto the floor and ruining them. No doubt, this imaginary incident provided her with a convenient explanation for being unable to produce images of Ashberry House or of the Outram family and their home, or why, unlike most former debutantes she had no photograph of herself in court dress — a long white gown with a train and long white gloves.

The *Macquarie* docked at Tilbury in May 1894, in the midst of a hansom cab strike. Although Elizabeth Salter states in her biography of Daisy Bates that the passengers had to walk to their hotels in the centre of London from Tilbury, a distance of over forty kilometres, it's more likely that the shipping line provided horse-drawn omnibuses for the passengers and their luggage. Daisy elected to stay at the Arundel Hotel in the Strand, maintaining the illusion that this was where her father and grandfather used to stay when they were in London. (This, of course, was a pure flight of fancy.) Although Jack Bates had promised to send his wife money, none had arrived, which left Daisy desperately short of cash. In fact, she would discover their bank had crashed as a result of the severe recession of the 1890s in Australia, and she and Jack had lost their savings, small as they were. According to Salter, Daisy was able to obtain an overdraft to pay her way for a short while.

Presumably Daisy met up with her sister Kathleen while she was in London. With impeccable connections and respectability on her side, Kathleen stayed at the ladies' annexe of an elite military club when she visited London. Perhaps she invited Daisy to meet her there. The two sisters would have had a great deal to talk about, catching up with each other's lives and the events of the thirteen and a half years that had slipped by since Daisy left for Australia in late 1882. Kathleen's husband, Robert Brownrigg, had died from pulmonary consumption in 1884, leaving her with two small daughters to bring up — the second daughter was born posthumously. The pension of an army widow was not large and Violet (born 1884) and Adele Kathleen (born 1885), now schoolgirls, were doubtless supported by their wealthy Brownrigg grandparents, so it's unlikely Kate helped Daisy financially.

Four years later, in 1898, Kathleen would marry again. Her second husband, a widower named Graves Chapman Swan, was the son of the late Colonel Champney Swan, a wealthy landowner from the Channel Islands, from whom he had inherited Trinity Manor on the island of Jersey as well as other properties.[1] On her second marriage certificate, Kathleen would once more recite the fantasy invented all those years ago — that she was the daughter of James O'Dwyer Esquire, a member of the landed gentry of Tipperary.

Kathleen's second marriage was to be more advantageous than her first. Unlike Daisy, Kate succeeded in acting out the sisters' girlish fantasies of becoming rich and respected. After 1898, it would have been painful for Daisy to compare Kathleen's life to her own. Where Daisy was married to Jack Bates, a man she did not love or respect, who had failed to save enough money to provide a proper home for his wife and son, Kathleen had several homes and a rich second husband who presumably adored her. It's tempting to describe Daisy as the 'Ugly Duckling' floundering in the wake of her sister Mrs Chapman Swan of Trinity Manor. Strangely, Daisy never mentioned Kathleen's successful and genuine claims to upper-class gentility in *The Passing of the Aborigines*, in which she makes several false claims about the gentility of other relatives.

ॐ ॐ ॐ

While Daisy set out to enjoy herself in London, young Arnold, back in Australia, was unhappy at school and resented the fact that his mother had left him. His grandmother, Catherine Bates, considered Daisy a bad, selfish mother and possibly did not hesitate to say so. Daisy had originally said she intended to remain in Britain for a year. Instead, she would stay there for almost five years. As a result of her prolonged absence, Arnold's emotional development was damaged by lack of motherly care. He probably recalled Daisy principally as a governess-mother, vainly trying to impose strict discipline and to instil in him her own love of books and learning — and failing to hide her disappointment at his lacklustre progress.

As he grew up, he strongly rejected the intellectual interests and professional career she had planned for him and became a 'difficult' adolescent, preferring to follow a physically active life more like that of Jack Bates.

Daisy herself, of course, had experienced severe emotional deprivation as a child, including the death of both her parents and the spite of her stepmother, and she too had been a rebellious teenager. Later, in one of the articles collected together as 'My Natives and I', she would refer to herself as 'moody' and 'difficult'. Modern psychiatrists say that adults who have experienced such deprivation often repeat this cycle of 'quasi-abandonment' where their own children are concerned.

❧ ❧ ❧

Daisy finally left England to visit Ireland. It must have been with mixed feelings that she returned to Roscrea to meet the rest of her family. She was *not* coming back, as she had once hoped to do, with her head held high, the wife of some wealthy Australian grazier.

When she arrived in her home town she found that Main Street, where she spent her early years, was a thriving town centre, with busy shops and offices leading to the Market House and weighbridge and the handsome Italian-style fountain (later transferred to Rosemary Street).

Daisy's stepmother, Mary Dillon Dwyer, had died in 1884. Jim Dwyer, Daisy's younger brother, had then taken over the lease of Lot 17 Main Street, where he set up house with the youngest Dwyer sister, Anne. It was the quiet, patient Anne who had looked after her grandfather James Dwyer in his last years and to whom he left the lease of his house in his will, while Jim inherited an acre of land on the outskirts of Roscrea. This was the time when the new land laws were coming into effect, abolishing the previous system of very short leases for Catholic tenants and enabling them to own property. Soon Jim would acquire the freehold of Lot 17. He had followed the example of his uncle Joe Dwyer and was making good money as a cattle dealer. His grandfather James Dwyer would have realised that Daisy's eldest sister, Marian (by now Sister Maria Flavia of St Paul's Convent at Selly Park, Birmingham) did not need the bequest of a house.[2] As for Mrs Kathleen Chapman Swann, she certainly had no interest in her grandfather's small property.[3]

Daisy may have resented the fact that Anne inherited their grandfather's lease, together with his furniture and whatever money he had in the bank. She herself received only a few pieces of inexpensive jewellery and nothing at all from her mother's sister's estate.[4]

Daisy's eldest sister, Marian, now Sister Maria Flavia

It seems she went to stay with two of her many cousins, and also stayed for a while with her brother Jim in Main Street. She visited childhood haunts, including the Convent of the Sacred Heart and the old Norman castle towering above handsome Damer House. And she would surely have laid flowers on her mother's grave, and gone to Ballychrine to visit Granny Hunt's old cottage.

☙ ☙ ☙

Daisy had seen everything she wanted to see in and around Roscrea. Inheriting nothing, she was now short of money and decided to return to London, knowing that she had to find work. Ever since her encounter with Arnold Colquhoun and Thaddy O'Kane at Charters Towers, the craft of journalism had fascinated her. In London she moved into a cheap hostel for working girls while she tried to find a job on a newspaper or magazine. Without connections this was not easy at a time when there were very few women journalists.

There are differing accounts of how Daisy came to meet William Stead, the famous media baron, but it is likely that she enlisted Kathleen's help and that of her social network. Stead was a controversial figure who was well known as a campaigner for social justice — he had succeeded in securing the right of an accused person to give evidence at his own trial, and he was a crusader against child prostitution. Stead was also one of the pioneers of investigative journalism. As well as being a powerful newspaper and magazine tycoon he owned a flourishing book-publishing business, producing cheap editions of the classics along with a series of far more sensationalist publications. Stead was respected for his literary magazine *The Review of Reviews*, and was closely in touch with the leading literary figures of the day.[4a]

Stead was apparently charmed by Daisy when she came for an interview at his offices in Mowbray House, Norfolk Street. Later she described their first encounter.

> 'Mr Stead, I want work.'
>
> 'What kind?' he asked.
>
> 'Any kind. I once got ten shillings for one poem and fifteen for another in Australia.'
>
> 'We don't accept poems for *The Review*.'
>
> 'But you have a library and an office. I'll dust one and scrub out the other until I can learn enough to fit in somewhere. Try me, please ... I can pay my way until Thursday, no longer ...'[5]

This account may or may not be true, but Daisy was a born journalist and always loved a good story.

Daisy had Irish charm as well as good looks, but she lacked typing skills or journalistic experience. Nevertheless, Stead gave her a job dusting and shelving books in his offices on a tiny wage. He advised her that if she kept her eyes and ears open, she would learn a great deal about journalism.

She became friendly with Stead's son Willie, his fiancée Lottie Royce, and a Bohemian composer called James Gru, who befriended the homeless and showed Daisy the darker parts of London — alleyways and courts off Fleet Street and stretches of the Thames that she had read about in Charles Dickens's novels.

As always, once her interest was aroused Daisy proved a hard worker. Her keen intelligence meant she soon escaped from dusting and shelving books into more congenial work. She learned to type at nightschool and, to improve her speed, worked at the typewriter keyboard 'till her fingers were sore'.

Years later in Australia, when she gave talks at Perth's Karrakatta Club to women's organisations, Daisy would tell her audience that she had met literary luminaries such as Rudyard Kipling and George Bernard Shaw while employed by W.T. Stead.[6]

Believing the 'little Irish girl' showed potential as a journalist, Stead had her taught interviewing techniques and eventually gave her a minor editorial job on *Borderland*, a spiritualist journal he published. Spiritualism, mediums and séances were all the rage in England at this time. This was an ironic step for Daisy; unlike the lady editor of *Borderland*, Daisy was convinced that spiritualism was a gigantic confidence trick. However, she applied herself to her new post with her usual ability. She had an article published on the ghosts of Leap Castle in Tipperary, which pleased her.[7] In due course Stead would pass on his opinion that Daisy Bates had showed real talent to Louise Mack, a Sydney journalist who had also escaped to London from an unsatisfactory marriage in Australia.[8]

'I was the odd man out, the prim little blue-serged, sailor-hatted maid of all work,' Daisy wrote demurely about her time at Stead's office.[9]

This description of herself was far from accurate. On the contrary, it seems that in this last decade of the nineteenth century, the years of the *belle époque* when so many men — both bachelors and husbands — kept mistresses, Daisy became something of a *femme fatale*, finding wealthy escorts who showed her all the delights London had to offer. She told everyone she was a widow — a very merry widow, it would appear. She seems to have acquired a number of admirers and a lover or two to provide expensive presents.

Professor Bob Reece, in his book on Daisy, states that in London she managed to live cheaply at St Gabriel's Hostel for Young Ladies in fashionable Mayfair, where young women's accommodation was subsidised by the philanthropic Countess of Meath. Fellow boarders included Hester Layley, niece of a peer and cousin of the now deceased Philip Gipps.[10] It is possible Daisy's entry to this privileged world came through her sister Kate. St Gabriel's gave Daisy a chance to observe the dress and manners of the landed gentry more closely and made her assertions she came from the upper classes more credible.

Both Elizabeth Salter and Julia Blackburn, biographers of Daisy Bates, refer to Daisy's curious story of 'Lady Mary' (Lady Rose Lindsay, from a distinguished Scottish family), who was listed as another member of W.T. Stead's office staff. Ernestine Hill repeated Daisy's description of how she befriended this 'elegant, aristocratic and frail young creature', desperately short of money — only to discover that Rose was working as a high-class callgirl. Having tried in vain to 'rescue' the girl, Daisy claimed that she ended the friendship.[11]

Julia Blackburn writes of Lady Mary that she 'would accompany wealthy men to hotels or their grand country houses . . . and receive whatever gifts they decided to give her'.[12] Blackburn speculates that perhaps this is the closest Daisy ever came to describing the sort of life she herself lived at this time, to enable her to survive.

Daisy, always a great hater, disliked Miss Freece, editor of *Borderland*, and eventually handed in her notice. She claimed then to have worked as a librarian for Jarrolds publishers in Norfolk. Elizabeth Salter examined their staff records and found no mention of a Daisy Bates, Dwyer or Murrant.[13] Perhaps she worked as Baglehole, or perhaps she had some other means of support.

Could Daisy, who had been paid only a modest wage by Stead, and now was most probably unemployed, have been some kind of high-class callgirl at weekend house parties, a member of the *demi-monde*? Daisy certainly described attending what sounded like *louche* upper-class country house weekend parties given by a man she named as her cousin, John Turner-Turner. (This name seems to have been a figment of her imagination, designed to sound aristocratic.) Elizabeth Salter wrote that John Turner-Turner owned Avon Castle, but there is no documentary proof of this. She talked grandly of fox hunting and of spending the evenings dancing, card playing and acting as a social hostess at weekend parties attended by wealthy men who were members of the snobbish Hurlingham Club and others whom she described as the *crème de la crème* of London society.[14]

She who was normally teetotal now developed a taste for French champagne. Years later she told Anthony Bolam, station master at Ooldea in South Australia, it was the best cure for a stomach upset, if sipped slowly.

Bed-hopping house parties with obliging married women, widows or actresses were a feature of English upper-class life at this time, with Edward, Prince of Wales (later Edward VII) as the chief 'bed-hopper'. Daisy wrote about a Richard Attwater, allegedly the owner of 'Ratfin Hall' — although no references to such a place have come to light — and he may have been, albeit briefly, Daisy's lover. According to Daisy, she met 'Attwater of Ratfin' at one of these dubious weekend country house parties, but this side of her life remains mysterious in her memoirs. She did say that Attwater's house was so beautiful and that he lived in such luxury, surrounded by servants, she could willingly have married him to become the mistress of Ratfin Hall.[15] But marriage with Richard Attwater never eventuated. Attwater was no doubt a pseudonym masking the name of a well-known married man who amused himself with Daisy.

The bachelor who undoubtedly *was* her lover and whom Elizabeth Salter described as may well have wanted to marry her was an Irishman as long on charm and as short of cash as Daisy. His name was Carrick O'Bryen Hoare. Little is known about him except that it seems he and Daisy had much in common: they both enjoyed riding, reading poetry and dancing. But Daisy was wary and did not take seriously her Irish lover's protestations of undying love. She may well have recalled her mistake in taking Breaker Morant at his word. 'I liked to fall in love and part,' she would tell Professor Grant Vere Porteous years later.[16]

༄ ༄ ༄

Parting was on Daisy's mind. She wanted to return to Australia, and for this she needed a large sum of money. Perhaps Daisy hoped that Kathleen, after marrying a very rich second husband twenty years older than she was, might help her financially, and possibly Kathleen did take pity on her and provide something. Daisy had accepted that she would not be receiving a legacy from her grandfather. What was she to do?

My own theory is that in 1899 Daisy decided to confront widowed William Baglehole, Ernest's father, whom she believed to be very wealthy. His situation had changed, however. Though still far from destitute, he had lost a large amount of his capital through unwise investments. Now retired from business, he was living in a house on Old Poole Road, an affluent area of the seaside resort of Bournemouth. Daisy may have discovered his address and set off to see him. Elizabeth Salter mentions a visit by Daisy to Bournemouth in 1889 to 'stay with a cousin', and Daisy's correspondence refers to trips to Bournemouth with her niece to meet Lady Jane Barlee, widow of a former Colonial Secretary of Western Australia.[17]

There was an important reason for taking such action. Daisy had recently received a letter from Jack Bates, in Western Australia, in which he said that he wanted a reconciliation and hoped to set up a secure home life with Daisy and Arnold. At long last he was actively looking for a cattle property to buy or lease in order to make a home for the three of them. But although Jack had saved some money he still needed more capital, which he hoped Daisy would be able to supply.

Jack had gone to Western Australia in response to the growing prosperity of that region (thanks to its gold rush) and its demand for more cattle. He had earned himself a reputation as a tough but well-respected drover, willing to risk the rough seas of the Bight accompanying cargoes of cattle from the east. He had also helped one of the richest cattlemen in the west, Sam Mackay of Roy Hill Station near Ethel Creek, to prevent the spread of dreaded pleuropneumonia among his beasts. The grateful Mackay had then offered to help Jack get established in the Ethel Creek district, and told him about 180,000 leasehold acres (450 hectares) of good pasture that were available there. Ethel Creek is not far from Mount Newman, a thousand or more kilometres north of Perth as the crow flies, in what is regarded as the fringe of the Pilbara region of Western Australia, now famous for its iron-ore deposits but then scarcely known.

Jack's letter must have changed everything for Daisy. Would she finally achieve her dream of a home for her son, herself and her husband? Was it possible that she and Jack could finally become the owners of a cattle station? This was the lure that led so many Irish emigrants to Australia — families such as the Duracks, who came from Galway to New South Wales in 1849, after the Great Famine, and whose epic trek across Australia to the Kimberley was described by their descendant Mary Durack in her book *Kings in Grass Castles*. Daisy must have envisaged Jack and herself as king and queen of a vast cattle empire which would one day be inherited by her son.

Since I'm putting forward a theory about an approach to William Baglehole, perhaps I can speculate further.

The socially ambitious Daisy was desperate for money to establish herself as a member of the landed classes and of Perth's Government House set, and to buy grazing leases and cattle. She may well have felt that securing money for land and Arnold's school fees justified her actions. And she may have still felt some resentment that she had been rejected by the family in favour of Jessie Rose.

Daisy's interview with Baglehole would have been carefully planned. She would have revealed that Ernest had entered into a bigamous marriage with her in Sydney — perhaps holding her marriage certificate to prove it — and that she had fallen pregnant, whereupon he deserted her. She might well have made out that Jack Bates had then nobly stepped in and married her to save her reputation.

But the most important part of her news would have concerned the birth of Arnold, William Baglehole's only grandson. Daisy would have been able to show him the appealing photograph of Arnold as an adorable little boy with long fair curls.

With a little research, Daisy would have realised that the people dearest to William Baglehole had died: his wife, Sarah; Ernest; his baby son, William; and his eldest and favourite daughter Maude, who had married the Rev Edward Dorling of Salisbury, who would eventually inherit Baglehole's money. (William's second daughter, Florence, had upset her father by defying his wishes and performing in public as a concert pianist. As a result, he had cut her out of his will.)[18]

Shocked as the elderly Baglehole would have been by Daisy's revelations, it is plausible that the news of his Australian grandson filled a gap in his lonely life. In showing Baglehole her son's photograph and perhaps relating some creditable stories about him, Daisy may have given the retired man new hope for the future.

She may have gone on to explain that Jack Bates had subsequently lost his money in the Australian bank failure, which made it impossible for him to continue to provide for both her and her son, and that she urgently needed money to ensure that the old gentleman's grandson received a suitable upbringing.

Daisy was ruthless when she wanted something badly. Did she also subtly imply that if she did not obtain a certain amount of money, she would apprise Jessie, Ernest's widow, of his bigamous marriage and the fact that his son was alive and well in Australia? Jessie would surely have been devastated to know that her husband had committed bigamy and that Daisy had had a healthy son by Ernest. If this story got out, it could prove very embarrassing to the reputation of the respectable Baglehole family. If Daisy's reunion with Ernest Baglehole had sounded like a plotline from a romantic novel, the possibility of her subsequent interview with his father seems to hold almost Dickensian overtones.

Daisy had married Ernest (admittedly committing bigamy herself) and in return he had deceived Jessie and deserted Daisy when she was expecting his child. She would have thought it only just that William Baglehole should provide money as compensation for the way his son had treated her. Economical with the truth as always, she would not have admitted to Ernest's father her own deception of Jack Bates while he was on the droving track.

Whatever transpired during that interview with William Baglehole at Bournemouth, assuming it took place, one thing is certain. A short while later, Daisy arrived back in Australia with what she called her 'mystery money'. It was a sizeable amount, enough to buy the lease of a large area of grazing land in the vicinity of Mount Newman along the remote upper reaches of the Fortescue River, as well as several hundred head of cattle and a block of land in Fremantle. She never did reveal its source.

Jack Bates in mid-life, on horseback

TO THE NORTHWEST AND ON TO BEAGLE BAY

*Sunsets blaze and fade . . . in these great empty wilds and dawn
sets her diadem over them . . . But all these places that once
echoed with song or war-cry are now left to birds and animals
whose forebears witnessed the arrival of humans and who are
now witnessing their passing.*

DAISY BATES, *THE PASSING OF THE ABORIGINES*

After several years abroad and enriched by a considerable
amount of money, Daisy returned to Australia on board the SS
Stuttgart, bound for Perth, for her reunion with a man with whom
she had little in common and from whom she had sought to escape
a life of boredom.[1] It was a demonstration of the triumph of hope
over experience.

On the *Stuttgart* Daisy met someone else who was to influence
the future direction of her life. In fact, this meeting with a man
fascinated by Aboriginal culture was to prove a watershed between
all her previous experiences and the very different way of life she
would soon embrace. Father Martelli was an elderly Catholic priest,

dean to Bishop Matthew Gibney of Perth, and he gave Mrs Bates Italian lessons during the voyage. Daisy had probably delighted him with her flair for languages and rapid progress. She learned that Father Martelli had come to Australia from Italy when he was young, and had worked with Bishop Gibney in an ongoing campaign to help Aboriginal people. Bishop Gibney himself, who was born in Ireland, was renowned as the humane priest who gave the last sacrament to Ned Kelly.

Father Martelli outlined for Daisy the history of white settlement in Western Australia, which began, tentatively, in 1826. At first, he told her, the Europeans and the Indigenous population appeared to be on good terms. Many of the Aborigines believed that the dead became white-skinned when they reached *konnarup*, the place of afterlife, and at first thought the white strangers were the spirits of their ancestors. But soon their hunting grounds were fenced in by the new arrivals and the native people were treated as trespassers in their own country. A few settlers were killed and a punitive expedition was sent against the black people. By this time some of the settlers had begun to regard the Aborigines as dangerous wild creatures, to be hunted down and shot; to other settlers they represented free labour to be exploited. The Aborigines, for their part, could not understand the ways of the white man.

Since those early days, Martelli told Daisy, laws had been passed to protect the Aborigines. But as the powerful European settlement grew, the native tribes had declined — and continued to do so. They died from the white man's diseases and failed to respond to medical treatment. A fatal despair seemed to have overtaken them. Martelli quoted the words of Sir John Forrest, Premier of Western Australia: 'With grief I admit the native race is disappearing.'

Before Daisy left England, a number of letters alleging ill treatment of Aboriginal people by white settlers had been published in *The Times*. Never shy about coming forward and proud of her new-found journalistic skills, Daisy had written to the editor of *The Times* and offered her services to investigate 'the Aboriginal question', as it was called, after she reached Australia. *The Times* editor was cautious and merely agreed to publish a letter to the editor if she sent one — which eventually she did. To begin with, this had been mainly an opportunistic gesture on her part.

During the years she had spent in Queensland and later in New South Wales, Daisy had never evinced much curiosity or compassion concerning Aboriginal people. Only when she first visited Tasmania did she allude indignantly to the infamous clearance of Aborigines from that island.

Now, Father Martelli had aroused Daisy's curiosity. She began to feel a genuine interest in the original inhabitants of Australia, the oldest known race on earth. To study and write about their culture seemed tremendously worthwhile.

By the time the *Stuttgart* neared Perth, Daisy Bates had intense sympathy for the 'dying race' of full-blooded Aborigines (whose number was falling at an appalling rate through disease and alcoholism). She asked Father Martelli whether anything was being done to record the language, customs, beliefs and legends of the remaining Aboriginal tribes. He told her that the abbot of the Catholic Mission at Beagle Bay, just north of Broome, was compiling a dictionary of tribal language there. He went on to describe the Beagle Bay Mission, which was run by Trappist monks and offered help and protection to the local Aborigines in the reserve established there. Martelli said he planned to visit the mission with Bishop Gibney. Recognising Mrs Bates's real interest in Indigenous people, he tentatively suggested that it might be possible for her to join this expedition. Daisy was intrigued and excited by this idea but put it at the back of her mind as the *Stuttgart* reached its landfall. At this moment, there were more immediate things that concerned her.

ॐ ॐ ॐ

At Perth, one can imagine Daisy, described by Elizabeth Salter as looking several years younger than her age (she was now forty), bubbling over with energy and ideas, peering over the ship's rail and scanning the waiting crowd to see Jack and Arnold. Memory can play strange tricks. Perhaps she remembered Jack Bates as the tall handsome drover who had won her heart at the rough-riding show all those years ago.

The reunion disappointed them both.

After years of living on campfire meals, working in the Australian sun and drinking in bars that stocked cheap alcohol, Jack was no longer the handsome 'wild colonial boy' who had swept Daisy off her feet at a bush dance long ago. Unlike her, he had aged badly. He was overweight, with a beer gut, and going bald. And standing beside him — could that unkempt boy in his shabby clothes really be Arnold, her thirteen-year-old son?

In contrast to Jack, Daisy had always looked after her figure, eating sparingly, avoiding alcohol and engaging in regular callisthenic exercise with the dumb-bells she kept in her shipping trunk. She came down the gangplank wearing an elegant costume and hat, designed in the latest London style.

It wasn't only the outward appearance of her husband and son that dismayed Daisy. She soon found that Arnold resembled Jack in every way: he had no interest in reading, had lamentable table manners and lacked other social graces, including conversational skills. Horrified by his lack of education and manners, she enlisted the help of Father Martelli to enrol him in a Catholic school in Perth run by the Christian Brothers. It was agreed that Daisy would pay half Arnold's fees from the mysterious sum of money she had brought back from London. Jack promised to pay the rest. Daisy also arranged for Arnold to board with a Catholic family in Perth. Jack planned a long outback trip to the north for Daisy and himself. There they intended to settle their purchase of the leasehold land on offer at Ethel Creek.

Meanwhile, Daisy soon established connections with Perth society. She enjoyed consorting with the governor and his wife and the upper-crust women she met through the city's exclusive Karakatta Club for ladies. Her Irish charm ensured that she made friends easily. Never at a loss for words, she was an amusing dinner guest and soon became a social success. She falsely claimed she had worked for Stead's leading journal, *The Review of Reviews*, rather than the spiritualist magazine *Borderland*, which she had once described dismissively as 'that spooky little quarterly'. Daisy also gained prestige by claiming that she had been appointed a freelance correspondent for *The Times*, London, which was untrue. All she was to do was write a letter to the editor describing the treatment of Aborigines in Western Australia.

She was distressed that at dinner parties with people who were well read and discussed interesting ideas, her husband either sat silent or said things that made him appear boorish. In contrast, Daisy, fresh from London and dressed in elegant clothes, talked wittily about famous authors such as H.G. Wells and George Bernard Shaw or the empire builder Cecil Rhodes and the other luminaries she claimed to have met at Stead's Christmas parties at his Westminster home and may well have done so.

Daisy found an instant rapport with the Resident Magistrate of Fremantle, Robert Fairbairn, and his family. Fairbairn, who was very interested in the welfare of the Aborigines, invited Daisy to visit the Rottnest Island jail for native people. She also met the Premier, Sir John Forrest, formerly an intrepid explorer, who had made public his concern for the rapidly declining numbers of Aborigines in Western Australia. He urged Mrs Bates to make a study of them while this was possible.

At the Karakatta Club she became acquainted with the formidable Dr Roberta Jull, who had qualified in medicine in Glasgow then emigrated to Western Australia, and who was the first woman doctor to set up her shingle in Perth. Roberta Jull, married to a Perth public servant, was to become involved in research on Aboriginal women and the age at which they started to menstruate. Later, during her Aboriginal linguistic research, Daisy would help Dr Jull by asking Aboriginal women questions about this topic. Dr Jull was a friend of fellow women's rights campaigners Edith Cowan and Bessie Rischbieth and over the course of her career initiated many reforms concerning the education, welfare and health of both white Australian and Aboriginal children. Daisy's important research paper titled 'Marriage laws, customs etc. of Aborigines in relation to women' would eventually be read by Dr Jull to a medical congress in Glasgow.[2]

As an orphan herself, Daisy had a soft spot for assisting schemes to help orphans receive an education.[3] Receipts among the Daisy Bates papers show donations to the Fairbridge Society's Farm School for orphans set up by her humanist friends Mr and Mrs Kingsley Fairbridge. Daisy donated money and practical help to the Fairbridge Emigration Society, which brought children who had been told they were orphaned out to Australia from Britain. In Perth Daisy also helped clean the houses in which the children would be living. This shows that she could be extremely warm-hearted to those in need. Like the other volunteers, she believed that orphans, who were living under miserable conditions in Britain, would be given the chance of a new and better life in Australia and wanted to help them.

Some of these children did have their lives changed by the 'vision splendid' of Fairbridge Farm Schools, which provided a haven for orphans from Britain's overcrowded industrial cities. Others were not so lucky. One celebrated example of a Fairbridge boy made good was twelve-year-old orphan John Ernest (Julian) Hay, who would stay at the Pinjarrra Farm School, eighty-six miles (137 kilometres) south of Perth. Julian Hay would become a schoolteacher and headmaster and later the father of John Hay, former Vice-Chancellor of the University of Queensland.[4]

Unfortunately, in later years many abuses would occur at Fairbridge homes and schools, but of course Daisy could hardly have foretold this.[5]

ॐ ॐ ॐ

Jack wanted to set off for their trip to the northwest without delay. He knew that the cyclonic monsoon season would soon arrive and was anxious to avoid as much of it as possible. He waited impatiently in Perth to please Daisy, who had gained an invitation to a reception at Government House, which Jack attended with reluctance. Then while the city celebrated the start of the new century, he at last set off by himself. Daisy, who had enjoyed all the festivities, waited until Arnold was settled in his new school and boarding with the family of a school friend, then left early in March

1900 to join Jack. She boarded a coastal steamer, the *Sultan*, bound for the pearling port of Cossack, where she and Jack had agreed to meet.

They then embarked on a rigorous journey by horse-drawn buggy to the town of Roebourne. From there they would travel in the same fashion to Port Hedland, spending rest periods at pastoral stations they passed along the way. By now the monsoon season had well and truly arrived. Ruined houses, their interiors open to view, were surrounded by sheets of corrugated-iron roofing. Electrical storms, with jagged lightning that could set the bush alight or strike trees where they sought shelter, were a recurrent hazard. There were no made roads, only rough dirt tracks.

During this hazardous marathon journey, undaunted by the warnings she received of snakes, giant centipedes and mosquitoes, Daisy revelled in a new-found sense of freedom. She had changed out of her fashionable city clothes, and wore a bushman's straw hat with fly veil, an ankle-length leather-bound skirt, white high-necked shirt and tie, kid gloves and high button boots — adjusting to the outback in a new persona.

One of the cattle stations they stayed at on the Sherlock River near Roebourne belonged to a family called Meares, relatives of Daisy's friends the Withnells. There they endured a fierce tropical storm, and the threat of monsoonal flooding meant that the family had to decamp to high ground. From the hilltop Daisy watched the floods destroy the Meares's homestead and sweep away the furniture and even some of the livestock. Mrs Meares's youngest child, not yet a year old, developed pneumonia and died a few days later. Daisy provided what comfort she could.[6]

Throughout their long journey Daisy observed as much as she could about the Aboriginal groups they encountered, recording their ways of treating sickness, hunting methods and the artefacts they made. She made a point of talking to Aboriginal women on the stations where she and Jack stayed. Daisy also made notes about how the various station owners treated their Aboriginal workers, observing how on the Withnells' and Meares' stations 'the black servants are treated as part of the family'. Daisy supported the system of providing rations to families, believing that it ensured that the Aboriginal children (always her prime concern) would not go hungry in times of drought.[6a]

Mrs Bates was stoic about the trials and tribulations of travelling through rough country in searing heat and dust.[7] The fact that Jack's name is absent from her account indicates the reunion of such disparate characters was proving a trial — no doubt to both of them. Above all, she marvelled at the countryside she travelled through, the deep red cliffs seamed with blue asbestos towering above the grasslands, and spectacular gorges where Aboriginal rock art abounded: 'On smooth faced rock, in every gully, animals, birds, fish and man have been chipped for countless ages', she wrote in what was undoubtedly the hottest part of Australia, where at Jack's insistence she had invested much of her mystery money in three large grazing leases.

At last they reached journey's end and she looked across the huge tract of grazing land called Ethel Creek, on the banks of the Fortescue River to the south of the Pilbara. Besides raising their own beasts, it would be an ideal run on which to fatten beef cattle brought from further north — a halfway station en route to the booming cattle markets of Perth. As she gazed across those far-flung acres, Daisy must have been tremendously excited to think that, at long last, her dream of joint ownership of a large cattle station was coming true.

What should she and Jack call their property? She thought back to her happiest time in Ireland as a child, living with Granny Hunt at Ballychrine, and decided on the name Glen Carrick. She might have thought wistfully of 'the green, green hills of Carrick' but in reality, there could scarcely have been a greater contrast between the emerald green of Ireland and the sunburnt grasslands beside the Fortescue River in the middle of nowhere.

Then it was time for Daisy to leave. Jack stayed at Ethel Creek to finalise his arrangements with the cattleman Sam Mackay, plan their cattle run and (as Daisy thought) the homestead they would build. She agreed to give Jack a further 1200 pounds towards the land. Daisy and Jack took weeks to drive the buggy on the hot, dusty journey to Port Hedland, where she rejoined the *Sultan* to return to Perth. The trip had lasted six months and Daisy realised how little she and Jack had in common.

❧ ❧ ❧

Back in the city, she visited Bishop Gibney and learned that he and Father Martelli were planning to leave for Beagle Bay in August to help Father Nicholas and the other three Trappist monks at the mission there to improve their land. The bishop had been warned that if this upgrading was not carried out to the satisfaction of a government inspector, they would lose the lease of the mission and the property would revert to the government. Help was needed right away.

Daisy always enjoyed a challenge and it was agreed that she would join them and the team of carpenters and other tradesmen who had volunteered assistance. They would travel to Beagle Bay via Broome, where the expedition planned to stay for a few weeks.

❧ ❧ ❧

Broome proved to be a melting pot of races, where the population included Chinese, Filipinos, Indonesians, Japanese, Malays and Pacific Islanders as well as Aborigines and Europeans. It was also the pearling capital of the north, where the average working life expectancy of an Aboriginal or Malay diver, male or female, was about two years. The master pearlers were mainly unscrupulous men who grew rich on the labour of those powerless to protest over their treatment. New recruits were often natives kidnapped by 'blackbirders' (as unscrupulous sea captains were called), and sold off to the pearlers to replace divers who had died from 'the bends' as a result of being brought up to the surface too quickly. The Broome pearling industry, with its fine pearls known as 'tears of the moon' for their beauty, took a terrible toll on human life.

Daisy was horrified that, during the off-season when the pearling boats were laid up, local Aboriginal women were traded for alcohol. She wrote: 'Practically every man who had a woman took her down to trade her with the Asiatics. These women returned dying and diseased [syphilitic] after the boats had resumed pearling.'[8]

In Broome Daisy was able to make further observations about the treatment of Aboriginal women who were kidnapped and forced into prostitution by the sea captains or bought as 'temporary wives' by Filipinos working in the pearling industry. She discovered that these women, each supposedly married to one man, were used as sexual conveniences by a group of fishermen or pearl divers and could not escape.

Eventually Daisy would succeed in getting such 'marriages' banned after she enlisted the help of Bishop Gibney, who reported this practice to the West Australian government. Daisy now took up the struggle for helpless girls and women who were sexually abused. The bishop confided how he had gone with a priest to visit a house in the Filipino quarter of Broome and found one Aboriginal woman, wife to a Manila man, in a bedroom with five of his brothers waiting outside the bedroom door to take turns having sex with her. Daisy wrote:'Having seen for himself the abuses of the system, Bishop Gibney when he returned to Perth issued orders that the clergy were to stop marrying Aboriginal women to Manila men.'[9]

From Broome a pearling lugger, the *Sree-Pas-Sair*, once the property of the 'White Rajah' of Sarawak, took the expedition members northwards on a three-day passage to Beagle Bay, where they unloaded their stores onto the beach. Nearby was the cemetery, where a row of wooden crosses commemorated French monks who had died far from their own land.

Daisy worked hard at Beagle Bay, from a genuine wish to help the mission and the local Aboriginal people, and to further her knowledge about their customs and language. She offered help to women from groups as varied as the Nyool-Nyool, the Lombadina, the Koolarbolo and Koalgurdi. Many were suffering from malnutrition, as well as from diseases that included leprosy, yaws and syphilis given them by Europeans. She took food to the sufferers lying in tiny wooden huts, too ill to leave their beds.

A pearl-fishing boat like those that visited Beagle Bay

At night she heard the monks chanting the 'Ora pro nobis' and their 'Kyrie eleison', mingled with the sounds of Aboriginal clicking sticks or boomerangs beaten together. The wailing of a corroboree and the stamp of bare feet on the earth came faintly to her as she fell asleep exhausted by the day's work.

Daisy managed to motivate a group of younger Aboriginal women to help her establish a market garden, digging the rock-hard baked earth and planting cabbages, lettuce and other vegetables, keen to improve their diet. They also helped in the kitchen and bakery, and milked the goats. She noted 'their child-like eagerness to please, their lack of acquisitiveness or ambition, delight in music and dancing . . . their happy natures underlying their grievances'. Daisy managed to turn hard work into a game. And so the Aboriginal women gradually grew fond of her.

She was grieved to discover that the practice of hiring out Aboriginal wives which she had observed at Broome was being repeated at Beagle Bay. She wrote:

> Some boats [had] laid up at Beagle Bay . . . and to keep
> the women and girls away from [the crew], the Bishop

told Father Nicholas to lock them in the store for the
night [for their own protection]. There was only one
small opening high up in the wall, fifteen or twenty feet
above ground and no ladder. Even so, at daybreak when
we went to the store there was not a woman there. They
had piled up the store cases and climbed through the
little window, dropping without hurt on the soft sand.
The Bishop hurried down to the seashore to reclaim the
girls, and ordered the coloured men away.[10]

She described how four of the Manila men (native Filipinos)
who worked at the mission were married to Aboriginal
women, and Daisy soon learned that their husbands made money
by hiring out their wives for the night sometimes to as many as
five or six men. Daisy grieved anew for those who were so
abused.

Meanwhile, the aid team led by the charismatic Bishop Gibney
gathered 'the natives' to help repair buildings, to dig and fence off
wells, and to muster, brand and yard the wild cattle.

Father Nicholas Erno was one of four remaining Trappist monks
who'd journeyed to Western Australia from the monastery in the
small French village of Soligny-la-Trappe. Initially the Trappists
had been displeased that a lady was included in the working party
helping to restore the mission. But Daisy's willingness and her
amazing capacity for hard work won them over.

Out of gratitude for her months of back-breaking work, Father
Nicholas showed Daisy his own special recipe for salve, which he
made to soothe the ulcerated sores arising from yaws and syphilis
and which she was then able to use for her treatment of the abused
women. Father Nicholas was fascinated by Aboriginal lore. He told
Daisy that the best way to gain information from Aborigines was
to ask questions when tending the sick and elderly, who out of
gratitude were more likely to respond truthfully.

As a result of Daisy's visit to Beagle Bay, that shrewd Irish
Catholic Bishop Gibney became one of Mrs Bates's keenest
supporters in her future work with Aboriginal people, but had no

idea Daisy had been baptised a Catholic. When he himself contracted a tropical fever and seemed about to die, it was Daisy who nursed him back to health.

By March 1901 Daisy, Bishop Gibney and Father Martelli were back in Perth. The bishop was so appreciative of her help that he gave Daisy a gold watch inscribed with a grateful message. His letter of thanks to Daisy contained the haunting words: 'I saw with my own eyes how devoted you were [to Aboriginal women] and how attached they became to you.'[11]

Daisy about to be presented to royalty at Perth's Government House in July 1901

CHAPTER 10

AT GOVERNMENT HOUSE AND
OFF THE BEATEN TRACK

There are a few fortunate races that have been endowed with
cheerfulness as the main characteristic, the Australian Aborigine
and the Irish being among them.

DAISY BATES, NOTEBOOKS, NATIONAL LIBRARY OF AUSTRALIA

Daisy's return to Perth came at a time of feverish excitement over the July visit of His Royal Highness Duke and Duchess of York (the future King George V and Queen Mary) for the celebration of Australian Federation. Her sojourn at Beagle Bay had made her something of a celebrity, and she received an invitation to a garden party to be held at Government House on 24 July 1901. Daisy had a linen tea gown with a silky fichu around the neck and silk organza sleeves specially made for the occasion. With her hair swept up on her head, in a photograph taken before the big day she looks slim and elegant.

As 'a member of the Protestant Anglo-Irish ascendancy' rather than the bootmaker's daughter and former charity child, Daisy was presented to the royal couple by Lady Lawley, the governor's wife.

The day was overcast and Daisy took an umbrella–cum-parasol with her. After the presentation, when the assembled throng was taking afternoon tea in the garden, Daisy dropped the umbrella, which rolled away from her and finished at the feet of the young Duke of York. With a smile and a kind word he picked it up and handed it back. Daisy was overcome by this royal gesture. For the rest of her life she took the umbrella with her wherever she went, regarding it as a talisman.

❦ ❦ ❦

Daisy's article titled 'From Port Hedland to Carnarvon by Buggy', which covered her observations of the Indigenous people she had encountered, aroused interest among scientists at a time when women rarely published in scientific or academic journals. She also sold 'popular' articles about Beagle Bay Mission and its work with the Aboriginal people to English papers and to *The Australasian*. Then, at the end of 1901, just as Daisy was beginning to make a name for her research, Jack was asked by wealthy Edwin Streeter to manage his West Australian cattle station, Roebuck Plains, some thirty kilometres from Broome. Streeter, a prominent London jeweller who had substantial pearling interests in Broome and in South-East Asia, had now diversified into cattle in country where, as Daisy wrote, 'brolgas danced and kangaroos roamed'.

One consolation for leaving Perth, her Aboriginal investigations and the pleasant social life of the city was that Streeter's company paid for a Japanese cook and other domestic staff at Roebuck Plains homestead, so she was free to study books about the Aboriginal people to her heart's content, as well as exploring the outlying countryside to observe them at first hand.

By now the Bates marriage was at a very low ebb indeed, a union in name only, lacking both a sexual relationship and true companionship. Daisy and Jack spent as little time together as possible. About to turn sixteen, Arnold infuriated his mother by insisting on leaving school that year and came to work for a while at Roebuck Plains. Whenever Daisy and Jack had rows, Arnold would side with Jack.

One incident in the past should have warned Daisy that Jack would have no sympathy for her plan to study the Aboriginal groups of Western Australia and write a treatise on them. During their brief courtship at Pyree they had been caught in a storm while they were out riding, and took shelter under a tree. A sudden flash of lightning illuminated everything and high above them in the tree they saw the silhouette of a mummified Aborigine whose bones were protruding through his skin. Placing corpses stripped of their intestines in tree branches was a common method of burial for Aborigines in that area. Jack had sworn in fright and berated Aborigines as 'savages' for not burying dead bodies as white people did. Daisy hotly defended them, insisting that different cultures had different burial rites. They had argued bitterly. Daisy's interest in Aboriginal culture increased as a result. (Perhaps, too, Daisy was unaware of Jack's dismissal from Jim Tyson's Tinnenburra for attacking an Aboriginal stockman.)

During their time on Roebuck Plains — the better part of a year — the main reason for the quarrels between husband and wife was Daisy's determination to continue her Aboriginal studies. Daisy had plenty of time to continue the reading plan she had begun in Perth and was absorbed in reading everything that was being written about the various groups of Aborigines. She devoured information concerning Aboriginal kin relationships and totemism, as well as different aspects of the culture, including painting, rock carving and body art. Whenever she rode out on horseback she would find Aboriginal people who would sit down with her and talk. In times of drought these nomadic people came from far afield to seek the underground water in the soaks of Roebuck Plains. Daisy was captivated by their nomadic way of life, their songs and dances, and their unwritten language. She took more and more notes on their customs and started to record their language in vocabulary notebooks.

She learned about the intricacies of Aboriginal marriage laws, including which relationships were forbidden, and about the marriages arranged between young girls at birth and old men which meant the men could take their wives by force as soon as the girls reached puberty, something Daisy deplored. She noted down the totems that belonged to different groups and individuals, and other laws concerning hunting and the sharing of food. She saw the welted scars on the men's chests and backs, and other scars on women's upper arms, often made during rites of mourning. She watched Aboriginal men carve spearheads with sharp stones, shape their boomerangs, and weave conical spinifex fishing nets with extraordinary deftness and delicacy; and she observed how they would rub the hair of possum or wallaby into a fine string along their thighs. She attended corroborees performed by women, entranced by the rhythmical clicking of the music sticks and the drone of the didgeridoo.

Daisy would continue taking notes and adding to her knowledge for the next forty years. In time, she became the leading expert on the Aborigines of this part of Western Australia. Her expertise equalled that of Francis Gillen, one-time Superintendent of the Alice Springs Telegraph Station, who studied the Aborigines of the Central Desert. He imparted his knowledge to Professor Baldwin Spencer, who wrote the classic textbook on the subject. Unfortunately, Daisy had no academic collaborator with whom to write a book. She was on her own, mocked by her husband for her efforts.

There is no doubt that Daisy managed to establish a rapport with Aboriginal people that few others would match — often talking to the tribeswomen while she held their babies on her lap. Many seemed to believe that Daisy, with her pale skin, was a spirit from their Dreaming and would respect their laws. In a similar way, the novelist, anthropologist and biologist E.L. Grant Watson recorded that at Sandstone the Aborigines allowed him to attend a male corroboree, believing him to be a *djanga*, a returned spirit from the dead.

Daisy came to feel that Aboriginal people she got to know possessed many of the characteristics of the Irish: they were light-hearted, quick to take offence, quick to forgive. A stand-off between the men could start in an instant, with the males rushing for their spears. Like the working people of Ireland, she found, Aborigines were hospitable, quickly jealous but lacking in malice; Daisy, inclined to mysticism herself, described them as having the true 'spirit of Celtic mysticism'. She drew parallels between the elderly Aboriginal women she talked to and Allie, the superstitious old woman at Ballychrine who had taken little Daisy to the priest rather than the bone-setter when she broke her leg and told her Irish tales and legends.

For his part, Jack worked hard, remained taciturn and still drank too much. He made little effort to understand that Daisy wanted something more than being the wife of a drover or cattle station manager. She wanted to succeed on her own merits, and the area she had chosen was a small but fascinating corner of the world of social anthropology — the study of the Australian Aborigines. But Jack made it abundantly clear that he despised native people. His denigration of them and his jibes at Daisy for trying to become an expert in the growing field of ethnology led to more arguments that only widened the gap between them.

Daisy had no wish to convert the Aboriginal people, educate them or change them in any way — in that respect she differed from the prevailing attitudes of the time. She simply wanted to observe, to try to understand their way of life, and to write down her findings.

With great sensitivity in an era dominated by the white man's belief in Christian supremacy, Daisy would later write:

> The one great fault in our attempt to Christianize the Australian aboriginal lies in our violent snapping of their own traditional beliefs, in our endeavours to replace these by teaching them the rudiments of that special creed to which we ourselves belong, or rather to the beliefs which we have reached in our present state of culture . . .
>
> The animism and totemism of the aborigine are his religion . . . and are there not sacred pagan places in our own Catholic Ireland? The waved lines, concentric circles,

zigzag patterns, dotted rings found in Australian rock-
drawings have their counterpart in the rock-drawings
discovered in England, Scotland, Ireland . . . [Daisy
doubtless meant the La Tene patterns at New Grange and
other prehistoric sites in central Ireland.][1]

According to the *West Australian Year Book*, on 23 April 1902 'a
cultured, frail-looking lady set off on one of the most arduous trips
that any lady has ever undertaken'. The plucky woman who
accomplished a journey on horseback which most men would have
hesitated to undertake through the hottest, most isolated part of
Western Australia was, of course, the unsinkable Daisy Bates.

From Roebuck Plains, Daisy and Jack, accompanied by Arnold,
set off on a mammoth ride of more than 1000 kilometres, with
700 head of their own Herefords purchased by Daisy and a
further 200 for Edwin Streeter — the money Jack the drover
would receive for this would be used to build a large and
comfortable homestead — Daisy's dream home. Their destination
was Peak Hill on the Murchison. Daisy rode side saddle, wearing
a long-skirted riding habit; at that time European women did not
wear breeches or ride astride. She had ordered three riding habits
to be specially tailored for her, and three pairs of pigskin gloves.
She also took along plenty of veiling with mesh fine enough to
keep out the swarms of flies.

To save money Jack employed six amateur stockmen, paying
them very low wages. This would turn out to be a disastrous
decision. The main mob was owned by Edwin Streeter's company,
which paid Jack for taking the cattle. The fees from this gruelling
overland trip were intended to set up the Bateses on leasehold land
they had both purchased at the place Daisy nostalgically called Glen
Carrick. She assumed that Jack (who had not set about planning a
homestead yet) would have made sure there was an adequate
dwelling of some sort, erected by the previous owners, where they
could live in the meantime.

They were accompanied along camel routes by a head drover, a
Maori cook, and a dray loaded with provisions, Daisy's

Daisy accompanied Jack Bates overlanding cattle thousands of miles on horseback

portmanteau and the drovers' swags. The men were forbidden to swear or tell dirty jokes in Daisy's presence, and she insisted they washed as often as possible. There was no 'double bed swag', for the men to snigger over. Jack slept by himself, while Daisy and Arnold retired to their respective tents. Arnold was making this trek before setting off for New South Wales to study to become an engineer, the profession he had been pressured into by his mother but would never follow.

Clouds of dust arose as they rode behind the huge triangle formed by the mob of cattle, with the strongest beasts at the head and the stragglers at the rear. Riding behind the mob, Daisy's face became streaked with dust, her hair matted with filth. She had to keep on riding as she was the 'tailer' at the end of the procession, making sure that the stragglers kept going. She hated the fact that they were forced to kill newborn calves too weak to stand the pace of the journey. It made her sad to hear the mothers bellowing distractedly for days afterwards, searching in vain for their calves. Later she wrote to her friend William Hurst, editor of *The Australasian*: 'I do not think a romantic account could be worked up of a real droving trip if the principal actors who make the romance have been tailing behind a mob of cattle over dusty plains.'

In fact, Daisy was so appalled by the outcome of this journey that it would be another twenty years before she wrote about her days as a drover, in an article she called '3,000 Miles on Side Saddle' — a somewhat romanticised account of the marathon droving trip, in which, as usual, she omitted any mention of Jack Bates.

All went well until they reached Battle Hill Well, adjoining Sam Mackay's Roy Hill Station. Here the huge mob of beasts, maddened by thirst, stampeded. The bulk of them broke down the fences and surged into the distance in search of water, mostly never to be seen again. Jack's stockmen hunted for them for days with scant success. Some may even have been 'duffed', or stolen. Daisy would never know exactly what happened.[2] Daisy's capital was exhausted. It was impossible to restock.

This financial and emotional disaster would mark the end of her marriage. Daisy never forgave Jack for the loss of the cattle, which meant the end of her dreams of wealth and her longed-for status as the wife of a cattle baron.

When they reached Ethel Creek and the Glen Carrick cattle run, Daisy discovered there wasn't even a bush hut there — only a miserable rough shelter made from boughs and with a dirt floor. She burst into tears of anger and frustration. She was so upset she couldn't eat for days. She swore that she never wanted to see Jack again. She was convinced it was his fault that she had lost her capital. She blamed him for not employing trained stockmen with dogs instead of rank amateurs. Daisy had a fierce temper when roused and one can imagine how she sobbed, screamed and yelled at him while Jack sought refuge in alcohol.

After the insecurities and miseries of Daisy's orphaned childhood, her efforts to achieve something so that people would respect her had been nullified by her hard-drinking husband. She had returned to Australia, tried to manage some sort of reconciliation with Jack and set up a business relationship with him, but it had failed. All her relationships with men had been a disaster; now the only thing she wanted was to live by herself.

This was perhaps the strongest reason for Daisy's later decision to live in the desert as a researcher into Aboriginal languages and culture. She no longer aspired to marriage. She wanted a different kind of status, to be taken seriously at a time when academic credibility in science was routinely denied to women.[3] Perhaps, too, there was an element of contrition in her whole-hearted adoption of this new way of life. Did she wish to atone for certain incidents in her past: such as a string of marriages, liaisons and deceptions — and perhaps her failure as Arnold's mother?

Ironically, it was not until Daisy finally left Jack that she learned their marriage could be regarded as legal. Early in 1902 in South Africa, Breaker Morant was court-martialled on a controversial charge of murder and was executed by a British firing squad, three months before the end of the Second Boer War.

᠅ ᠅ ᠅

In that hot little bough hovel at Ethel Creek, arguments raged over who was to blame for the loss of the precious beef cattle and who had put more money and effort into what had become a failed project. At last Daisy gave up on the hopeless situation and packed up, ready to leave, taking off for Port Hedland in a buggy owned by a local contractor. From Port Hedland she travelled by steamer to Broome, and spent considerable time there searching for the missing cattle. It was a fruitless task. She was by now a stone lighter in weight than when she set out for Glen Carrick. From then on Daisy never set eyes on Jack again. She told everyone he was dead and only ever referred to him as 'my late husband, a wealthy cattleman', which was untrue.

Aside from Daisy's habit of embroidering the facts and burying unpleasant incidents in her life, there was good reason why she should maintain that Jack Bates had died. Western Australia, like Queensland, had very harsh laws concerning divorce and marriage separation, favouring the husband and punishing the wife. Women were supposed to obey their husbands without question, and husbands had the legal right to strike their wives if they did not do so. A divorced or separated wife had no legal rights where her children were concerned and could claim no part of her husband's property. In any case, divorce was an extremely costly process, which Daisy could not have afforded to instigate. If it were known that Daisy had left her husband, she would have had no chance of working in Western Australia and her reputation would have been severely damaged. In Daisy's case, too, she was well aware of the fact that she had contracted a bigamous marriage with Ernest Baglehole after she became the wife of Jack Bates, and she may well have feared legal punishment for that.

Jack, meanwhile, very much alive, stayed on at the property at Ethel Creek with the remaining cattle, most of which belonged to Sam Mackay. After they had fattened up nicely on the lush grass, he delivered them to Perth as promised. He would eventually attempt, unsuccessfully, to sell the run in its unimproved condition. Daisy would demand her share of the property, claiming that she had put her own money into the cattle and her blocks of land which proved hard to sell. She was now asset rich but cash poor and without a husband. Eventually Jack took a job managing a cattle property at Humpty Doo, outside Darwin.

ৡ ৡ ৡ

Back in Perth by 1902, Daisy managed to survive by writing articles as a freelance journalist. Many of these warped the truth to appeal to the popular press. They contained sensationalised tales of corroborees and references to cannibalism, two sure-fire sellers in that era. It would be wrong, however, to assume that Daisy was the only European to make such claims. A missionary named R.D. Joynt, who spent ten years in the Roper River area of the Northern Territory, from 1908 to 1918, lists 'human flesh' in his report under the heading, 'What The Natives Eat' and the Norwegian scientist Carl Lumholtz who visited South Australia and Queensland described his experiences in his book *Among Cannibals* in unemotional and scientific terms.[4]

But Daisy also retained her scientific ambitions: she wrote articles for quality journals such as that of the Royal Geographical Society of Australia (1905 and 1906) and *The Science of Man* (1910 and 1911), as well as compiling a detailed statistical account of the proposed Trans-Australian railway in conjunction with the West Australian Minister for Works. This gave her credibility in certain circles. She wrote well, but her notebooks reveal how much she needed to pare down and polish her prose before sending it away for publication.

Daisy learned to use a camera and took photographs of Aborigines of the northwest of Western Australia on a research expedition there. Hoping to make money she published them in a series of postcards, but few people were interested and she lost money she could ill afford on the venture. Only her sensational stories of cannibalism and sorcery made money although they enraged many people trying to help the Aboriginal cause.

On 8 April 1904, a settler called Malcolmson had raised 'the Aboriginal question' again, writing to *The Times*, London, and claiming that Aborigines were treated worse than black slaves in America's Deep South. In response to his letter the *Western Mail* paid Daisy Bates to go to the Peak Hill district to investigate the treatment of Aborigines there. She journeyed through harsh country to waterless Meekatharra and on to Nannine, ignoring snakes, spiders and the lack of bathing and toilet facilities. A month later *The Times* published Daisy's spirited reply, a long letter from her (not an article, as Daisy would later claim) regarding the treatment of Aborigines. She must have sent this letter by overland telegraph. In it she claimed that Malcolmson's story was ridiculous. She added that she found the behaviour of most settlers as well as the Western Australian government exemplary, and described how she had talked with property owners such as the Withnells and the Meares, who did their best to help the Indigenous people. At the time Daisy believed this was true, but she learned there were many other settlers who were doing the opposite. She claimed that many European owners helped their stockmen when they fell ill. She knew they were not 'plaster saints' but to compare them to the American slave owners was untrue.[5] Daisy wrote a statement she would later retract: 'No State is doing more for its Aboriginal population than this one,' referring to Western Australia.

Daisy produced her article for the *Western Mail* and was clearly capable of holding a research or administrative post connected with her chosen subject. She desperately wanted to work with Aborigines, in whom she had a genuine interest and for whom she felt compassion. Her tragedy was that for the rest of her life she would continue to seek a paid post in this area but as a woman in a man's world whose scholarship was larded with sensational and controversial statements she would never be offered one.

In 1904 there were no academic courses in Australia in social anthropology, let alone Aboriginal studies. Daisy read everything that had been written on Australia's Indigenous people, beginning with observations made by Charles Darwin when he sailed to Australia aboard the *Beagle* in 1836. Darwin had been convinced that the full-blooded Aboriginal people would soon die out and many shared his views. Daisy read accounts by explorers and observers of Aboriginal people such as Ernest Giles, Edward (E.M.) Curr, Sir George Grey and Sir Augustus Gregory (later a trustee of the Queensland Museum), and corresponded with one or two of them. And she continued to discuss Aboriginal affairs with the explorer turned politician, Sir John Forrest.

Daisy now accepted an invitation from the Department of the Registrar General in Western Australia to take part in a research project designed to document the different Aboriginal languages spoken in the State. It was agreed that she could broaden the project to include serious and detailed studies of Aboriginal customs and mythology. For this labour-intensive work the department would pay her the princely sum of eight shillings a day. The arrangement lasted from 1904 till 1912 but gave her so meagre an income she needed to supplement it by journalism.

Contrary to received opinion, it is Daisy Bates rather than the much better known Margaret Mead, an American, who should be celebrated as the female pioneer of social anthropology. Mead did not sail to Samoa and live with the Samoan people to make her famous study of them until the mid-1920s. Two decades earlier, Daisy Bates had already been acknowledged by the Parliament of Western Australia as an expert on Aboriginal culture. Along with her controversial articles, she would produce some excellent anthropological research, and had she been a man she might have been given a research or lecturing post, leading to a flourishing academic career.[6]

CHAPTER 11

CONTRADICTIONS, COMPLEXITIES
AND RESEARCH

Daisy was a puzzle of contradictions and complexities . . .
impetuous, extravagantly generous . . . a rebel with a warm
heart.

ERNESTINE HILL, *KABBARLI*

The years 1895–1903 saw Australia in the grip of the 'Great Drought', Australia's worst ever to that point. Hundreds of Aboriginal people were forced to leave their traditional hunting grounds and walk long distances in search of drinking water and game. The government of Western Australia, aware that pastoralists were driving Indigenous people away from their traditional waterholes in order to preserve water for the cattle, set up Aboriginal reserves around piped water supplies.

Daisy continued to write articles for popular newspapers in order to gain much-needed extra income. The Glen Carrick property remained unsold, and Jack Bates provided no alimony for his wife. Then, as we have seen, a new opportunity arose for her: the West

Australian government's offer over the next eight years to compile a record of all the languages spoken by Aborigines in the State and list the most commonly used words in them with appropriate translations.

The severe shortage of drinking water saw many Aborigines flocking to the recently established reserves. It was on these reserves that Daisy intended to defy convention and camp while she carried out her research, considered a very daring thing for a European 'lady' to do.

Daisy had agreed with Malcolm Fraser, an elderly public servant and dedicated amateur anthropologist responsible for employing her, that in addition to language studies she would also study Aboriginal customs, lore and legends: her studies would form part of the report which she would hand in at the end of the project. Fraser assured her that the West Australian government would eventually publish her findings as 'a book of reference for ethnologists and philologists in their study of our interesting Aborigines'. Unfortunately, he failed to draw up a written contract to this effect.

She began her fieldwork in May 1904, at a time when very few women had well paid jobs outside the home or were involved in research of any kind. With no university department of anthropology to refer to, she taught herself the rudiments of this new science sometimes also known as ethnology, while maintaining an extensive correspondence with other amateurs working in the same field, as well as an intensive reading program of published material.

Convinced that she now had a real chance to enter her chosen profession, Daisy set to work with enormous enthusiasm, proving herself an excellent researcher, well organised, hardworking and efficient. To start things off she sent out questionnaires to graziers, policemen and others who had contact with Indigenous people, asking them to write down all the Aboriginal words they had learned, together with the English translations.

As a female ethnologist/anthropologist she broke new ground in Australia when she went to live beside the Ma'amba Aboriginal

Reserve, some ten kilometres from Perth. Here wooden and stone huts had been built to accommodate drought-stricken Aborigines and there was a constant supply of fresh water. Many different groups of the Bibbulmun people arrived here, driven from their nomadic way of life on lands now claimed by pastoralists.

The Bibbulmun would become the linguistic group that most interested Daisy. She was saddened to realise the impact that Western civilisation had had on these handsome people she called in admiration 'the once proud wanderers of the desert'. She was saddened to see remnants of that formerly huge tribe, which had once occupied a large part of Western Australia, living at Ma'amba among what she described as 'shanties and shacks of wood and iron, kerosene tins, hessian bags, crawling with dogs, black with flies'. Accustomed to a nomadic life, they had no proper sanitation, no access to medical treatment, and were badly affected by European diseases such as mumps, measles, kidney diseases and rheumatic fever, as well as varying degrees of blindness caused by ophthalmia (of which conjunctivitis is one form). Many of the people had walked for hundreds of kilometres to reach the Ma'amba Reserve, and their feet were torn and damaged. She listened sympathetically as the older Aborigines told her that many of their families had died from starvation and thirst in these drought years.

Daisy's own living conditions at Ma'amba were primitive, but she did have the luxury of a clean tent with a bed, and always wore a hat with a fly veil. She would set up her small tent for a week or so at a time, returning to Perth at frequent intervals. Daisy Bates was the first woman in her field in Australia to camp near her subjects (never right among them) in order to carry out fieldwork. She did her best to form good relations with her Bibbulmun informants, offering food as a way of gaining acceptance. Out of her modest government salary (she received only two-thirds of the male salary for identical work) she paid for sacks of oats and flour and made damper and porridge for them, recalling the words of Father Nicholas at Beagle Bay: 'A good present will almost always elicit information.' Several religious bodies were delighted to know that Daisy was there to give out food to hungry Aborigines, who in the drought had trouble finding game to hunt, and offered help. But Daisy distrusted their motives. She did not believe in converting Aborigines to Christianity; she was convinced they should live according to their own cultural beliefs.

Daisy also visited nearby Katanning Reserve, where another Bibbulmun-speaking group, the Wardandi, had arrived in search of food and water. Here she nursed many of them during a measles epidemic. It was at this time Daisy claimed that she had been accepted into the kinship system of the Bibbulmun and had received a 'skin' name. She also claimed to have persuaded certain Aborigines that her native name was 'Kallower', and that she was a magic woman.

She 'sat down' with old Aborigines who had been born before the first Europeans arrived to settle in Western Australia. Daisy asked questions in their own language, which she now spoke reasonably well, and noted down their answers. In return she provided them with porridge, damper and treacle, bathed their swollen eyes with a solution of borax and water, bandaged cut feet and applied ointment to the burns children often suffered after falling into the embers of the campfires.

Many of the surviving members of Indigenous groups had lost family members killed by white men; they had no reason to love Europeans. Over cups of sweet tea Daisy gradually built up a relationship of trust. Elderly Aboriginal men and women provided details of tribal initiation ceremonies, and some of the women showed Daisy how bodies and faces were painted with white and red clay for corroborees. When she didn't know the name of an item of body decoration she would call it a 'giggleywick'. In return for these favours she would dispense a special mixture of boiled rice and Bovril, which she christened 'hobble gobble' as she enjoyed inventing her own words.

Living in a tent beside the Ma'amba Aboriginal Reserve and on other camps and reserves, Daisy became something of a nomad herself, sleeping in a small tent she took around with her from place to place. She soon found that the nomadic life suited her and came to enjoy the freedom of her new life with its lack of housework and escape from mundane domesticity and routine. Living at close range with Aborigines allowed her to visit and study various Aboriginal groups and travel round the State of Western Australia carrying out her research in areas like Guildford, Bunbury, Albany and the Vasse River.

In 1904 when 'nice women' were usually chaperoned whenever they travelled, Daisy's new life was daring indeed. Her conduct caused unfavourable comment among white settlers, amazed that a white woman was living in such circumstances surrounded by half naked Aborigines, who might rob or even rape her. What were this woman's motives, some people wondered, and crude jokes circulated about her.

A desire to live in desert areas and observe different desert cultures motivated several exceptional women travel writers. Mary Kingsley, Daisy Bates, Gertrude Bell and Freya Stark are now regarded as pioneering the art of travel writing. Daisy Bates was one of the first women to have published articles about hazardous journeys through the outback, including 'Through the Murchison Ranges' for the *Western Mail* (July 1904), 'Across the Bight by Camel Buggy' for William Hurst's paper, *The Australasian* (July and August 1918), and '3000 Miles on a Side Saddle' in *The Australasian*, (23 July 1924).

Daisy felt a new sense of purpose and excitement enter her life as she learned more about the language, customs and myths of such ancient peoples, research she believed could make her a name in scientific circles. She hoped that by entering a scientific publishing her research she might finally gain acceptance as a scientist.

Daisy's work at Ma'amba and Katanning Reserves would set a pattern for the rest of her life — studying and supporting Aborigines in whatever way she could. If her attitude appeared condescending, it arose from the fact that she merely reflected the approach of white people of her era in Australia.

In 1905 the West Australian government, alarmed by a rapid growth in the part-Aboriginal population, passed the *Aborigines Act*, which had far-reaching consequences. At the time, part-Aborigines were despised by full-blood Aborigines and Europeans alike, labelled 'yeller fellers' or 'coconuts, white inside but black outside', (a term cited by Xavier Herbert in his novel *Capricornia*). The 1905 Act made it a criminal offence for a white man to have sexual relations with an Aboriginal or part-Aboriginal woman — which had the effect of punishing the women rather than the European men who pursued them. In some States the law provided for the forcible removal by police of children born of such unions.

During the cooler season of 1907–08, intent on carrying out fieldwork, and paying for tea, sugar and tobacco as 'gifts' for her informants, Daisy travelled east to Esperance by horse and cart, stopping along the way to talk with various Aboriginal groups. She later presented Governor Frederick Bedford with a series of sketches by a crippled Jukun-Ngumbari man called Billingee, a skilful rock carver of animals and humans who came from near Broome. Daisy was familiar with great art from her time in London in the 1890s; she became a firm admirer of Aboriginal art at a time when most Australians regarded it as crude work designed for tourists, and unworthy of admission to State art galleries. She encouraged Billingee to provide drawings of local ceremonies, body ornaments, hunting scenes and tribal shields, providing him with wax crayons — yellow, green, pink and red. Then, in consultation with the artist, she wrote notes on the objects he depicted — an interesting example of cooperation between an Aboriginal man and a European woman.

Billingee told Daisy that his country stretched from Beagle Bay, 120 kilometres north of Broome, to Roebourne, and helped her to compile a vocabulary of his language. Their linguistic collaboration lasted from 1907 until 1912. The result was a vocabulary of a Western Australian Indigenous language that was dying out as members of Billingee's family group passed away, and without Daisy's intervention would have been lost.

Daisy's successful collaboration with Billingee resulted in her cooperating in a project of great importance for future generations of Aboriginal people. She gave some Aboriginal men, who were expert hunters, writing and drawing materials so they could create maps of their hunting territory, supervising all thirty-five maps, mainly of the Murchison district and the Kimberley. She was the first social anthropologist to tackle this work, but she did not claim credit for the maps herself; instead, she listed the names of all the hunters — Maju, Moaji, Ngulyibongu, Jangari, Muri, Womburu, Jilguguru and Yingilit, among others — as the creators of these very significant documents, now used as evidence in land rights claims.

Daisy was also helped in her gathering of information by her close friendship with Ngiligi, a Wardandi Bibbulmun woman from the Busselton area. The story Daisy related was that as a baby Ngiligi had been found abandoned in a field after her mother fled in terror when she was discovered stealing potatoes. Ngiligi claimed to have worked for pioneer Alfred Bussell as well as the Forrest and

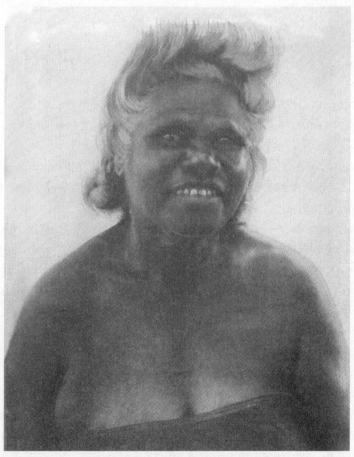

Daisy's friend, the much-married Ngiligi,
a Bibbulmun woman

Fairbairn families, and learned to speak English. Daisy maintained that she was the last of her family group. When they met, Ngiligi had 'thirty-two dogs, seven goats and a dozen fowls, four Aboriginal suitors and a half-caste aspirant'. A kindly government had given her a plot of ground, fenced for flower or vegetable growing, a hut, a double bed and a spring mattress — 'for Ngiligi's dogs were her blankets at night and thirty-two dogs and a hefty woman require a full-sized double bed'.[1]

As a result of her life experiences, Ngiligi had become a bridge between two cultures. She helped Daisy to see elements of Aboriginal life from the woman's viewpoint, including topics that male anthropologists had ignored, such as the strict laws against menstruating women mingling with their men. Daisy's insights into the daily life of Aboriginal women differentiated her work from that of many anthropologists of her era.

☙ ☙ ☙

This period in Western Australia seems to have been a happy time in Daisy's life. Disillusioned by her unsuccessful relationships, she filled in the gap in her life by becoming a dedicated fieldworker. No doubt she did not miss Jack or Arnold; she did not envy her elder sister Kathleen her luxurious homes, nor her younger sister Anne her property in Roscrea. Instead, she became fully engaged in researching Aboriginal culture. She described herself as in the grip of 'the virus of research'. Her field studies covered a wide range of topics, from women's work and birthing procedures to burial rites and the initiation ceremonies of Aboriginal boys, which she described years later in a 1942 radio interview with Russell Henderson of the ABC as 'very sexual indeed'; although in spite of her prim attire Daisy proved to be unshockable.[2]

Mrs Bates, as she insisted her work colleagues must call her, maintained her persona as a respectable widow, and firmly sidelined scurrilous gossip that she was over-fond of Aboriginal men. Daisy had shocked the prim and proper ladies of Perth when she went off to live in her tent, alone and unchaperoned. It was considered scandalous for a lone European woman to live near a fringe camp filled with unwashed natives. Daisy's own harsh childhood meant that, unlike most 'respectable women' of her era, she had grown up able to endure conditions they would have baulked at in polite society. Sometimes she made capital of this, enjoying the results. Forward-thinking as many of the lady members of Perth's exclusive Karrakatta Club undoubtedly were, did they ever forgive Mrs Bates bringing along an Aboriginal woman called Fanny Balbuk-Yooreel as a luncheon guest — and then proclaiming that Fanny Balbuk was actually their landlady, since she was the original owner of the land on which the Karrakatta Club stood?[3]

But Daisy Bates was never a political activist. She genuinely cared for Aborigines and especially appreciated their sense of humour in the face of grim tragedy. However, she had no time for 'half-castes', somewhat cruelly blaming the sins of the fathers on those unfortunate children who at the time were shunned and despised by Aborigines and Europeans alike. This was the era of Federation in Australia, an outpost of Empire where the deeply ingrained assumptions about the superiority of whites over blacks and perceptions of British superiority affected all those who attempted to help Aboriginal people. Daisy Bates has sometimes been denigrated by today's Aboriginal activists, yet viewed alongside many others of her era she was a progressive humanitarian.

In 1907 Daisy was created a Fellow of the Anthropological Society of Australasia and a member of the Royal Geographical Society of Australasia, Victorian Branch. Her first published scientific work, a study of Aboriginal marriage relationships and burial rites, appeared in the prestigious *Journal of the Royal Geographic Society of Britain and Ireland*. This was a great honour, which helped to bolster Daisy's confidence. Later she published another paper on Aboriginal languages in France's *Revue d'Ethnolographie*.[4]

Given the lack in Australia of any university department of anthropology, in order to exchange ideas and information, Daisy corresponded with a number of male enthusiasts who were, like herself, all self-taught from intensive reading and their own observations. These highly intelligent men took her work very seriously. One of her regular correspondents was a friend from

North Queensland days, British-born Frank Hann. Frank had been very taken with the beautiful, flirtatious Miss Daisy O'Dwyer when she stayed at the Maryvale property. After his brother William drowned, disease and drought brought bankruptcy to Frank Hann, who was forced to walk off his land. 'Do not give way to despair,' he wrote bravely in letters to friends and accepted a job as an explorer and mapmaker with the West Australian government. He would correspond with Daisy for years, and at one point she asked if he would 'name something' after her. He discovered 'a prominent peak' and named it Mount Daisy Bates. It lies in West Australia's remote shire of Ngaanyatjarraku, near the borders of the Northern Territory and South Australia.

Another Australian woman also interested in studying Aboriginal life at this time did not have to live in a tent like Daisy. Her name was Catherine (Katie) Langloh Parker, who lived in a comfortable homestead at Bangate Station, on the edge of

Frank Hann and an Aboriginal servant, c. 1900. Hann was an amateur anthropologist and a pastoralist.

sandhill country in western New South Wales. For Katie Parker ethnology was a hobby conducted in comfort. Her husband employed Aboriginal servants and, as she was childless, Mrs Langloh Parker was able to devote herself to writing a book, *The Euahlayi Tribe*, covering many of the same topics that interested Daisy, including kinship systems, totems, Dreaming legends, initiation ceremonies, and sorcery practices such as 'pointing the bone'. Like Daisy she was interested in Aboriginal women. One chapter of her book she described an elderly

Aboriginal woman who sat immobile with grief on the lawn in front of Bangate homestead, muttering to herself and claiming she was a witch. In fact, the poor woman had literally gone mad with grief over the death of a child.[5]

※ ※ ※

From 1909 to 1910 Daisy was in Perth, writing up the results of the field studies she had been undertaking for the Registrar General's Department. It was an anxious time for Daisy, who worked in a government office that she was under notice to vacate. A new government had been elected and Aboriginal studies were no longer regarded as a priority. By now into her fifties, Daisy had developed an ear for the phonetics of various Aboriginal languages and she recorded lists of words — virtual mini-dictionaries — in over two dozen different Aboriginal languages, a task she would continue in the future.

Over the past seven years Daisy Bates had also been hard at work producing a vast manuscript, half a million words in length, which she titled *The Native Tribes of Western Australia*. Much of it was written in longhand, though sometimes she used a battered portable typewriter. Her academic study included sections on Aboriginal language, legends and myths, kinship laws, hunting grounds, initiation ceremonies, and special practices relating to women. Daisy emphasised that Aboriginal tribal customs and rituals differed from group to group, and observed how they were breaking down under the impact of European settlement.

Daisy's enthusiasm meant she badly needed a sympathetic editor with a knowledge of social anthropology to shorten the work and pull it into shape. She obtained estimates of the cost of having her manuscript published in London or Edinburgh, where costs were cheaper, but the newly elected Scadden Labor government in Western Australia considered the project far too expensive to sponsor. There was no way Daisy could afford to publish herself. As a last resort she sent a copy off to Andrew Lang, a well-known Scottish authority on folklore and primitive peoples, hoping he might offer to edit it for her.

In fact, seven decades were to pass before her major work, *The Native Tribes of Western Australia*, was eventually published, long after Daisy's death, by the National Library of Australia. It was edited by Isobel White, a scholar and retired anthropologist, who commented that there was 'no reason to doubt the accuracy of [Daisy Bates's] first hand observation'.[6]

In 1910, at this critical juncture in her life, Daisy received a visit from an up-and-coming British academic, the ambitious, young Alfred Brown, who changed his name to the more aristocratic Radcliffe-Brown in 1926. He would become the first Professor of Anthropology at the University of Cape Town, South Africa then move to London. Not quite thirty when he met Daisy, the charismatic professor had recently conducted a successful expedition to the Andaman Islands, whose inhabitants had regarded him as a god — something that only served to increase Radcliffe-Brown's already excellent opinion of himself. Now he was planning an expedition to the Australian outback, jointly funded by the Universities of Oxford and Cambridge, and was keen to find a good interpreter. Knowing of Daisy's language skills, he invited her to join him. He also told her that Andrew Lang had (unbidden) passed on to him the copy of her rambling and overly long but interesting manuscript. Lang claimed he was unable to edit it due to ill health, but Radcliffe-Brown intimated that it might be possible to publish an edited version of *The Native Tribes of Western Australia* as part of the overall report on the expedition.

Daisy accepted with alacrity the young university lecturer's invitation to join him, believing she had found the very man to edit her huge manuscript. And his objective appeared similar to her own: to research Aboriginal lore and customs before the Indigenous people died out.

Her hopes rose once more. Would this expedition and the research it produced help her to break through the academic barriers that held her back in science? Could she prevail on Professor Radcliffe-Brown to edit her manuscript?

CHAPTER 12

TO THE ISLES OF THE DEAD

The work that Mrs Bates has done among Aborigines, the interest that she has created among those quaint, lovable and primitive people, to whom, when all is said and done, Australia really belongs, entitles her to rank among women who have accomplished great things.

WESTERN MAIL, PERTH, 10 MAY 1910

The news that an anthropological expedition from Oxford and Cambridge was about to carry out fieldwork in Western Australia and that a woman would be a member of it was exciting. The *Western Mail*, interviewing Mrs Bates shortly before the expedition departed for Sandstone, reported that she was 'anticipating the journey with intense eagerness'.

In Perth Daisy showed tremendous kindness to young Professor Alfred Radcliffe-Brown, and obtained additional funding for the expedition from the wealthy pastoralist Sam Mackay, who had always admired Daisy's keen intellect and her looks. The professor, however, showed Daisy no gratitude at all, claiming that Sam Mackay had given *him* the money when slightly drunk following a public lecture he delivered in Perth's town hall. Daisy took pains to smooth his path in other ways, explaining to Aborigines she knew well that the professor was her son: aware that they would then accept him into their kinship system, just as they had accepted her. As yet she was unaware of the difficulties others had experienced with the opinionated Radcliffe-Brown.

Armed with a supply of notebooks and pencils, high button boots and fly veiling, Daisy took off for Bunbury with the 'Prof' and his assistant, Elliot Lovegood Grant Watson, a pleasant young academic with a Van Dyck beard.[1] They sailed by steamer to Geraldton, where Radcliffe-Brown employed a Scandinavian cook and hired horses and a groom to look after them. From there they would travel east to a place called Sandstone, some 500 kilometres from the coast.

Even at this early stage, Radcliffe-Brown had begun to display those unfortunate traits of character that others had experienced when they tried to work with him. He was supremely egotistic, with a mercurial temperament that impeded his ability to function as a member of a team. Daisy herself could be difficult, but in the case of this expedition the fault lay with Radcliffe-Brown. (Much later, when he lectured Margaret Mead at the University of Sydney, Mead found him intellectually stimulating yet arrogant and obsessional. 'Any disagreement, tacit or uttered against his ideas, he takes as a slap in the face,' she declared.)

Radcliffe-Brown remarked unkindly to Grant Watson that Mrs Bates's mind resembled 'a sewing basket in which kittens had played'. He scorned her weaknesses and ignored her strengths. When the professor finally returned the copy of her manuscript that Andrew Lang had sent him, Daisy was upset to find whole sections scissored out of it. Like Mead she began to realise that Radcliffe-Brown was an autocrat who brooked no opposition to his own ideas.

✿ ✿ ✿

Excellent horsewoman that she was, Daisy had no trouble riding to Sandstone, where they pitched their tents some distance from the town, near an Aboriginal camp where they planned to interview as many of the older members of the group as possible.

They were unlucky. A band of native troopers arrived at Sandstone to investigate the case of an Aboriginal man who had been speared to death as punishment for breaking tribal law. The troopers fired their revolvers at the native dogs and behaved so objectionably that all the Aborigines fled from the camp. The troopers did not catch those who had speared the victim, who were by now sheltering in Radcliffe-Brown's tent. The professor was furious that his carefully laid plans had been ruined by this police intervention. He told the rest of his party that they would now leave Sandstone for Aboriginal lock hospitals — places for the treatment of sexually transmitted disease — on remote Bernier and Dorré Islands to interview patients, where there was no possibility they would be disturbed, since the police would be too scared to follow them. Both islands were gazetted by the Western Australian government as isolation areas for syphilitic Aborigines, with an all-male hospital on Bernier and the female hospital on Dorré.

Daisy argued that if they waited at Sandstone the Aborigines would return, but Radcliffe-Brown resolutely fixed his eyes on the horizon and refused to listen. Next day he curtly informed her that he, Grant Watson and the expedition's cook were leaving straight away for Bernier Island. If Mrs Bates wished to follow them, she was free to do so — but the professor offered her no help in reaching the islands. He hoped Daisy would give up and return to Perth.

Grant Watson found himself in a quandary. Daisy had shown him kindness and he wanted to support her (he described her as 'a woman of charity and compassion'), but did not want to risk angering his chief, as he was at the start of his academic career. Later he would declare that Mrs Bates and the professor had personalities that were totally incompatible. So Daisy was left to make her own way to Shark Bay and its islands by horse and cart and by ferry boat.

At that time there was no effective cure for syphilis. The disease is transmitted by sexual intercourse or through contact with open wounds. It has a long incubation period and can also be passed from parent to unborn child, who may be born blind and deaf. Victims of the disease develop weeping sores as the syphilis spirochete gnaws away at bone structures and destroys the brain. The final tertiary stage of syphilis is characterised by what was known as 'general paralysis of the insane' — paralysis complicated with insanity. Syphilis was the scourge of the Victorian and Edwardian eras, often spread by sailors and soldiers. Winston Churchill's father, Randolph, died of syphilis, as did Schubert, Beethoven, Delius and Gauguin. Patients were treated with Salvarsan ointment or mercury, neither of which was really effective. Not until 1940, following the discovery of penicillin in the late 1920s, would a successful treatment be found.

On these remote islands off the West Australian coast at Shark Bay the only treatment offered was nursing and palliative care — morphine, or laudanum, was effectively the only painkiller then available. Bernier Island had a small tented hospital with a doctor's residence, nurses' quarters, and a laboratory and dispensary. The doctor periodically crossed the strait between the two islands to attend to the women patients on Dorré, but a storm or heavy swell often made it impossible for him to set out.

In *The Passing of the Aborigines* Daisy was so moved by their plight she would write some of her most emotive prose describing them:

> When I landed on Bernier Island in November 1910,
> there were only fifteen men left alive there, but I counted
> thirty-eight graves. The doctor's assistant and the orderly
> staff occupied a wooden building on a rise, the hospital
> was a tent, and the sick were housed in three-sided huts
> of canvas, each with a half-roof of corrugated iron. The
> natives on both islands preferred the open bush to all the
> hospital care and comfort.
>
> Deaths were frequent — appallingly frequent,
> sometimes three in a day — for most of these natives
> were obviously in the last stages of venereal disease and
> tuberculosis. Nothing could save them, and they had been

transported, some of them thousands of miles, to strange and unnatural surroundings and solitude. They were afraid of the hospital, its ceaseless probings and dressings and injections were a daily torture. They were afraid of each other, living and dead. They were desert people and were afraid of the ever-moaning sea.[2]

There was a severe shortage of food on the island and the authorities failed to send in sufficient supplies. 'They were strangers to the island, and the seeds and berries and fish food it could have yielded them,' Daisy observed. 'There were plenty of wallabies, but most of the natives were too emaciated and ill to go hunting.' She described Bernier and Dorré as 'sad islands of death'.

She was acutely aware of the way in which tribal beliefs, lore and customs were disregarded on the islands. She described how:

When the bleak winds blew, the movable huts were turned against them, facing each other, regardless of tribal customs, which meant mistrust and fear. Now and again a dead body would be wrapped in a blanket and carried away to burial in the sands, and the unhappy living could not leave the accursed ground of its spirit. Some became demented, and rambled away and no one of an alien tribe would go to seek them. One day an old man started to 'walk' back over thirty miles of raging waters to the mainland. These shores are infested with sharks, and he was never seen again.[3]

Daisy then crossed to neighbouring Dorré Island, where:

There were seventy-seven women on Dorré Island, many of them bed-ridden. I dared not count the graves there. A frightful sight it was to see grey-headed women, their faces and limbs repulsive in disease, but an even more frightful sight to see the young — and there were children among them. Through unaccustomed frequent hot baths, their withered sensitive skins, which are never cleansed in their natural state save by grease and fresh air, became like tissue-paper and parted horribly from the flesh.[4]

Daisy pointed out the difficulties of dealing with women from different tribes who were traditional enemies:

> Some of them were alone of their group, and they could not give food or a firestick to a possible enemy or a stranger for fear of evil magic. A woman would be called upon to bath and feed or bury another woman whose spirit she knew was certain to haunt her.
>
> Restlessly they roamed the islands in all weathers, avoiding each other as strangers. Some of them cried all day and all night in a listless and terrible monotony of grief. There were others who stood silently for hours on a headland, straining their hollow, hopeless eyes across the narrow strait for the glimpse of . . . a far lost country . . .[5]

Daisy was horrified by the suffering of these syphilitic Aboriginal women, bartered by uncles and cousins to European men in exchange for alcohol and tobacco, or else raped, and infected. Her attitude towards the hospital inmates was in stark contrast to that of Professor Radcliffe-Brown, who regarded them with the chilly detachment of an academic, as statistics for his research. He never became involved with the Aborigines as fellow human beings. He was determined to elicit replies to the questions he posed at any cost, yelling at the patients if they did not respond. Daisy was appalled at his callousness.

By now she and Radcliffe-Brown disliked each other so much that it was impossible for them to continue working together. She left him and Grant Watson on Bernier Island when she went on to Dorré, where she did her best to relieve the sufferings of the Aboriginal women. She made up quantities of the salve for which Father Nicholas had given her the recipe at Beagle Bay Mission and used it to treat their ulcerated sores. She always wore cotton gloves, which Father Nicholas had insisted were essential to minimise the risk of infection through small cuts in the hands. In gratitude, the women of Dorré Island gave Daisy Bates the name she would use for the rest of her life: 'Kabbarli' (pronounced 'Ke-bahlee'). This was a term of respect, roughly translated into English as 'kindly grandmotherly person'. Daisy wrote:

> . . . it was at Dorré Island that I became *kabbarli*,
> Grandmother, to the sick and the dying there, and *kabbarli*
> I was to remain in all my wanderings for the name is a
> generic one, and extends far among the western-central
> and central tribes.
>   Our Expedition parted company in March 1911.
> Professor Radcliffe-Brown continued his researches,
> taking a northward route through the sheep and cattle
> stations of the mainland. Grant Watson sailed for Perth . . .
> Not very long after our visit, the costly hospital project
> and the islands of exile were abandoned.[6]

After leaving Bernier Island, Radcliffe-Brown conducted more research among the Kariera people, while Daisy interviewed Aboriginal groups in the Peak Hill area before she returned to Perth. As a result of the expedition on which she had pinned such high hopes, she had in fact made a bitter enemy and ruined any chances of an academic career for herself. For Radcliffe-Brown, who would make his name from his research into kinship systems and social organisation, the expedition led to more academic recognition — later he would be offered the position of Foundation Professor of Anthropology at the University of Sydney. Before taking up this position he returned to England, taking with him Daisy's manuscript *The Native Tribes of Western Australia*. She believed he took material from it which he used in talks he gave on the Aborigines of Western Australia, but had no proof of this.[7] For years the professor ignored all the letters Daisy sent him asking for the return of her manuscript.

Fortunately she had her own copy of the manuscript and did her best to edit it herself, but the task proved too time-consuming when she desperately needed to earn money. As a woman alone, unsupported by any husband, she had now reached a critical point in her life. She still had grazing leases on the Glen Carrick run. Doubts have been expressed that Daisy ever owned grazing land — that claiming to be a landowner was part of an act to impress her contemporaries. However, records in the Lands Office of Western Australia contain a sketch map of four large parcels of grazing land, together with their measurements, that Jack Bates had assigned to Daisy. For years now she had been unable to pay the rent on the original parcel of land whose lease she had bought with her 'mystery money' when she returned from England. Eventually it was repossessed by the government.

In 1912 she again offered for sale those four large blocks of grazing land near Mount Newman. The four parcels were oblong in shape with water access, and marked on survey maps as 'transferred to Mrs Daisy Bates'. The advertisement of sale stated that the land had no improvements. Minimal fencing was required, as the Ophthalmia Ranges acted as a natural boundary. The advertisement also detailed 'two hundred lost and branded cattle'. Were these the Herefords Daisy had bought, also out of her mystery money? Now she was reminded once more that land in the Pilbara, one of the hottest parts of Australia, was difficult to sell. The land was beautiful, but so isolated, and with such a harsh climate, that no one wanted it. Stubbornly Daisy refused to lower the asking price for years, hoping the market would improve, even though paying rent for the leases kept her perpetually short of money.

Finally, she came to a decision that would ultimately define her proud and singular lifestyle for posterity. She would abandon civilisation to live in a tent and pursue her Aboriginal research, first at Eucla, where the Western Australia–South Australia border meets the shore of the Great Australian Bight, then later near Fowlers Bay, on the eastern reaches of the Bight. It seems apparent that Daisy reached her decision for a variety of reasons. She had failed in all her relationships with men, fallen out with her son, Arnold, who she may have hoped would support her in old age, and failed to establish a home commensurate with her 'ladylike' status. She had failed to publish her research study on the Aboriginal tribes of Western Australia and had lost her hope of an academic career in anthropology due to her sensational journalism and controversial utterances. All her former hopes of a brilliant new life in Australia had disintegrated.

A tent in the desert would provide cheap living, provide her with further valuable research material, and give her time to think about what she should do once the prices of grazing land increased and could be sold at a profit, bringing her much needed capital.

CHAPTER 13

EUCLA AND THE NULLARBOR PLAIN

My tent is so small, 8 x 10 [feet], and so crowded that I haven't
room for . . . more than the necessaries plus my mss. and letters
and Dickens. I have two big tables in my tent, both covered with
my ms. papers etc. etc. and I've just room on one of them to put
down my writing pad or my typewriter or my little breakfast
tray. All three couldn't be placed on the table at one time, only
one of them. My floor space within my tent is 7 x 4 [feet] so
you see how cramped my little home is.

DAISY BATES TO E.W. CROUCH, A COLLECTOR OF ABORIGINAL

ARTEFACTS. FROM THE PAPERS OF ELIZABETH SALTER,

NATIONAL LIBRARY OF AUSTRALIA

In 1912 Daisy boarded a coastal steamer for Eucla. She was
chaperoning a young girl called Beatrice Raine, who was
travelling to stay with her elder brother on his cattle property,
Nullarbor Station, 190 kilometres east of Eucla. Brother and sister
were both well educated and loved books, and Daisy stayed at
Nullarbor Station until October 1913, before setting out for Eucla

to set up her tent to study the Mirning, an Aboriginal group in the area. She would remain friends with Beatrice Raine for the rest of her life, and eventually stay with her in old age at her house in Adelaide.

Eucla, hundreds of kilometres from civilisation and bordered on its seaward side by a semicircle of cliffs, was now a virtual ghost town, a single street of wooden houses with tin roofs, the street itself half buried under shifting sands. It had grown up around a wooden jetty built to service the Overland Telegraph Station, some twenty-four kilometres from the border of South Australia and Western Australia. This was part of a network of telegraph stations that, among other things, connected Adelaide, Katherine, Darwin and London. By now, however, the telephone had come into wider use and Eucla had declined with the demise of the telegraph. The only remaining inhabitants were the station master, the storekeeper, and a few linesmen to service the telegraph line. To the west and east stretched the vast expanse of the Nullarbor Plain. On the shore the decaying jetty received a coastal steamer once every three months. The ship brought mail from Albany or from Fowlers Bay to the east and was the lifeline of those who remained in this isolated place.

Letters from Ireland kept Daisy in touch. As Mrs Swan, Kathleen led a pleasant life with a doting wealthy husband. Marian, as Sister Maria Flavia, continued to find contentment in convent life in Birmingham. (Daisy was convinced that one day her eldest sister would become a Mother Superior.) Little Anne, Daisy's youngest sister (now Mrs O'Connors), whom she had never taken seriously, had become a successful businesswoman, owning property in her own name. Using her grandfather's house as collateral, she had managed to purchase Uncle Joe's former house and shop in Main Street, which she rented out. And curly-headed Jim, who had rambled over the hills of Ballychrine with Daisy, was living in his father's old house in Main Street. He was happily married with two children, and remained a successful cattle dealer. Considering the burning ambition to become rich and secure that had brought Daisy to Australia in the first place, she must have felt that compared with all her siblings she was the least successful in worldly terms. Small wonder she felt depressed.

The final blow came when the South Australian government refused her request for a salary to accompany her new title of Honorary Protector of Aborigines (proclaimed on 11 September 1912): there would be no income or pension to cushion her old age. Seeing her reflection in the looking-glass, Daisy must have observed how she was ageing. Lines were etched around her mouth and eyes. Ever since leaving school at Roscrea she had done her best to associate with educated people and improve herself. All she had to show for those years were a few well-worn reference books, a trunk of antiquated hand-tailored clothes and a set of novels by Charles Dickens. The taste of failure must have been bitter in her mouth.

It was some comfort for Daisy to discover that Eucla had a wild beauty of its own. From her tent, which she pitched amid sandhills close to the telegraph station, she looked out over the huge waves of the Southern Ocean as they rolled into the shore. To her amazement she realised that a single wave could stretch two miles or more in length.

To begin with, Daisy was able to use the outdoor shower and toilet at the telegraph station. Impoverished she might be, but her fierce Irish pride refused to allow her to ask for help, financial or otherwise, from the residents of Eucla. They viewed her with suspicion, even though she insisted, as usual, that she was a member of the Anglo-Irish gentry who had come to study Aboriginal people as a 'hobby'. Among themselves the residents speculated on why an educated white woman was camping out like a tramp or vagabond. Ladies did not do such things. It was even rumoured that Mrs Bates intended to take an Aboriginal lover. To counteract gossip, Daisy was careful never to be seen alone with an Aboriginal man and always wore her ankle-length skirts and high-necked blouses, emerging from her tent with scarely a hair out of place. At a time when most white women would not go near an Aboriginal camp for fear of rape or robbery, Daisy was fearless for her own safety, although she was aware that sleeping alone in a tent, she could encounter problems from white men as well as Aborigines. She was careful to keep a pistol by her bedside for 'emergencies'.

From an account she wrote of 'dogging' or dingo hunting with Aboriginal friends, it appears she was a good shot. Had she been taught by Breaker Morant or Jack Bates? Jack had certainly demonstrated to her various survival methods in the outback, drawn from his long experience as a stockman.

Remnants of desert Aboriginal groups affected by drought and disease had crossed the desert to reach Eucla, with its large soak of underground water. It is thought that for more than 40,000 years Aborigines had roamed the Nullarbor, one of the harshest places on earth. They survived by catching and roasting snakes, goannas, small lizards, wombats and quail-thrushes, but in severe, extended droughts like the one happening then, many such creatures, as well as wallabies and kangaroos, died of thirst. In addition to lacking food, some of the Aborigines at Eucla had become addicted to alcohol given to them by white men in return for the sexual services of Aboriginal girls. Daisy found many of the tribespeople badly affected by European diseases to which they had no resistance: measles and whooping cough as well as venereal diseases including gonorrhoea and syphilis. She realised, too, that the authority of the elders was waning under the stress of colonisation. Respect for tribal lore and the marriage laws which had held together the framework of their society was gradually being eroded; the old taboos were breaking down.

ॐ ॐ ॐ

After a settling-in period, and reconnoitring the area, Daisy introduced herself as 'Kabbarli' to the Aboriginal elders of the Mirning, explaining that as their Lady Protector she had come to help them. She promised that she would supply their sick, elderly and crippled people with billy tea, porridge and damper and with her homemade cough mixture, and would use the salves and ointments in her medicine chest to soothe their sores. In return, she would ask them questions about their previous nomadic way of life. She planned to use the information she obtained in another study on desert Aborigines, their way of life and their ceremonies, myths and legends.

She obtained help to pitch her canvas tent three kilometres from the telegraph station, out of sight of prying eyes, beyond the gossip and much closer to the survivors of the semi-nomadic Mirning, Kokata and Pindini family groups. To her surprise she found there was only one survivor from the original Eucla clan. This old man explained that the totem of the Eucla group was the wild currant, or *ngoora*. The currant bushes stood about a metre high and bore berries that other groups came to feast upon each year. This year the harvest brought new groups to the area for Daisy to study. As each new clan arrived, she stood beside her mulga fence and politely offered them tea and damper.

Daisy had arranged for a brush fence to be erected around her tent and never allowed any man, Aboriginal or European, to come beyond it. The woman who had had three husbands and at least one lover, who had claimed that she enjoyed 'meeting, loving and parting', now reinvented herself as a stickler for respectability, the very model of propriety. Doubtless she feared that if anything from her past leaked out, no one would take her scientific aspirations seriously. In a remarkable volte-face, Daisy Bates, once a free spirit, now became critical of the sexual behaviour of others.

She overcame loneliness by keeping herself busy and befriending the Aborigines she interviewed. She continued to correspond with anthropologists and ethnologists and write long letters to friends. In a letter to surveyor-turned-anthropologist R.H. Mathews, an expert on desert Aborigines, Daisy wrote that she had gone to live in the desert because she was motivated by 'the virus of research'. Other anthropologists and explorers also regarded her research as very important. Working as a trainee journalist in London, Daisy had learned interviewing skills that most male anthropologists lacked. They would make a long trip to a remote area, find a group of Aborigines, stay there for a few days, ask their questions and depart. Since they neglected to win the confidence of Aboriginal people before interviewing them, they often failed to achieve the in-depth responses that Daisy Bates received or to learn about tribal ceremonies the way she did — the barrier of her gender notwithstanding. Daisy also kept in contact with newspaper editors such as William Hurst of *The Australasian*, a popular and rather sensationalist weekly, and British-based Arthur Mee, who produced a *Boy's Own*-style newspaper for children. They both bought articles from her.

She was happy to find a pet, a basking lizard that became so tame it would answer her call and sit on her lap. She tied a skein of red wool to its leg so that none of the Aborigines would harm it. During the day she enjoyed playing with the tousle-haired, dark-eyed Aboriginal children and invited them inside the sandy enclave around her tent where adult visitors were banned.

But night and darkness brought a greater sense of loneliness. Eating her evening meal in her tent, Daisy would often lay extra places for distinguished guests she would have liked to invite to a dinner party. Sitting alone at her card table, she would place photos cut out of old newspapers on the empty plates of her imaginary guests. Poignantly she described how this made her feel she was enjoying their company. Such guests reflected her obsession with British royalty and its Australian representatives, the State governors and their wives. Guests included Queen Mary; Edward, the Prince of Wales; Prince Henry, Duke of Gloucester; Sir Francis Newdegate — who became governor of Tasmania in 1917 — and his wife; former governor of Western Australia, Sir Frederick Bedford and Lady Bedford; and former premier of Western Australia, Sir John Forrest, and his wife. Wearing her antiquated clothes from another era, her tent lit by candlelight, thousands of kilometres away from civilisation, Daisy held conversations with her guests, chatting away about details of her life or books she had read. She said it helped to keep her mind active.

In hindsight, however, it appears that this somewhat delusive practice signalled the start of a very long and slow decline in Daisy's reasoning power. The problem for Daisy was that, as a result of her experience of living in isolated fringe camps from 1904 onwards, only broken by short trips to the city, her diet was inevitably low in fresh vegetables and fruit. This, of course, was long before refrigerated trucks brought a range of food to the outback. Her spartan diet, which she always maintained was healthy, lacked essential vitamins, especially thiamine, as well as niacin and iron. Her staple fare in the desert consisted of billy tea with powdered milk, oat porridge, damper with jam and treacle, and a few potatoes baked in her campfire, all foods that could be stored easily. In season, she ate nutritious scarlet quandongs and wild blackcurrants, but they only fruited for a short time. As a treat she enjoyed an occasional piece of roast goanna, bush turkey, mallee-hen or snake given to her by the Mirning or shot by Daisy herself.

Slowly and relentlessly the lack of vitamins and essential minerals would harden her arteries and slow down the flow of blood to her brain. She was afflicted by an insidious disease known as vascular dementia, which over the years would cause specific clusters of brain cells to die, resulting in aberrations of thought processes and obsessions. (It is likely that Daisy's obsessions with Aboriginal infant cannibalism, which she wrote about in her popular articles, as well as her illogical prejudice against half-caste children, arose from this disease.) Physically she was tough and loved taking long walks, which kept her very fit; it was her mental health that was affected.

※ ※ ※

In time Daisy learned to love the freedom of her life on the edge of the desert, in her 'blackcurrant camp' with its superb view across the sandhills, the only sound the distant roar of the surf. Gradually the beauty of the area soothed her and she started to feel happy once more, refreshed mentally and physically by her tranquil surroundings. She was content with her new research project on desert Aborigines, which would extend across the rest of her career as a pioneer ethnologist or anthropologist — depending on your point of view — the occupation that had brought meaning to her life. Later, in her book *The Passing of the Aborigines*, Daisy would write, 'A glorious thing it is to live in a tent in the infinite — to waken in the grey of dawn, a good hour before the sun outlines the low ridges of the horizon, and to come out into the bright cool air, and scent the wind blowing across the mulga plains.'

She described the Nullarbor as a vast limestone plateau covered in reddish sandy soil, freckled with mallee scrub and blue-grey saltbush. Beneath an arc of brilliant blue sky was some of the most dramatic scenery in Australia. The Nullarbor, with its wind-blown ridges of reddish sand, covered more than 200,000 square kilometres extending into Western Australia and north to the Great Victoria Desert. Originally a gigantic seabed, it was now honeycombed by limestone caves that contained supplies of fresh water. Rain was a rare event. When it fell, the water penetrated the porous limestone and trickled down into huge underground lakes known as 'soaks'. In the course of the long drought these lakes were now drying up, which spelt disaster for the desert people and the game they lived on.

Her days developed a regular pattern. Each day she wrote down the new words she was learning from the various Aboriginal languages spoken around her, pinning the slips of paper around her looking-glass to help her to learn them. Morning duties to 'my natives' consisted of taking billycans of sugary tea to the sick and elderly, together with small bowls of porridge. As they drank and ate she asked them questions about Aboriginal lore, initiation ceremonies and kinship systems, jotting down their answers on scraps of paper. She always noted the identities of her informants.

Then she would crouch beside the elderly Aborigines in order to treat sore eyes with borax and rub her special salve into the wounds that had erupted on their bodies. She also treated the children's eyes, in order to prevent them becoming victims of 'sandy blight', a form of ophthalmia, and did what she could to help the Aboriginal people during epidemics of measles and influenza. Daisy had never received any nursing training, but she remembered simple remedies her grandmother had used at Ballychrine. The medicine chest in her tent contained Condy's crystals for bathing sores, insecticides for treating body lice, eucalyptus oil, Epsom salts and senna pods. Her cough mixture was based on an Irish recipe: a tablespoon each of honey, brandy, lemon, olive oil, sugar and vinegar. Many a doubt has been voiced about the effectiveness of her nursing, but she did her best with minimal resources.

During the hottest part of the day Daisy slept in her tent. Once it grew cooler she would go out again with more tea and food late in the afternoon. Returning to her tent, sipping water and lemon juice in a vain attempt to keep cool, she would sit at her work table and transfer the jottings she had made to her notebook. Then, after a simple meal, she would sit quietly on a chair in front of her tent to watch the sun set.

Amid the silence of the desert, Daisy's insecurities and her former desire to impress everyone with tales of her youth at Ashberry House and with the Outrams of Hallans Hall faded into insignificance. 'Her' Aborigines knew nothing of the British class system. Daisy was aware that they liked her for herself and what she did for them. They were totally uninterested in who her father was or how many husbands she had married. They simply accepted her as 'Kabbarli', a compassionate, grandmotherly person who had come to help them at a time when few white Australians seemed to care whether they lived or died in one of the worst droughts ever experienced.

Thinking of her childhood in Ireland, Daisy found parallels between the Aborigines and the impoverished and dispossessed Irish who had slowly recovered from the Great Famine. She recalled how Granny Hunt had also acted as 'Kabbarli' to the wretched souls at Ballychrine.

At Eucla, Daisy wrote down legends the Aborigines told her about giant serpents that crawled out of gullies or star-crossed lovers who disobeyed tribal law and were turned to stone. Some were their creation legends of the Dreaming; others sought to explain how the Aborigines had discovered fire; there were totemic tales of birds and animals that sought to explain how they had acquired their characteristics, and others that taught tribal beliefs. Outstanding were the stellar legends, related to the bright stars and constellations in the clear night sky above the desert. Sometimes the myths and legends were incomplete or misremembered: Daisy might hear the beginning of a legend from one storyteller and its conclusion much later from someone else.

She recalled the Gaelic tales Allie and her grandmother had told of heroes, giants, demons, witches, banshees and leprechauns, conjuring up a world of magic creatures in which the wind and the rain were endowed with the power of speech. Because of her Irish upbringing, Daisy accepted Aboriginal tales of unquiet spirits who could not rest but stayed close to the spot where they died. She found nothing unusual in the fact that the Aborigines refused to utter the name of the recently dead, fearing that if they did, the spirits of the dead would haunt them. She knew that storytelling provided an outlet from the harshness of life, an escape into the rich world of the imagination that respected the spiritual aspects of life.

Daisy loved the quick wit of Aboriginal people, their gift for mimicry, their lack of malice. In return they accepted her lack of personal possessions as a normal state of affairs. In her heart Daisy grew very grateful for the warmth and friendship that Aboriginal people showed her at what was possibly the lowest ebb of her adult life.

Without a regular income, Daisy managed to survive on the edge of the desert by spending very little and continuing to wear her outmoded clothes, an economy that helped to establish her iconic appearance and reputation for eccentricity. Freelance journalism was her only way of earning money, but from now onwards she wrote very little that was new. She recycled articles she had written when she first came to Western Australia in 1899 — her most productive period. She knew that most editors still wanted sensational stories about circumcision rites and wholesale infant cannibalism and she obliged, doubtless salving her conscience by reasoning that the money paid by newspapers she was spending on feeding ailing Aboriginal people and clothing adults and children. *The Australasian*, the *Western Mail* and the *Adelaide Observer* continued to buy this sort of material from her until she reached her late sixties, by which time Mrs Bates received complaints that her articles had become repetitive and were rambling in style.

Whenever Daisy received a cheque for one of her articles, she would place an order for sacks of oatmeal and flour and crates of jam, treacle and tea to be sent to Eucla by steamer. She would continue this pattern when she moved to Ooldea, on the Trans-Australian railway line, via which her supplies were sent. In addition to the 'Kabbarli tucker' she supplied, various community groups to whom she had lectured in Perth sent her parcels containing bandages, cough syrup and Vicks Vapour Rub. She always insisted that these organisations should send brand-new clothes, fearing that second-hand clothing could spread 'white man's diseases' such as measles. Perhaps, too, Daisy recalled her own humiliation when she was forced to accept hand-me-down clothes from wealthy boarders at the Convent of the Sacred Heart in Roscrea, manifested in her lifelong hatred of the very word 'charity'. What she most wanted at this stage in her life was to be paid a salary by the State or Commonwealth government in return for her work as Lady Protector of Aborigines — surely not an unreasonable desire for someone doing unpaid aid work and spending her own money on Aboriginal people.

Photograph from The Passing of the Aborigines *of a group of desert Aboriginal men
whose ceremonial patterns were first traced on the skin in blood
and then picked out with down taken from small birds. Daisy made detailed notes
of traditional customs, language and ceremonies.*

CHAPTER 14

CAMPING AT JERGALA CREEK
ON THE EDGE OF THE DESERT

*All you boggli [grandsons] bring your spears to me . . . I will sit
down and take care of them, and then you can go a little way
and have a good fight, and come back for food.*

DAISY BATES DEFUSING A TENSE SITUATION IN THE DESERT

Once Daisy had obtained all the material she needed on
Mirning customs and language, she decided to move her tent
sixteen kilometres away to a new campsite beside an isolated
waterhole on Jergala Creek, where there was a much larger
Aboriginal group. The totem of the Jergala inhabitants was the bush
turkey. As none of the European men at Eucla offered to help Daisy
to move her camp, men from the Mirning set up her tents at Jergala,
and Jergala people built her a windbreak and a bough shed.

Daisy was a good organiser. She made sure her dunny was kept
clean and sweet with phenol disinfectant and disposed of food
scraps by burying them in a trench to avoid flies, techniques she had
picked up from Jack Bates on their journeys in Western Australia.

Cooking in a camp oven over the ashes of her fire while wearing a long skirt had problems (in pioneer days numerous women found their skirts caught alight). As the numbers of Aborigines coming to Jergala increased dramatically, she delegated to some of them the task of making the damper or oat porridge each day for those unable to feed themselves.

The water she fetched from the waterhole for herself and ailing Aboriginal people who lacked relatives to care for them was kept in an earthernware crock in her tent. But in summer it became too hot to drink. Sandstorms and winds constantly blew grains of sand among her possessions. In mid-winter the winds blew cold and temperatures could drop below freezing point. Carting water for herself and the Aborigines, she staggered beneath two heavy buckets she carried on a yoke. She refused to lower her standards and always took her daily 'canvas-bag shower'. The Aborigines used water only for drinking; instead of washing, they oiled their skin until it gleamed in the sun.

At Jergala, Daisy claimed she attended traditional male initiation ceremonies, giving the men to understand (as she had done previously) that she was in fact *Kallower*, a 'male spirit' returned from the dead, with a special *kabbarli* magic of her own. This questionable practice has attracted her a good deal of criticism in recent years and implied that Aboriginal women did not invite her to watch their ceremonies.

She noted that each family made unique and beautiful body paintings in various designs, using red and white ochres, pipe-clay and animal fat to adorn them.

She gave detailed descriptions of the rituals of initiation that she observed, in all their stages. One stage she claimed to have observed involved relatives squeezing blood from cuts in their arms which was sprinkled on the initiate. The ceremony was an elaborate process that took place over several days.[1] Daisy wrote:

> The last manhood ceremony of Eucla was held in 1913,
> when Gooradoo, a boy of the turkey totem, was initiated
> at Jeegala [sic] Creek . . . A great crowd of natives straggled

in by degrees, remnants from all round the plain's edge,
from Fraser Range, Boundary Dam, Israelite Bay, as far east
as Penong, and as far north as Ayer's Rock . . . 700 miles
and more of foot-travelling. There were numbers of
women among them, as in all these gatherings an
exchange of women is an important part of the ceremony.

. . .

In physique the border natives were fine sturdy fellows
. . . 'We are Koogurda,' they told me, and frankly admitted
the hunting and sharing of kangaroo and human meat as
frequently as that of kangaroo and emu. The Baduwonga
of Boundary Dam drank the blood of those they had
killed.[2]

Although Daisy claimed in her often unreliable memoir that
cannibals were camped all around her tent, this was another
fantasy encouraged by her more sensationalist publishers to sell
newspapers.

Not all was peace and harmony between the different family
groups at Jergala Creek. When a contingent of Wanji-wanji dancers
arrived, no fires were lit to greet them; instead, the men at Jergala
waited for them with spears and clubs, ready to fall upon them.
Daisy believed she must do something, otherwise bloodthirsty
carnage would ensue. She stayed calm and maintained that in her
role of *Kallower* she could interpose herself between the two groups.

'All you *boggli* (grandsons) bring your spears to me,' she said
quietly, attempting to defuse the situation. 'I will sit down and take
care of them, and then you can go little way and have a good fight,
and come back for food.'[3]

To Daisy's relief, the belligerent men, their body language
expressing rage and hostility, respected her air of authority and
handed over their spears, which she arranged according to their
totem groups. 'Now go and have plenty talk,' she said firmly, treating
them like the children to whom she had once acted as governess.
They walked away into the distance, where she heard them yelling
out their grievances at each other. Then, without rancour, they

returned, hungry for the damper she was cooking over the campfire and the sweet jam that would accompany it.

The Wanji-wanji were famous for dances and songs concerned with their Dreamings. At the Jergala Creek corroboree, which lasted a fortnight, they gave three performances each day. Daisy wrote that she attended all the (all-male) ceremonies. However, many anthropologists, knowing that certain parts of the dances were forbidden to be seen by any woman on pain of death, did not believe her assertions she was allowed to watch. Yet night after night Daisy heard the music and chanting and described the 'orgies' as they continued. She described how one man, having danced himself into an overheated frenzy, lay down on the damp ground and went into a rigor that led to paralysis and death. Was she exaggerating? At this remove and with no other recorded witnesses, who can say.

The grand finale of the initiation ceremonies was the introduction of the new initiates into the totems and the addition of new totem boards to the sacred store. At Jergala, Daisy claimed that she was initiated into the freedom of *all* the totems, including mallee-hen, curlew, native cat, wild currant, kangaroo, emu, dingo and bush turkey.

On the last day she was woken by the clicking of boomerangs outside her tent, where some fifty men had gathered in a half-circle. They carried spears and were naked except for painted stripes of red ochre and white pipe-clay, cockatoo feathers, and belts or girdles spun from human hair, some coloured with human blood. They had arrived to escort their 'Kabbarli' to the place where the presentation of the totem boards would take place.

Daisy's sense of humour made her appreciate the bizarre spectacle as they set out in procession. Here was she, an elderly woman in a straw hat with fly veil, a long skirt and high-necked blouse, walking along to a site called Beera, about eight kilometres west of Eucla Telegraph Station, surrounded by Aboriginal men whose naked bodies gleamed with oil. Two of the men, Wirrgain and Karndung, ran beside the procession uttering blood-curdling 'eaglehawk' screams that echoed among the cliffs.

The men reached a cleared space where a large bonfire had been lit and danced around it chanting the songs of the totems. Suddenly, at the far end of the clearing, a tall bearded elder named Wardunda appeared, holding a giant *koondain*, a totem board over four metres high, carved and painted with the sacred markings of Maalu, the kangaroo. Daisy and the young initiates were touched with smaller totem boards carved with the same symbols as more songs were sung. Remembering the Catholic Masses of her childhood, Daisy described how Wardunda lifted the giant board as though he were the priest elevating the host. After the ceremony was over all the boards were placed in a little storehouse built from mallee branches, its opening hidden by fresh mallee leaves and the procession returned to the camp.

ॐ ॐ ॐ

At such gatherings for male initiation corroborees, Daisy would ask the different family groups questions about the Aboriginal trade routes that traversed Australia. She discovered that Aborigines from the north bartered pearl shells — which in the south were thought to have magic properties — as well as precious red ochre and flint knives. Other traded items included various grades of hardwood spears, stone heads, fur-string belts, tails of the rabbit and bandicoot, clubs made from strong roots, carved and painted shields from the people of the Murchison Ranges, and bull roarers from Central Desert people. Daisy even saw what she took to be a Neolithic stone axe from the eastern Kimberley. All these diverse objects found their way over immense distances along recognised trade routes, increasing in value as they travelled.

Daisy continued to feed the elderly natives in her care, to tend their body sores and bathe their eyes, aware that they could go blind. Although she herself wore dark glasses, her eyes were starting to suffer from the sun's glare. At night she used to write by candlelight, but now she found this too much of a strain. On one occasion she suffered so badly from 'sandy blight' (ophthalmia) that she was virtually blind for two weeks, and was glad of the pieces of roasted goanna and snake that her Aboriginal 'grandchildren' gave her until she recovered.

She loved going outside her tent at night to look at the stars, so bright in the clear sky. When the wind came from the right direction, the blowholes in the limestone caves created an eerie music she enjoyed hearing. During the day she appreciated the beauty around her — the vivid colours of the white or reddish sandhills, the green of the saltbush, and the vivid blue sky.

Sometimes she would join the Aborigines around their campfire, sitting down with elderly women whom she regarded as her friends, learning more legends from them, aware that the entire Eucla area had spiritual significance for the local people. She also realised that many of the Aborigines' ancient traditions, their complex kinship systems and the marriage laws that had underpinned their culture and nomadic way of life for thousands of years were collapsing.

Each month brought more deaths. On her daily rounds of the sick and elderly, she found many of the people in great pain as they waited stoically for the mysterious end to life that they called *nalba*. More and more often she heard Aboriginal women keening for their dead.

Winter was a dangerous time at Jergala, bringing the threat of infection transmitted through small cuts or sores. On winter nights the Nullarbor Plain was extremely cold, and Daisy developed chilblains on her hands. Whenever she treated ailing Aborigines she wore a white overall over her clothes and kept up her permanent order for white cotton gloves to be sent out to her from John Martins department store in Adelaide. These were vital for her treatment of those suffering from syphilis, who would turn to her in their despair and confusion to ask what was happening to them. Mrs Bates was unusually frank about sexual matters for a woman of her era. She had no qualms about discussing venereal disease and used words such as 'penis', 'scrotum', 'testicles' and 'vagina', which most ladies of that era genteelly avoided.

When she first lived alongside Aboriginal people, Daisy had been surprised to discover that they did not relate the sexual act to pregnancy: instead, they believed that children came to them through their spiritual life — their Dreaming. What Daisy never fully grasped was how important family life was to 'her' Aborigines — and how much they pitied Kabbarli for living alone without any relatives, which may have made them kinder and more tolerant towards her often autocratic ways.

ৡ ৡ ৡ

On Christmas Day 1913, in extremely hot weather, Daisy recorded cooking a special meal of damper with jam, tea and plum pudding for fifty-three Aboriginal friends. The 'plum pudding' mixture was a recipe Daisy invented specially for desert conditions. It consisted of a huge bucket of crumbled Weetabix cereal moistened by condensed milk to which boiled currants and raisins were added and tinned peaches with even more condensed milk poured over the top and then left to set solid in the sun. The pudding was very sweet and sticky. Daisy knew that Aboriginal people were very fond of sweet food, in particular the blind and elderly and the smiling Aboriginal children who flocked around to receive a slice each.

The success of this Christmas lunch by Daisy, who freely admitted she was a mediocre cook, prompted her to continue the custom each Christmas. Acting the role of cook-hostess helped her overcome a lonely time.

No letter or card arrived from Arnold, whose continuing rejection of his mother must have hurt her a great deal but was never mentioned in her Christmas letters to friends, such as Ainslie Fairbairn, a daughter of Robert Fairbairn, former government resident at Roebourne. The fact that she had left Arnold for the years she spent in England had formed a barrier between Daisy and her son that nothing could ever bridge.

With Jack Bates working as manager of a cattle station near Darwin, Daisy had no contact with him either. In fact, she and Jack would never meet again. When he retired he stayed with a nephew, or lived in cheap lodging houses. Jack would die almost insolvent in a hotel room at Mullawa, near Geraldton, around 1935. Daisy did not attend his funeral.

ৡ ৡ ৡ

In her many notebooks and on scraps of paper Daisy recorded that the Mirning — like most Aborigines — did not believe in the concept of private property and held all possessions in common. For them belief and ritual were far more important than possessions. She observed how hard Aboriginal women worked as the gatherers of roots and bulbs, grubs, seeds and fruit, going out with their coolamons and digging sticks and using grinding stones to make food palatable. Strict laws regarding the distribution of food meant that the hunters must be fed first with the choicest cuts of any roast creature before the women received mainly offal and skin. While pure-blood Aboriginal children were fed on meat scraps and offal, along with the elderly, mixed-race children would be fed last of all, and if there wasn't enough to go around they were the ones who went hungry.

At Sandstone and in railway workers' camps, Daisy had been horrified and saddened by seeing Aboriginal girls bartered for grog to white men. At this time, Aboriginal fringe camps were regarded by white men as a source of 'black velvet', the pejorative term for sexual intercourse with black girls. Daisy herself experienced one distressing night when drunken men, probably rail or telegraph workers from Eucla, jumped the fence and burst into her tent while she was sleeping. They waved bottles of alcohol, demanding Aboriginal girls in exchange. Waking in the dark, Daisy thought they had come to rob or assault her. She screamed for help and Mirning men rushed to defend her. A fight ensued. The Mirning men won and the drunken Europeans departed, vowing vengeance on the 'bloody boongs'.

From her knowledge of Aboriginal lore, Daisy learned that if a European man had sex with either a full-blood or part-Aboriginal woman, he was expected to regard her family as his close relatives, and must share food and tobacco with them. Since the European was occupying Aboriginal land, it was natural that the Aborigines expected him to honour their laws. When such expectations and obligations were not fulfilled, his Aboriginal 'relatives' would feel cheated, and bitter fights often took place. Neither the Europeans nor the Aborigines could understand the other group's point of view.

Now Daisy was shocked to learn that pubescent 'half-caste' Aboriginal girls with European fathers, some only ten or eleven years old, were given as sex toys to white men, bartered by their Aboriginal 'uncles' or half-brothers in return for tobacco, grog and sugar. Just as these part-Aboriginal girls were the last to receive food, so they were always the first to be abused or prostituted, because they occupied such a lowly position in Aboriginal society.

One might imagine that Daisy would have been sympathetic to the plight of these part-Aboriginal girls, but in common with many people in her era she developed an obsession against so-called 'miscegenation'. As part of this obsession, possibly exacerbated by her slow slide into dementia, she banned part-Aborigines from any camp she ran. Such was Daisy's virulence in opposing child abuse that she misguidedly believed these half-caste girls, who would always be the first to be bartered for, would have a better life if they were sent away to homes or missions. She was also aware of the terrible consequences of contracting venereal disease; she would never forget those slow, painful deaths from syphilis she had witnessed among women on the 'Isles of the Dead'.

At that time neither Daisy nor many other people of goodwill realised the misery and suffering these 'stolen children' endured, grieving for their mothers and missing the world in which they had grown up. Nor were such people aware of the abuse and cruelty that so often took place in missions or government-run homes. Having benefited so greatly from her education by nuns, Daisy thought homes and missions would provide an acceptable solution. But these unfortunate girls did not receive a proper education, and were merely trained to become a source of cheap child labour. Their wages were taken by the government; only rarely did they receive the money due to them. When the girls went out to work, white men continually pestered Aboriginal and part-Aboriginal girls for sex, and if they became pregnant the cycle continued. The girls' babies were promptly removed from them, allegedly for their own protection.

Daisy Bates has also incurred disfavour among Aboriginal people today for her assertions that widespread infant cannibalism took place. Aboriginal laws often seemed harsh to Europeans, but they had been formulated for a nomadic lifestyle in unforgiving territory where white explorers died of hunger and thirst. Australian anthropologists A.P. Elkin and Charles Mountford, who were working around the same time as Daisy or slightly later, described how in certain groups Aboriginal lore sanctioned the deaths of deformed babies who would not stand up to long treks through the desert, and how the weaker infant of twins was killed for much the same reason. Findings like these may have influenced Daisy to form her own theories about the subject.

CHAPTER 15

JOINING THE HIGH AND MIGHTY

The entire scientific world is a hierarchy of snobbery. Each science looks down on the new ones . . . the old ones being seen as far more complicated and difficult than the newer ones . . . while male scientists tend to look down on women in science.

MARGARET MEAD, AS CHAIRMAN OF THE AMERICAN ASSOCIATION
FOR THE PROMOTION OF SCIENCES

By 1913 Daisy Bates had been appointed an honorary member of several scientific societies, a rare honour for a woman of her era.

Then, early in 1914, she was thrilled to be invited to Melbourne to present a paper, 'The Social Organisation of Some Western Australian Tribes', at the conference of the British Association for the Advancement of Science, and to attend smaller, associated conferences in Adelaide and Sydney. The main anthropology conference was to be chaired by Professor Baldwin Spencer, an authority on the Arrerente and other linguistic groups of Central Australia. Daisy hoped that at such a conference she might at last make contact with a publisher for her magnum opus, the later

Gauera and her husband Balgundra accompanied Daisy on the trek across the Nullarbor to Yalata, the first leg of Daisy's journey to the Adelaide opening of the 1914 Australian meeting of the British Association for the Advancement of Science.

*Gauera beside the camel buggy
in which they crossed the Nullarbor*

published *Native Tribes of Western Australia*. In order to attend the conference she sought financial assistance from Georgina King, a talented amateur geologist and sister of the eminent businessman Sir George Kelso King.

Miss King was sympathetic towards Daisy, as she believed her own research had been plagiarised by the New South Wales government geologist, Edward Pittman, and by Professor Edgeworth David, and she objected to the fact that women were rarely asked to address learned societies. She kindly provided Daisy with sufficient money for a gruelling journey across the desert.

Daisy set out on the long trek across the waterless Nullarbor Plain, with only a compass to steer by. There were no maps. From an Afghan driver in Eucla she hired a buggy and camels to pull it, and chose two Aboriginal friends to accompany her: Gauera and Gauera's most recent husband, Balgundra. It was mid-winter and at night the temperature in the desert fell below freezing. In a series of photographs taken by Daisy, Gauera and Balgundra wear warm sweaters and coats she had bought them. At the last moment Gauera's former husband, Ngilallilea, announced he would come too. The fact he was naked except for a string penis cover worried Daisy. She was quite used to naked Aboriginal men but feared that he would fall ill and ruin their chances of reaching their destination. However, it was too late to obtain more clothes so Daisy added extra blankets to the luggage.[1] Photographs show the buggy piled high with Daisy's suitcase, sacks of tea, flour and sugar, and in one of them, the wheel of a bicycle, which Daisy planned to ride around Melbourne, protrudes above the sacks. Fat, jolly Gauera in her new overcoat and felt hat, and Daisy wearing her long coat and skirt and a hat with the inevitable fly veil, sat in front of the sacks. Gauera sang some of the corroboree songs she'd learned from the Wanji-wanji, while Daisy, who loved Aboriginal chants, did her best to join in and jot down the words in her notebook.

Progress was slow. Sometimes both women got down and walked beside the camels. Fortunately Daisy had allowed two months for the 240-kilometre trek, travelling from waterhole to waterhole. The camels padded on day after day over the reddish-gold sand and eventually the little party arrived at Yalata, near Fowlers Bay, in good time. There Daisy sent her three Aboriginal companions back with the buggy to Eucla, while she stayed at Yalata Station with Mr and Mrs George Murray so she could recuperate and become accustomed to white civilisation again before attending the conference.

From Yalata, Daisy wrote to thank Georgina King for her help and told her about the trip. She found the Murrays very kind to the Aboriginal people: many old and sick Aborigines from the eastern and northern edges of the plain found shelter on the property, where they sat behind the woodshed 'mostly gossiping and loafing, always sure of a sympathetic understanding with plenty of good food and kind treatment from Boonari (as George Murray was known), notwithstanding the fact that the native dogs played havoc with the sheep'.[2]

Leaving Yalata, she took a steamer around the Eyre Peninsula to Adelaide. There she gave evidence before staff of the South Australian Department of Home Affairs that the Mirning and other Aboriginal groups were suffering from syphilis and ophthalmia. She also pointed out that providing help to 'her' Aborigines had drained her funds. Daisy was finally given an unpaid appointment as Travelling Protector of Aborigines, with a special commission to conduct inquiries into Aboriginal problems such as working conditions on cattle and sheep stations and the bartering of young Aboriginal women for alcohol and tobacco.

Daisy's land remained unsold and her financial position remained bleak; she asked the South Australian government for a salary to go with her new title, as well as funding for Aboriginal health measures, but her requests were ignored.

ॐ ॐ ॐ

The 1914 Australian meeting of the British Association for the Advancement of Science was spread over several weeks and held at different geographical locations. It opened in Adelaide and was attended by over 300 British scientists and 5000 locals. Luminaries such as Professor Baldwin Spencer, William Bateson, W.H. Rivers and the famous European anthropologist Professor Bronislaw Malinowski, who had carried out research in Papua New Guinea, were all speakers at the anthropology session in Adelaide. Daisy soon found many male academics who practised 'veranda

anthropology' rather than using direct interviewing techniques as she did. The fact that these men were content to observe Aboriginal people from afar rather than conducting fieldwork amazed her.

However, the warmth of the reception for her scientific work by some of her male colleagues revived her confidence that the research she was doing was important. Professor Radcliffe-Brown delivered a paper based on his experiences in Western Australia, and Daisy claimed that

Daisy in 1914

she heard many of the points made in her unpublished manuscript read out. Years later she would describe how she ironically congratulated the professor for presenting her material so well. She didn't record his reply so we cannot know whether it was withering or explosive. Since the published conference papers contain only brief extracts of the work of each speaker, at this remove it is impossible to judge how much of Radcliffe-Brown's paper was really based on Daisy Bates's research.[3]

Then, on the third day of the Adelaide conference, a telegraphed message arrived bearing the momentous news that the forces of Kaiser Wilhelm of Germany had invaded Belgium. Britain, which had pledged to defend Belgium, immediately declared war on Germany and its ally Austria, which had now invaded Serbia following the assassination of Archduke Franz Ferdinand at Sarajevo. Australia followed suit, pledging to raise a fighting force against the enemy. World War I had begun. The delegates were so shocked by the news that the conference ended in disarray. Everyone had sons, brothers, fathers who might enlist. Aboriginal problems and the need for more money to help solve them slipped off the agenda. Daisy had hoped to use the conference to plead for more humane treatment of Aborigines and increased medical funds to help them. Now this proved impossible.

But there were further conference sessions in Melbourne and Sydney. At one session in Sydney Daisy met an artist named Olive Pink, who told her that she too wanted to help Aborigines. Daisy invited Miss Pink to stay with her in the desert, an invitation which would be accepted several years later. She also received news that having dropped the price substantially, her land on the Fortescue River had sold.

After returning to Adelaide, Daisy found herself stranded there by a desert sandstorm. She discovered that she liked this elegant city with its bluestone houses, neatly laid out streets and excellent State Library and museum. She hoped that one day she might buy a house for herself in the Adelaide Hills. During her stay she formed significant friendships with kindly Miss Kathleen Kyffin-

Thomas, from an old pioneering family, and the wealthy, philanthropic Barr-Smith family, as well as the Duttons. These were people of goodwill who donated money anonymously over the long term to help Aboriginal people. From Daisy's contact with the Barr-Smiths would stem her future friendship with their young daughter Ursula, a warm-hearted girl who was fascinated by art and felt she should use her trust fund to help others. Ursula Barr-Smith would eventually marry wealthy department store owner Bill Hayward and both would become staunch supporters of Daisy Bates's work.

Finally, Daisy returned to Yalata Station, where she intended to study different Aboriginal family groups. She arranged for the Eucla telegraph station master to send on her tents and other possessions to the nearest railhead. From Yalata she subsequently travelled to another fringe-dwellers' site at Wirilya, west of Fowlers Bay. Here she studied Indigenous customs and legends, and engaged in the 'participant research' in which she excelled, preparing series of questions and taking down the answers. At Wirilya she encouraged local Aborigines to make hand-drawn maps of their hunting territories, as she had previously done in Western Australia, and wherever possible she added the European names of places. Few other anthropologists did this, and today such information is extremely important.

Even with the sale of her land, Daisy did not have enough money to buy a house in the Adelaide Hills, as she had hoped. Nevertheless, she was able to pay off worrying debts and invest the remainder to provide a very small annual income.[4]

Meanwhile, all the newspapers were filled with accounts of armed conflict on the beaches of Gallipoli and in the trenches of France. Few people wanted to read anything about Aborigines, and there was no market for the freelance articles that had provided a small source of income.

The only person to whom Daisy confided her disappointment was Georgina King, but Daisy's fierce Irish pride would not allow her to ask Miss King for more money to help with her work. The topic of Daisy's outdated clothes arose only when Miss King in a letter politely inquired why Daisy clung to the fashions of a vanished era. Daisy replied that her hand-tailored garments had acquired a timeless charm. Pride prevented her from saying that the reason she continued to wear them was lack of money to buy new ones.

֍ ֍ ֍

Some time towards the end of the war Daisy suffered a nervous breakdown, something she covered up when she later recounted her memoir to Ernestine Hill. All she ever revealed about the stress and anxiety, no doubt caused by the disappointing prices she was receiving for her grazing blocks, was contained in these words: 'In 1918 a bad breakdown in health brought me to Adelaide for medical attention.' She went on: 'When the beautiful Mount Lofty Hills had restored my vigour I was asked by the authorities to take charge of the Returned Soldiers Home at Myrtle Bank, which needed reorganising . . . Although I knew comparatively little of matronship as such, I did know a great deal about mothering.' In view of the fact that Daisy had virtually abandoned her son to go off to England, this seems a highly questionable statement.

Patriotic fervour meant that most women had carried out some sort of war work, and Daisy naturally wanted to record that she had done her bit — as well as concealing the episode of her nervous breakdown. Returned soldiers with tuberculosis were treated at the war veterans home in the suburb of Myrtle Bank, which was administered for the Repatriation Commission, under Dr Bedlington Morris. Daisy's slowly advancing vascular dementia was damaging some of her cognitive powers and she found working as a matron a great strain, and resigned after two months.

This and other fantasies would be incorporated into the memoirs recorded by Ernestine Hill and into the biography written by Elizabeth Salter. Ernestine Hill later excused herself from checking facts by saying: 'Of her private life, I asked no questions, writing only what she wished me to write.'[5]

After the armistice that ended World War I, Daisy must have been encouraged when a paper she had written years earlier — 'Aborigines of the West Coast of South Australia: Vocabularies and Ethnographical Notes' — was finally published in the 1918 edition of *Transactions and Proceedings of the Royal Society of South Australia*, Volume 43. No doubt this acted as the spur she needed to return to the desert to continue her research.

꒞ ꒞ ꒞

In mid-September 1919 Daisy Bates decided it was her duty as Protector of Aborigines to take the train across Central Australia and stop off at an oasis called Ooldea Siding, where it had been reported that emaciated and starving Aborigines were leaving their drought-stricken traditional lands and clustering around the railway to beg for food and money from the passengers of the new Trans-Australian Express. She had already written to State and Federal government officials, telling them they should provide aid to desert Aborigines at various points along the new rail line, but they paid no attention to her demands.

Mrs Bates decided the time had come for action rather than pious talk. She enlisted the aid of several monied families in Adelaide including the Duttons who promised to provide financial aid if the situation proved to be as serious as press reports indicated. She was warned that temperatures at Ooldea could soar to 49 degrees Celsius for weeks on end. But once Daisy Bates made up her mind to do something, no amount of horror stories could scare her.

Mrs Bates purchased a rail ticket to Ooldea and boarded the Trans-Australian Express. Loaded into the goods wagon went her precious sacks of oatmeal and flour to make porridge and damper, and crates of tinned treacle which she knew Aboriginal people loved and which would keep without refrigeration.

Another reason for establishing a base at Ooldea was her ongoing linguistic research. For thousands of years, Ooldea (Yooldil Gabba) had been a trading place for Aborigines from different language groups, who celebrated their corroborees and initiation ceremonies in the magnificent natural amphitheatre around the soak. While feeding and nursing the elderly, Daisy hoped to learn new dialects and languages.

Daisy had previously attended one of John Martins' bargain basement sales and depleted her meagre bank account buying racks of new clothes. She had read in the press how the nakedness of adult Aborigines had shocked some prim lady passengers who had complained to the directors of the railway company. The company had hastily sent out a bundle of second-hand clothes from which unfortunate Aborigines, lacking resistance to European diseases, had become very ill with measles, mumps and various pulmonary infections. New clothes it had to be. Daisy had had enough of hand-me-downs in her own childhood.

On 26 September 1919, tightly corseted even in the heat, and clad in a long skirt of cream-coloured holland or fine linen, plus a high-necked blouse with a stiff collar, Mrs Bates regally descended the steps of the express train. Before her were miles on miles of reddish-gold sandhills stretching away endlessly to the horizon on which was a shimmering line of bluish-purple mountains. The red-gold of the desert was freckled with a few grey-green saltbushes and sun-bleached spinifex. Facing her was a row of small wooden houses for railway workers' families, and a few sheds on wheels, used as temporary accommodation by unmarried fettlers. There were no shops, no canteen, no amenities of any kind.[6]

She had brought two tents, one for a bedroom-cum-workroom, the second to house her stores and her large medicine chest filled with simple remedies, bottles of Eusol disinfectant and rolls of bandage, aware that native people who had walked for hundreds of miles weres bound to have cuts and sores on their feet.

Porters unloaded Mrs Bates's sacks of oatmeal and flour, and her crates of treacle and tea. A couple of sympathetic fettlers helped Mrs Bates set up her tents near station master Anthony Bolam's house. Some of the railways workers' wives thought she was mad coming to this isolated spot. They pointed with disgust at the row of *wurlies*, or spinifix huts, clustering further along the railway line where here and there the figures of Aboriginal people clad in rags huddled or shuffled around, no longer the proud dwellers of the desert. Most of the young, fit men had gone away to find work on cattle stations, leaving at Ooldea those too weak or ill to hunt, and who were now resorting to begging from passengers who halted here by train three times a week.

'Kabbarli' told the elders that all she asked in return for supplying food and medicines was that her 'patients' would help her by answering simple questions. Possibly Daisy showed the elders her carved *mobburn*, or magic stick, received from a dying *kadaicha* man who had been credited with curing the sick, as well as placing a curse on any who offended the stick's owner. In her trunk she also had another present from the dying *kadaicha* man, two 'pointing bones' and a pair of 'murderer's slippers' made from emu feathers held together by fibres of possum hair. The slippers left no footprints, making them ideal accessories for murder. Told by the fettlers that the Prince of Wales was scheduled to pass through Ooldea the following year she planned to present them to His Royal Highness as a rare and unusual gift.

Station master Anthony Bolam and his family arrived several days later and were surprised to find an elderly lady camping on their doorstep, doling out free supplies of porridge and damper to ailing, sun-blinded or crippled Aborigines.[7]

Along with her daily food distributions Daisy gently persuaded the siding's Aborigines to swap their filthy rags for brand-new cotton dresses, or shirts and trousers. Daisy described how their dignity had been affronted by having old clothes chucked out of the train with orders to put them on.

Daisy had little time to feel lonely. Her days were taken up caring for others and her evenings were spent writing by the light of a flickering candle. Just as at Eucla she continued to gain comfort from gazing at the stars. However, she found her camp at the siding too exposed, with passengers travelling in the Trans-Australian line often descending from the train while the engine was refilled and clustering around to watch her at work among the

Aborigines. So to ensure more privacy Daisy moved her camp closer to Ooldea Soak. There, in 'a sandy gully on the track that led to the Soak', Aboriginal men helped her build a windbreak from mulga wood. From the start she made it clear that she valued her privacy. Anyone wishing to enter 'her' fenced area should first call out 'Kabbarli' before being allowed to pass through the gate in the fence.

> I had a smaller bough shed on the crest of the [sand] hill, with a ladder leading to its leafy roof, as my observatory. Here in the bright, still evenings, I studied the skies . . . and compiled my aboriginal mythologies, many of them as poetic and beautiful as the mythologies of the Greeks. A prickle-bush . . . was my barred gateway . . . a barrier for privacy passed by very few in all my years of residence. Outside [my fence] natives would come to await my attention . . . They would make their fires on the sand-hills and camp contentedly while I sewed for them or obtained from my store the clothing they needed before they approached the siding, all too soon to learn the art of scavenging.
>
> . . . sometimes [Aboriginal people] were as long as two years on the journey, zigzagging through the desert for food and water . . . Each mob was more reckless and difficult to control than the preceding one.
>
> My duty, after the first friendly overtures of tea and damper, was to . . . clothe them and in simple language explain the white man's ways and white man's laws. Sometimes a group of forty or more would arrive . . . finding their way, across the desert, drinking water from tree roots.[8]

The fettlers gave Daisy a rusty water tank and she was delighted, writing how 'The upturned tank I utilised as library, storing my manuscripts and my books [and] a bough shed "storehouse" held everything from my daily provender and supplies for the natives to their most sacred totem boards'.[9] She tried carrying water for herself and her blind and crippled patients by using her *wanna*, or digging stick, as a yoke and carrying two buckets attached by chains from it but found the stick cut into her back.

Daisy's introductory talks to new arrivals warned them of the perils of alcohol. She remembered Gauera, her companion on the camel buggy trip, and how she had been bartered by her husband for a pipe and tobacco to another 'husband'. She found that the unmarried fettlers took advantage of the situation and bartered alcohol and tobacco for Aboriginal women, who were regarded as economic assets by the men who 'owned them and could exchange them ... for weapons or as payment.'

> Prostitution of native women was rife, sought by the blacks and encouraged by the lowest whites. When the first half-caste babies appeared the mothers believed they were the result of eating white man's food and rubbed them frantically with charcoal to restore their health and colour . . .[10]

Once word got around the Nullarbor and Tanami deserts that Kabbarli was providing free porridge and damper, Aborigines of many different language groups flocked to Ooldea. After feeding the crippled and the blind, Daisy found herself conducting morning clinics, treating cut feet and legs, the result of walking many miles through the desert. As she had done so many times, she donned her cotton gloves to protect herself while performing the unpleasant task of applying salves to the septic sores of syphilitics. Despite this precaution, she suffered from a very painful poisoned finger after preparing for burial an elderly Aboriginal man who had died of syphilis.

With no latrines in the Aboriginal camp, attacks of dysentery were frequent and while Daisy tried to be scrupulous about her own personal hygiene she often could not help becoming sick. She believed she could cure herself by sipping expensive French champagne, a habit no doubt learned in her 'party years' in England. She bought the champagne from the dining car of the Trans-Australian Express. On one occasion Daisy's dysentery was so severe the rail workers' wives feared she might die and she had to be carried unconscious from her tent to the station master's house, where Mrs Bolam nursed her back to health. Daisy hated the idea of being ill and chose to ignore this incident in her account of her time in Ooldea when she wrote her memoir.[11]

Once again, Daisy enjoyed the feeling of being needed. Here in the desert she was a mixture of queen and grandmotherly figure with magical powers. She described how 'My healing was unhygienic, perhaps, but effective because of mutual confidence and my cheerful bedside manner'.[12]

But Daisy was not just playing at being a Desert Queen. She genuinely *cared* about the ailing Aborigines she befriended and who talked to her about their creation myths and legends. As before, Daisy wrote down their stories in her notebooks or on whatever scraps of paper came to hand.

From each grateful patient she learned new words in various dialects from as far away as the Mann, Gosse, Everard, Petermann and Musgrave Ranges, Streaky Bay and even remote Kalgoorlie.

After many months of drought, some government aid for the Aborigines was provided by police at Tarcoola and Kalgoorlie, at the ends of the line, but no aid was provided at Ooldea. By now what little vegetation had survived in the desert was gone and game was in very short supply. As the months wore on and still no rain arrived, more and more desert Aborigines arrived to beg for money, food and tobacco from the passengers who made a three-hour stop-over at Ooldea for the train drivers to take on water for their engines.

A supply train was eventually provided once a month to bring 'rations' of essential foodstuffs to the railway workers at subsidised prices, but Daisy was not entitled to buy from it to feed her ailing Aborigines. Instead, she was forced to use her diminishing funds to purchase sacks of flour and oats in Adelaide and pay high transport costs to bring them to Ooldea by goods wagon. Deprived of milk she started buying powdered milk as well.

Occasionally she would sell an article to William Hurst's *Australasian* newspaper and she wrote Hurst long, chatty letters about life at Ooldea, and considered him one of her closest friends. On receiving a cheque from his newspaper one time she was able to buying fresh foods at high prices from the restaurant car of the Trans-Australian Express. But her normal evening meal was 'a potato in the ashes now and again, a spoonful of rice . . . and occasionally the treat of a boiled egg — and always tea, my panacea for all ills — were the full extent of my culinary skills'.[13]

The situation became grim during an eight-week strike of rail workers. All trains were cancelled, no mail arrived and food shortages ensured the workers departed as the opportunity arose. The indomitable Daisy, however, refused to leave her sick Aborigines. Each day she continued to provide bowls of porridge and drinking water, but by now there were signs that the bore at Ooldea Siding was slowly drying up, and the soak itself starting to turn brackish. Daisy described how:

> The next few weeks were indeed difficult. I existed on porridge, eeked out with damper or a potato. Once I made a meal of an iguana that two Aboriginal friends caught and cooked for me . . . As water was no longer needed for the fettlers, supplies were strictly limited. By the end of the [eight-week] strike I was on the verge of desperation, with no relief in sight. But when finally the first train came through, I was able to purchase one loaf and a pound of butter. Never did I enjoy such a simple meal so heartily.[14]

Once the train strike ended, life returned to its usual pattern of hard work with her elderly patients during the day and letter writing at night. Although Daisy always admitted she was not a good cook, she made daily vats of porridge and a soup or gruel to feed her charges.

At Christmas she made huge quantities of Christmas pudding mix in a disused washtub, using whatever came to hand, Weetabix, condensed milk, currants, sultanas, and as she had no means of cooking her pudding served it raw. This did not worry her Aboriginal patients, who loved it.

Station master Anthony Bolam found Daisy autocratic and stubborn, their views on how best to help the Aborigines conflicting. They argued frequently. Bolam wanted to use the Aborigines to make money by making and selling boomerangs, shields painted with ochre designs, and carved letter sticks to the passengers that passed through, and turn them into an attraction rather than an eye-sore around his rail siding.

Daisy objected. She hated seeing these once-proud people begging but she feared turning them into a tourist attraction. She also feared that mass production of their artefacts would degrade the quality of their work, and erode the spiritual meaning of their decoration. The boomerangs incised with traditional designs had taken them weeks to carve and paint. But as Aboriginal groups continued to arrive and still the government provided no relief, the situation became desperate. So station master Bolam's money-making schemes went ahead with Daisy's support.

Initially boomerang-throwing displays took place near the train but after a few broken windows it was decided to hold them closer to the soak. But the income earned from this was not enough to support all the Aborigines now camping near the siding and Daisy's help remained vital.

In his memoirs station master Bolam admitted that though they argued a great deal, he admired Mrs Bates for the courage with which she faced the harsh living conditions and the harrowing cases among her syphilitic patients that confronted her. Like many of the passengers on the trains he wondered what gave her the strength to stay in the desert.

In letters to friends Daisy claimed she found comfort in reading her Bible. Apart from her set of Dickens, the leather-bound Bible that Mrs Goode, the bishop's widow, had given her all those years ago, was another treasured possession that she kept all her life.

Daisy Bates was a paradox she believed in an all-powerful Christian God but insisted Christianity was irrelevant for Aboriginal people who, she thought, should maintain their unique culture and traditional way of life. Desperate for money to alleviate their situation she accepted funds from several churches in Adelaide, but the donations stopped once word got back that Daisy refused to preach any dogma before giving out food bought with church money.

For herself she accepted little at all. When a group of scientists passed through Ooldea by train en route to a conference, they walked across to Daisy's camp and were horrified to find a lady living in such primitive conditions. When they had a whip-round for her, instead of thanking them as they had expected, the former charity child was mortified and threw the money back at them.[15]

Daisy always claimed to be a Christian but resisted following any specific church or denomination. Even her good friend the Catholic Bishop Matthew Gibney did not know she had been raised a Catholic. But she may have had a lingering sense of guilt. The shock of her elder sister Marian's death during the Great War may have prompted a reassessment of her life.

Certainly Daisy's strength of character and native Irish optimism helped her continue in the blistering heat and the freezing cold of a desert winter, when her fingers became stiff with cold and so sore with chilblains she could not use her typewriter and had to write notes, letters and newspaper articles using pen and ink.

As she approached her seventies Daisy remained rigid in her ideas — a dedicated Empire loyalist and monarchist, she had always celebrated Empire Day at Ooldea by raising a Union Jack and giving 'her' Aborigines a huge feast.

Passengers peering out of train windows eager for a glimpse of the petite elderly lady in her old-fashioned clothes had no idea that the saintly Mrs Bates had once been an Antipodean Becky Sharp, ambitious for money and status.

To journalists who stopped off at Ooldea she told her usual stories of a privileged childhood. They believed her and described Mrs Bates as 'a daughter of the old sporting gentry of Ireland'. They gave her the title 'The Great White Queen of the Never-Never', a title Daisy liked and did her best to live up to.[16]

'Mrs Bates at home in the sandhills of Ooldea.'
A photograph taken by station master Bolam.

CHAPTER 16

'GREAT WHITE QUEEN OF THE NEVER-NEVER'

'I enjoyed my work in the desert. It's all in the mind whether things are hardships or not.'

DAISY BATES, TO BRITISH TRAVEL WRITER RODERICK CAMERON,

ADELAIDE, 1947

Perhaps Daisy's most outstanding characteristic was the stoicism with which she confronted the deprivations of desert life. Unlike most outback women of her era, who had no choice but to follow their husbands, Daisy went there voluntarily to study Aboriginal people and care for them. Unlike the majority of pioneer women, who were largely unaware of the dangers and difficulties they would face, resilient and resourceful Daisy Bates knew exactly what she was letting herself in for when she elected to live in a tent on the edge of the Nullarbor Plain.

Arthur Mee, in his Introduction to Daisy's 1938 book *The Passing of the Aborigines* compared Daisy Bates to the famous nineteenth-century English traveller Mary Kingsley, who spent time among the Fang tribe in Africa. She wrote about them as 'natives', as did other settlers in Africa. Most Australians simply called the Aborigines 'the blacks', without bothering to learn the names of their linguistic groups.

Living for so many years on the edge of the desert, Daisy Bates became a solitary and ultimately an eccentric figure without parallel in Australian history or anthropology. Her eccentricity, however, had much in common with that of Lady Hester Stanhope, another peripatetic self-appointed 'Queen of the Desert'.

Lady Hester, the daughter of the third Earl Stanhope, was born in 1776 at sumptuous Chevening, a stately home in Kent surrounded by a large park. Her mother died when Hester was four and like Daisy she acquired a stepmother who loathed her clever, moody stepdaughter. Hester's saving grace was the fact that she adored her bachelor uncle, the Prime Minister, William Pitt, who rescued her from her stepmother and installed her at Downing Street as his official hostess from 1803–06. In 1810, following his death and that of her fiancé, Sir John Moore, in the Peninsular War, Hester left England to travel through Greece and Turkey.

Three years later, at the head of a motley retinue, she made a spectacular entrance from the desert into the ruined city of Palmyra, in what was then Ottoman Syria. She wore a queenly robe with a turban, as depicted in her portrait at Chevening. Like Daisy, Hester Stanhope spent the rest of her life alone. She installed herself as queen and lawgiver at Djoun, in the Syrian desert, regarding herself as a semi-regal personage ruling over 'her' subjects. In a letter to a friend, Hester Stanhope related that she had lived in a tiny tent before retiring to the shelter of a ruined monastery surrounded by mile upon mile of sand. She admitted that one problem of living among natives was that 'it is vain to seek a bush or tree for any little purpose'. Instead, she relied on a chamber pot to relieve herself. In the desert she wore 'a shabby dress with a veil', with 'a warm Syrian camel-hair cloak in winter'. Both Lady Hester Stanhope and Mrs Daisy Bates had a restricted diet, with a long-term lack of essential vitamins and minerals. They both suffered from ophthalmia, succumbed to dementia and died almost destitute.

Daisy's increasingly eccentric behaviour included a contempt for modern inventions such as the radio and telephone, which she regarded as vulgar. Yet beneath her eccentricities she was *genuinely* fond of Aborigines. She especially appreciated their sense of humour; and also she showed orphaned Aboriginal children more love than she had ever shown her own son. She bought them chocolate and boiled lollies whenever she was in funds.

Daisy's mornings in the desert began when she went outside her tent to feed the birds and share her precious drinking water with them. She loved the dawns and the splendid scarlet and pink sunsets of the Nullarbor. There was the ring of truth in her words when she declared:

> Freedom . . . meant much more to me now than the life
> of cities. A glorious thing it is . . . to waken . . . before the
> sun outlines the low ridge of the horizon, and to come
> out into the bright cool air, and scent the wind blowing
> across the mulga plains . . . Before I retired at night,
> I invariably made a good fire and covered the glowing
> coals with soft ash, having watched my compatriots so
> cover their turf fires in Ireland.[1]

Every morning Daisy washed herself from head to toe, often using a canvas-bag shower suspended from the tree where she also hung her saucepans, inside her mulga fence. Nowadays she no longer had to fetch water using two buckets on a yoke. She had been given a small cart by the fettlers in the railway yard, who felt sorry for the woman they now regarded as an eccentric old lady. Tannin stained the water a deep reddish-brown, which meant that Daisy could not use it for washing her white blouses and other clothes, so once a week she sent off her dirty linen by train to a Chinese laundry in Adelaide, handing her laundry bag to the sleeping-car attendant, who returned it a week later. Her Friday visits to the train to collect her mail and her clean laundry were as regular as clockwork. The Trans-Australian Express was her lifeline to the world beyond the desert.

Daisy's Edwardian outfits must have been hot and constricting in summer. She'd had several light, oatmeal-coloured suits made up from holland, an inexpensive, durable linen-blend material generally used for window blinds. Kabbarli the Great White Queen never ventured beyond the fence until she was fully dressed.

శ్రీ శ్రీ శ్రీ

Some time while at Ooldea Daisy was visited by her son, Arnold. The visit was not a success. Whether or not Arnold was aware that Ernest Baglehole was his real father is debatable, but he certainly appears to have stored up bad feeling against his mother. Daisy refused to let him inside her compound, claiming that the Aborigines would not believe he was her son. It seems that she made him sleep outside the mulga fence. Judging from a remark made by Daisy thirty years later to British writer Roderick Cameron, this annoyed Arnold so much that he departed early next morning. After that, she said, he broke off all contact with her.[2]

In contrast, it must have given Daisy some pleasure when, in 1920, she was asked by the Commonwealth government to organise a corroboree in honour of HRH the Prince of Wales. There was tremendous excitement about his visit to this country, which was intended as a gesture of thanks to Australians for their heroic sacrifices during World War I. The prince was due to arrive in Melbourne in May, tour Victoria and South Australia, and arrive at the Nullarbor in early October aboard the Trans-Australian Express.

The prince had indicated his wish to watch a corroboree, with traditional Aboriginal dancing and singing, as well as a display of boomerang throwing. Daisy knew it would not be easy to organise a mass display involving hundreds of Aborigines from different linguistic groups, some of whom were traditional enemies. She would have to use all her tact and linguistic skills in rehearsals to persuade them to perform together and avoid fights breaking out. But this did not faze Daisy, who always loved a challenge. Her sole reward for this task would be her meeting with the Prince of Wales.

Meanwhile, those chosen to host the bachelor prince at different locations in Australia prepared luxurious accommodation for his stay. The Collinses at Nindoinbah House, wealthy graziers, built a ballroom onto their home to entertain HRH in style. Upper-crust girls dreamed of dancing with him. There was a popular song: 'I danced with a man who danced with a girl who danced with the Prince of Wales.' Office girls pinned his picture above their desks. Newspapers speculated on whether he might find a suitable bride in Australia. No one realised that Edward, a sex symbol to so many women, is widely believed to have suffered from sexual dysfunction and could only achieve orgasms with experienced women. Edward, Prince of Wales, had a romantic tryst with the flirtatious and very attractive wife of a New South Wales grazier. Nine months later, it is alleged, this amorous interlude produced a boy baby who in adult life bore a startling resemblance to the prince, by then Duke of Windsor. For this reason he was known as 'Duke' to his friends.[3] (In 1936, after just eleven months on the throne, Edward abdicated in order to marry a twice-divorced American, Wallis Warfield Simpson, who became his Duchess of Windsor.)

Canberra officials had decided the corroboree should take place at Cook Siding, four train stops west of Ooldea, which made the organisation even harder for Daisy Bates. She travelled to Cook over a week before the prince was due to arrive there, and was dismayed to find that all the railway workers' cottages had been requisitioned for high-ranking public servants. All that was available for her to use as a combined bedroom and office was a disused goods wagon that reeked of goat droppings and swarmed with fleas. No one was available to help her clean it; everyone was far too busy building and decorating a dais from which the prince would watch the corroboree, and making other preparations.

Instead of throwing a tantrum or bursting into tears of frustration, Daisy asked a fettler's wife for buckets of hot water, scrubbed out her quarters with disinfectant, set up her office, and carried on with the rehearsals of the various Aboriginal groups.

When the Prince of Wales arrived, Daisy watched the mass display of Aboriginal dancing from the dais. Standing by his side, she explained the significance of the different dances to him and he congratulated her on the excellence of the performance and on the boomerang throwing that followed. It was one of the high points of Daisy Bates's life. Royal approval made her feel she was gaining acceptance for her work of helping the Aborigines.

꙳ ꙳ ꙳

Daisy continued to feel distress at the havoc the Trans-Australian railway wrought on Aboriginal culture. As the 'Silver Snake' approached Ooldea Siding, half-naked Aborigines with flies swarming around their eyes and lips would come rushing to beg from the passengers, who amused themselves by throwing down sweets and tobacco from the train windows. They played cruel tricks such as offering the Aborigines a crisp pound note or a shining penny for their boomerangs or emu eggs, gleeful when the shiny coin was accepted instead of the paper note. It pained Daisy to witness how the Indigenous people, with their superb hunting skills and once so independent, had now become objects of derision to Europeans.

In an attempt to stop the begging, both Daisy and Sister Annie Lock, who set up a tiny Lutheran mission at Ooldea in 1933, urged Aboriginal people to sell small carvings made from mulga to the passengers, rather than just ask for money. Daisy thought this would give them a sense of self-worth. Some showed great skill; soon they were selling the passengers carved walking sticks and small decorated lizards, snakes and birds.

Daisy Bates was not alone in her outrage at the official treatment of Aborigines. There were others who shared her views. One of them was Olive Muriel Pink, the Tasmanian-born painter of wildflowers whom Daisy had met in 1914.

In May 1926 Olive Pink boarded the Trans-Australian Express to take up the invitation to stay at Ooldea given her by Daisy Bates more than ten years before, when the two women met at the conference of the Australian and New Zealand Association for the Advancement of Science. Over the years they had corresponded. This trip to the edge of the Nullarbor would open the forty-two-year-old Olive Pink's eyes to the possibility of a new and very different life from the one she had known so far. She felt the urge to help the Aborigines she saw living along the line, some half-starved and clad in rags, and began to understand what kept Daisy working in the desert.

At Ooldea, Olive discovered Daisy's library — a quite extensive one. Daisy had always protected her precious books as best she could against the desert sandstorms. Besides her beloved Dickens, she read and re-read old favourites such as Rudyard Kipling's *Kim* and his *Just So Stories*, as well as Andrew Lang's books on myth, magic and totemism and James Frazer's *The Golden Bough*, in which some of Daisy's observations on Aboriginal beliefs and myths were cited. Her reference works included books by celebrated anthropologists and ethnologists including Baldwin Spencer and Ernest Gillen, and works by Alfred Howitt, Walter Roth and Carl Lumholtz.

Daisy's own work was helped by reading the published papers of the amateur Australian anthropologist Robert Hamilton Mathews, another enthusiastic fieldworker and recorder of Aboriginal culture. Although Mathews lacked formal training, he is highly regarded today. He made a special study of the marriage laws and social structures of native tribes in New South Wales, Queensland and Central Australia.

Daisy was also influenced by John Mathew's book *Eaglehawk and Crow*, published in 1889, which like her own writings had failed to find favour with the scientific establishment. John Mathew, a teacher turned Presbyterian minister, was an amateur anthropologist who studied the Kabi and Wakka people of North Queensland. His studies in linguistics and of myth, magic and ceremony are regarded favourably today.

Olive became increasingly interested in Daisy's work. Later, she would study anthropology at the University of Sydney with Professor R.W. Firth and would also attend the lectures of Professor A.P. Elkin, who helped her obtain a research grant to work with the eastern Arrernte people of Alice Springs and the Warlpiri of the Tanami region. Later, she and Elkin fell out. Olive's artist's eye was enchanted by the purple peaks of the Macdonnell Ranges, the deep red earth and the remarkable clarity of the atmosphere.

When she spoke with Arrernte and Ngarlia people, Olive saw for herself how their tribal way of life was threatened by graziers who wanted to take possession of their waterholes for their cattle — whose cloven hooves broke the skin of the sand and churned it up, while their excrement fouled the water on which Aboriginal people had traditionally relied in times of drought. Olive was furious at the violation of human rights when graziers (as well as some mining companies) threatened to ban Aborigines from visiting their waterholes altogether under the terms of their pastoral leases. She raised the matter in Sydney with the Association for the Protection of Native Races, which had close links with the League of Nations in Geneva.

Olive came to love the desert areas. She visited Ernabella Mission, on the edge of the Musgrave Ranges in the northwest corner of South Australia, founded in 1937. At Ernabella, she purchased some *tjuringa*, Aboriginal spiritual artefacts, but was warned about doing this. She also visited the Hermannsburg Lutheran Mission in the Northern Territory, on the southern side of the Macdonnell Ranges, where Pastor Albrecht was in charge from 1926 to 1951. There she saw his valiant attempts to make the mission self-supporting by setting up a date palm grove and selling the fruit.

At an ANZAAS conference she attended later, possibly in 1935, the fiery Olive fell out with the academic Ted Strehlow (another of Daisy's critics) whose father, Carl Strehlow, headed the Hermannsburg Mission from 1894 to 1922. Their long-running disagreement concerned the Aborigines' selling of sacred objects and the fact that Ted Strehlow was buying them or accepting them as gifts. Strehlow was critical of Olive's lack of qualifications. Olive believed that Strehlow somehow used his influence to put paid to her hopes of receiving a salary as Lady Protector of Aborigines; he apparently claimed her health was not up to the work involved.

Like Daisy, Olive wrote often to State and Federal governments protesting about the harsh treatment of the Indigenous people. But where Daisy was courteous, Olive was strident. She pleaded for a large area of land, from which cattle must be banned, to be set aside as an Aboriginal reserve free from pastoral or mining interests. At Papunya, west of Alice Springs, she attempted to set up a reserve for the Warlpiri people, whose numbers were falling sharply, but the project failed.

At Papunya Olive followed a similar daily routine to that of Daisy Bates at Ooldea, taking food to the Aboriginal people, 'sitting down' to talk to them as she treated their ailments, and taking notes as part of her research. She noted that Aboriginal women were excellent mothers, very affectionate with their children, and rebutted Daisy's claims concerning the practice of infant cannibalism. She built up vocabularies of the Warlpiri language, with their Arrernte equivalents. She turned her observations into an ethnological study about the culture and language of the Warlpiri, but then decided not to publish the material as it contained information about secret rituals. Her decision to place a fifty-year embargo on her work was met with hostility from male academics.

Olive Pink gained the respect and friendship of many Aboriginal people, although (as with Daisy) some of them thought her slightly mad in her old age. She spent her last years amid the beauty of the Native Flora Reserve she had created on the outskirts of Alice Springs and died in 1975.

When Daisy met HRH Prince Henry, the Duke of Gloucester, at Ooldea, in 1934,
she still carried her talisman umbrella from 1901

CHAPTER 17

MRS DAISY BATES, CBE, AT CANBERRA AND OOLDEA

I am still not quite sure what powers of authority this medal gives me other than being able to write CBE after my name.

DAISY BATES, WRITING TO AINSLIE FAIRBAIRN

In November 1933, over fifteen years since she had first arrived at Ooldea, Daisy was thrilled to receive a letter from Buckingham Palace. It informed her that she had been nominated to receive the CBE (Commander of the Order of the British Empire) in the New Year's honours list.

Daisy had always cultivated the persona of an upper-class lady who believed in the British Empire, the Royal Family and their colonial representatives. Now the onset of vascular dementia meant that her interest in royalty had become obsessive. To receive that letter from Buckingham Palace must have seemed like a summons from Mount Olympus.

The following year she went to Adelaide to visit Government House, where she was presented with a gilded medal in a velvet-lined case by Sir George Murray, KCMG. The investiture was followed by a garden reception. Daisy stood out among the crowd in a black ankle-length skirt and stiff-collared shirt, surrounded by other ladies wearing shorter silk frocks in bright colours.

At Government House she was in her element. But what exactly did the medal signify? The title Commander of the Order of the British Empire was usually reserved for high-ranking men. Women normally received the lesser MBE (Member) or OBE (Officer). In any event, the honour her beloved King George V had conferred upon her must have provided some compensation for the years of isolation and hardship she had endured — as well as consolation for the fact that the large research study she had conducted in Western Australia would apparently remain unpublished.

Within a few months of her investiture, Daisy was informed that HRH Prince Henry, Duke of Gloucester, a younger brother of the Prince of Wales, would make a brief visit to Ooldea Siding in October 1934, before crossing the Nullarbor Plain as part of his royal tour of Australia. Apparently the duke had made a special request to meet Mrs Bates, 'the lady who lives with the Aborigines', and to see a display of Aboriginal dancing and spear-throwing like she had arranged for his brother.

However, Daisy was now in her mid-seventies and government officials feared that the strain of organising such a massive event would be beyond her. So they asked the Lutheran missionary Sister Annie Lock to organise it instead. Daisy was hurt and disappointed, but was promised an audience with the Duke of Gloucester after the corroboree. He duly arrived at Ooldea and rode out to the natural amphitheatre around the soak to watch the display.

A photograph of the duke standing beside Daisy shows him informally dressed in sports shirt, jodhpurs and riding boots. Daisy wears her best black suit (tinged faintly green with age) and carries her talisman, the black umbrella handed back to her by the Duke of York (now King George V), to whom she was presented at Government House in Perth at the official celebrations for Federation.

The prestigious English magazine *The Sphere* carried a photograph of Daisy and Prince Henry on the front cover of its

November 1934 issue. Copies were sent to every corner of the British Empire, showing Mrs Daisy Bates, CBE, in her Edwardian clothes. This award raised her prestige in the eyes of public servants in Canberra, even though by this time she was becoming known to some Adelaide residents as 'Granny Crackpot', following her recent visit there. Now she was invited to Canberra for consultation on Aboriginal affairs with government ministers, with her fare and hotel accommodation provided. She was to give them advice on how best to help the Aboriginal people.

The visit was not a success. By the time Daisy reached her seventies, she had begun to behave in irrational and inappropriate ways and make strange, even contradictory, statements at times. Those afflicted with vascular dementia remain unaware of what is happening as the disease gradually progresses and their modes of speech and behaviour are affected. Sufferers may 'plateau' at a certain stage, remaining at the same level for years, until some event triggers another sharp descent, in what is termed a 'staircase' effect. For Daisy, the stress of travelling to Canberra and meeting the Minister of the Interior and other officials seems to have precipitated one such 'staircase' descent.

For years now her behaviour had been regarded as eccentric; in Canberra it took a turn for the worse. The elderly Mrs Bates skipped around the Ministry of the Interior like a young girl. She asked the minister if she could be appointed High Commissioner for Native Affairs in charge of the Nullarbor area, and requested transport to take her there — a donkey cart would be ideal, she suggested. The minister was uncertain whether Mrs Bates was joking. (In fact, she was serious.) To demonstrate to the amazed politicians how strong she was, the normally dignified woman picked up her long skirts and ran up and down the stairs of Parliament House in a burst of energy. She also flirted outrageously with some good-looking officials in a way that was totally inappropriate for an elderly visitor on an official trip.

The politicians were confused by Daisy's bizarre conduct. At this time nothing was known about vascular dementia, but they realised she was more eccentric than they'd been led to believe. She wore strange, old-fashioned clothes and refused to use the telephone, claiming it was vulgar. They listened politely as Mrs Bates, CBE, told them they must spend more money on Aborigines, then nodded their heads and hoped she would soon go back to the desert. Politicians and public servants in Canberra echoed the opinion expressed in Adelaide, that she was turning into 'Granny Crackpot'.

Nothing was accomplished. The visit over, Daisy returned to her lonely tent, to the swarming flies, the heat and dust and poisonous snakes. In the desert her behaviour and outdated garments did not seem strange. She derived comfort from watching the glorious sunrises and sunsets, feeding the birds each morning and sharing her drinking water with them. Her pet lizard devoured the ants that thronged her tent as she settled back at her work table, wrote increasingly muddled letters, took bowls of porridge and drinking water to 'her' ailing and elderly Aborigines, and was reasonably content. So long as she followed her normal routines she was able to cope well on the edge of the Nullarbor. From the safety of her camp inside its mulga fence she saw herself as a queen returned to her own realm, and viewed the Aborigines she fed and clothed as her subjects.

Unlike other, more radical supporters of the Aboriginal people, including Olive Pink and another activist of the time, Constance Cooke, Daisy Bates never actively promoted Aboriginal land rights. She simply wanted the government to provide more medical supplies and food in times of drought. *Giving* was the only way she knew in relating to the Aborigines. And as her dementia progressed she produced several very impractical schemes to improve the condition of the Indigenous people, which she outlined at length in letters to various authorities.

❧ ❧ ❧

Daisy's obsessive interest in royalty was matched by her fixation concerning the subject of infant cannibalism among desert Aborigines. This became worse in her seventies and eighties as her dementia increased, and did much to destroy the good impression her previous publications in the field of ethnology had made when she was younger. Daisy used a twisted logic to justify the articles about infant cannibalism she wrote for the popular press: she said that writing them was the only way she could earn money to provide food for starving Aborigines. But, quite rightly, her academic critics derided her for the many references to cannibalism she'd been making. In the tabloid press articles concerned, there are more than forty such references.

A number of specific accusations sparked Daisy's allegations of infant cannibalism. A missionary pointed out to her an Aboriginal woman who had supposedly eaten her child — without supplying any evidence to support this claim. Another alleged incident concerned a pregnant woman who went into the desert to give birth, according to custom, but returned without her baby. Again no evidence was presented. As for Daisy's most sensational story, about Dowie, a Bardi man who was said to have eaten his four children and five wives, it is quite ridiculous and once more unsupported by any evidence. All these stories caused considerable distress to others who were trying to help the Aboriginal people. Daisy did make some efforts to support her claims of cannibalism, but they were completely unconvincing. Unfortunately, when her unreliable memoir *The Passing of the Aborigines* was published a few years later (based on her series of newspaper articles for the Adelaide *Advertiser* titled 'My Natives and I'), her allegations of cannibalism were repeated and further harmed her reputation.

Another of Daisy's obsessions sprang from her illogical views concerning 'half-caste' children. The 1905 *Aborigines Act* had made it an offence for a white man to have sexual relations with an Aboriginal or part-Aboriginal woman, but as noted already, this had the effect of punishing the Aboriginal women rather than the European men who pursued them. The law provided for the forcible removal of children born of such unions, while ignoring the conduct of the European fathers. This was a very racist era in Australia, with majority support for the infamous 'White Australia' policy.

Daisy described the Aborigines at Ooldea as 'fine upstanding people' whose young women she had to protect from 'low whites' working for the railroad and telegraph companies, to whom they were bartered in return for alcohol. With her knowledge of Aboriginal food laws, she had seen many half-starved part-Aboriginal children and knew the lowly regard accorded them by their full-blood relatives. She knew, too, that 'half-caste' girls were those most frequently bartered to Europeans. She was convinced that such children would be better off if they were taken away and cared for in missions and government homes. In most fringe camps there were high levels of leprosy, typhoid, yaws, kidney disease and trachoma, besides venereal disease. Perhaps she believed she really was doing the best thing by removing the girls from the camps, failing to realise that conditions could prove even more harrowing for them in many government homes. She herself was never involved with any of the homes, whether run by the government or by missionaries. After her visit to Sandstone in 1910 with Radcliffe-Brown and Grant Watson, she had written to the Protector of Aborigines about a part-Aboriginal girl in that camp, as follows:

> One half-caste girl named Rita was with the Sandstone
> people and ought to be taken away but it will be difficult
> to catch her . . . The day before the half-caste Polly and
> two [other] half-caste children went away in the train,
> I took the Sisters of the convent to the jail to see the
> poor creatures. As Polly had worked for them [the Sisters],
> when I told her they would all be taken to another
> Sisters' place she seemed to be more reconciled. After the
> train had gone I saw the mother of one of the children
> who had been taken away, but she seemed to believe my
> statement that the children would be happy.[1]

This letter provides evidence that Daisy was deluding herself with that impossible claim that 'the children would be happy'. Today her statements (as well as her use of the pejorative term 'half-caste') are considered highly offensive, and in hindsight seem to reflect badly on her. It was ironic that the West Australian Act which eroded the liberties of Aboriginal women under the guise of 'protecting' them was powerless to protect Aboriginal girls from rape and other forms of assault once they went to live in State homes or in missions.

Time would change Daisy's opinions. Perhaps she came to realise just what sort of places the children were being condemned to. Years later, at Ooldea, she would behave very differently. She is recorded as hiding part-Aboriginal children in her tent whenever police or government welfare officers came to take them away to homes or missions.

Daisy and Annie Lock, a trained nurse, provided the only medical services available at Ooldea. Measles epidemics killed many of the Aborigines, who easily succumbed to this disease introduced by Europeans. Daisy did what she could: she saw that the victims rested in their humpies and provided them with nourishing gruel. She also continued to alleviate the discomfort of those who were suffering from syphilis, rubbing her special salve into their sores on limbs and genitalia — a task so unpleasant and odorous that many army nurses during World War I refused to carry it out. In fact, at this stage all Daisy was capable of doing, as she said herself, was to 'ease their passing'.

Something that annoyed Daisy was the fact that, as a Lutheran missionary, Annie Lock received substantial church funding and was able to offer the Aborigines a much wider choice of food than Daisy could afford. Plentiful supplies of corned beef, coupled with rousing hymns and happy clapping gained Annie Lock many converts. Daisy, who had little time for

Daisy tending Jinnawillie at Ooldea

missionaries of any persuasion, detested these gambits. She felt strongly that Aborigines should guard their traditional beliefs (although she deplored practices such as infant betrothal, vaginal circumcision and wife lending). She did her best to stop new arrivals at Ooldea from drifting across to the Lutheran Mission, but to no avail; only those elderly and frail Aborigines who had known her for a long time remained true to her.

Daisy observed that Aboriginal women gave birth in an easier and more hygienic way than Europeans, at a time when childbed or puerperal fever caused a high childbirth death rate. Doctors and midwives in Australia often failed to implement the infection-control reforms of Hungarian physician Dr Ignaz Semmelweiss, and deaths among European settlers' wives were widespread, caused by unscrubbed hands and lack of hygiene. Daisy passed on her observations to Perth-based Dr Roberta Jull, noting that Aboriginal women who gave birth in a squatting position did not suffer puerperal fever. Daisy herself had experienced a difficult childbirth with her son Arnold and there seems to be a wistful tone in what she wrote:

> Motherhood came easily . . . Birth had no pangs for the
> young mother. She knelt down, rested her buttocks on
> her heels, pressed her breath, and the baby was born, so
> easily, so free from pain or obstruction, that there was
> rarely a cry. The operation performed upon young girls
> and their initiation to womanhood at an early age tends
> to this painless birth. The baby is left on the ground, a
> mother or elder sister will snip the umbilical cord with
> her strong and long nails, leaving two or three inches on
> the navel. This is tied in a loose knot and flattened down,
> and later, when it dries and falls off, hair is netted about it
> in a little ring, to be hung around the baby's neck and left
> there for weeks and months. It is supposed to contain part
> of the child's spirit existence, and when it withers off the
> baby has absorbed the spirit. The baby is massaged
> tenderly with soft ashes and charcoal.

On the day of the child's birth, the mother may go on
a journey of thirty miles if the group is travelling, but
throughout this period she must keep apart from the
men.[2]

At this point Daisy introduces the topic of infant cannibalism:

She is not punished if she elects to kill and eat the baby,
and returns to camp with or without it to resume her
work of vegetable food-gathering. A fire is always made
over the spot where the birth took place.[3]

After Daisy returned from her disappointing visit to Canberra,
she attempted to interview the prime minister, the Rt Hon Joseph
Lyons, as he stopped briefly at Ooldea on the train. She aimed to
ask for better medical and living conditions for the Aborigines, and
to request a paid position as their Lady Protector once more. All
through a long hot afternoon at Ooldea Siding she waited patiently
for the prime minister to arrive. She was a bizarre figure standing
there, holding Aboriginal artefacts and weapons, armfuls of
documents and photographs of Aboriginal women and children
with flies swarming around their infected eyes. She planned to ask
the prime minister that, in times of drought, regular supplies of food
and water be handed out all along the Trans-Australian line, not
simply at either end: a modest but important request.

Unfortunately, Daisy had not reckoned on the rigid protocol that
surrounded the head of government and had made no written
request to Canberra for an interview. Train compartments in this
pre-World War II era were not air-conditioned, and Joseph Lyons,
himself elderly and in poor health, was overcome by the heat of the
Nullarbor and fast asleep when the train arrived at the siding.
Although Daisy explained repeatedly to members of his staff that
she needed to see him, his aides refused to wake him. She felt
humiliated standing there in front of railway employees and their
wives, who had watched with interest as she waited for the train, no
doubt thinking she was acting more crazily than usual. Daisy

held her head high as she walked back to her tent, but her disappointment that both the Federal government and that of the Northern Territory had refused to appoint her as Protector of Aborigines, followed now by her abortive attempt to interview the prime minister, had upset her badly.

As her dementia worsened she became more paranoid and difficult; on bad days she would accuse the fettlers' wives at Ooldea of stealing her mail.

ॐ ॐ ॐ

Another continuing disappointment for Daisy was the fact that her detailed research into the customs, culture and languages of the Aborigines of Western Australia remained unpublished. Daisy was convinced, quite rightly, that between 1904 and 1919 she had carried out valuable research on various Aboriginal tribes in Western Australia, and that one day her work would achieve publication and she would be vindicated. She was sure that her lack of a university degree and understanding of academic method was not the problem: many 'gentleman' anthropologists were qualified in subjects that had no relation to anthropology or ethnology. Charles Darwin, renowned author of papers on botany and zoology, had studied divinity at Cambridge. Sir John Vanbrugh, who designed the magnificent Blenheim Palace as a grateful nation's tribute to the Duke of Marlborough, was a playwright who lacked architectural qualifications. Sigmund Freud was a neurologist who initially studied psychotherapy as a pastime. The phrase 'only an amateur' is a misleading, modern construct.

Daisy Bates's strength as an ethnologist was her wide knowledge of Aboriginal languages (although it was not as extensive as she would later claim in her book *The Passing of the Aborigines*). Her interviewing skills stemmed from journalistic experience — and she was one of the first researchers to note informants' names and to live close to the people she studied, a decade before America's Margaret Mead (who was thirty-eight years younger than Daisy) won acclaim for her ethnological research in Samoa, in particular for her book *Coming of Age in Samoa*, published in 1928. It is interesting to compare the differences as well as the similarities between Bates and Mead.

'I was a wanted child and when I was born I was the kind of child my parents wanted,' Mead wrote in her memoirs, *Blackberry Winter.* She came from an affluent background and had the advantages that Daisy had longed for. Her father, a professor, was happy to pay for his daughter to study with the famous anthropologist Franz Boas. In contrast to Daisy's traumatic childhood, Margaret Mead always felt loved and financially secure.

Like Daisy, Mead had three husbands. Her first husband was a theological student; her second a New Zealand anthropologist, Rheo Fortune, who was Radcliffe-Brown's prize student in the Department of Anthropology at Sydney. Then Mead fell in love with Gregory Bateson, one of Fortune's postgraduate students, whom she married in 1936. They both went to Bali to begin fieldwork there. Eventually Bateson was appointed Visiting Professor of Anthropology at Harvard, while Mead secured a well-paid position as a museum curator, with the financial security and prestige that Daisy Bates always hoped to achieve but never obtained. Mead survived the break-up of her third marriage without difficulty.

Margaret Mead's memoirs too were unreliable like Daisy's would prove. Both women skated carefully over their marriage break-ups to avoid damaging their image. Both were alternately venerated and denigrated by critics. Mead's research in Samoa, especially the fact that she may have been purposely misled by two young Samoan girls into accepting statements that were not true, has been the subject of considerable controversy.

Daisy's own unreliable memoirs would soon be ghostwritten for her by the Australian journalist and author Ernestine Hill, at a time when Kabbarli's vascular dementia had taken another downward step in its 'staircase' progression. The meeting of Daisy Bates and Ernestine Hill was about to take place.

Ernestine Hill

CHAPTER 18

BIRDS OF A FEATHER

Daisy's voice was soft, gentle and low. In all the years I knew
her I was never to hear it raised . . . but it was never
monotonous. Of course, she was Irish . . . that explained
everything, the idealism, the endurance, the self-sacrifice, the
prejudice and the pride.

ERNESTINE HILL, *KABBARLI*

Ernestine Hill and Daisy Bates had much in common, even
though Daisy was forty years older than Ernestine. Both had
worked in the competitive male-dominated world of 'popular' or
sensational journalism. Both had had clandestine relationships with
men that brought them grief. And both were destined to become
eccentric in their later years.

Like Daisy, Ernestine had a great deal to hide. She became a single
supporting mother in an era when single motherhood was
considered shameful and single mothers were regarded as 'fallen
women'. They were forced to enter special homes to give birth,
away from acceptable married mothers, and were offered every

inducement to give up their babies for adoption. So it is understandable that Ernestine simply invented a husband to cover the fact that as an unmarried working woman she was pregnant by a man who could not be named.

Ernestine Hemmings, born in Brisbane in 1899, was the daughter of a schoolteacher and a factory manager. Young and inexperienced, she moved to Sydney, ambitious to enter the world of journalism. There she lost her heart to a man, believed to have been married, who promised to leave his wife for her but didn't keep his word. Ernestine refused to have a back-street abortion and was determined to keep her child, something very atypical of the time. Doubtless her parents tried to persuade her to have the child adopted, then the normal procedure for a child born out of wedlock. But Ernestine resisted such advice. After her baby was born she changed her surname by deed poll to Hill, telling everyone that Mr Hill had died and that she intended to raise his child alone.

Ernestine Hill's entry into sensational journalism was unusual for her day, when most women only wrote about hats, parties and cake recipes. Ernestine did not attend university but learned shorthand and typing at a commercial college in Brisbane. She had always longed to become a journalist.

In Sydney her first job was in the typing pool of *Smith's Weekly* magazine, where her undoubted writing talent was noticed by the famous editor of *The Bulletin* Jules Archibald (who, in his will, established the Archibald Prize at the Art Gallery of New South Wales). He appointed Ernestine as his secretary for the few months left before he retired and recommended she be promoted to sub-editor. What Ernestine yearned to do, however, was to do interviews and write riveting stories. Convent-educated, this nineteen-year-old girl from provincial Brisbane with her large brown eyes and wide mouth emphasised with cherry-red lipstick bore some resemblance to the young Audrey Hepburn.

Ernestine's big break into journalism came from another powerful editor, Robert Clyde Packer, a renowned yachtsman and father of future media baron Frank Packer — and grandfather of

Kerry Packer. R.C. Packer also recognised Ernestine's talent and made her a journalist. She had a natural talent for finding unusual stories and writing them in an interesting way, although she sometimes neglected to check facts.

Then Miss Ernestine Hemmings fell pregnant and left Sydney. Her son, registered as Robert (Bob) Hill, was born on 30 October 1924. According to *The Australian Dictionary of Biography*, R.C. Packer was rumoured to have been the father of Ernestine's son, although this was never acknowledged publicly by him. However, there were whispers that Bob's father could have been R.C. Packer's son Frank, dubbed the Don Juan of Sydney's Eastern Suburbs and well known for his numerous liaisons with women before and after his marriage.

Ernestine's 'marriage' of convenience to the elusive Mr Hill was as mysterious as the marriages of Daisy O'Dwyer to Breaker Morant and Ernest Baglehole. But early in 1924 young Frank Packer left Sydney to work as a jackaroo on a property at Boorowa, north of Canberra. If indeed the charismatic Frank was Bob's father, it is a closely guarded secret.

Both Daisy and Ernestine, clever, independent women, had secrets they hid from the world. Ernestine was not averse to mystery: she used an indecipherable shorthand code for many of her private papers. After returning to Sydney and working for R.C. Packer's Associated Newspapers as a freelancer, she became their outback reporter, travelling throughout the bush with swag and notebook to discover the 'real Australia' beyond the towns and cities. With her much loved son in boarding school, she established herself as a 'literary legend'. Ernestine was described as 'this slim, dark-eyed girl who appeared seemingly out of nowhere with practically nothing except her horse, her saddle, her typewriter and books and the makings of billy tea and some frugal food . . . and a passion for the land'. She hitched rides on mail trucks, camel trains and river boats to gain her stories. Her roving life and single motherhood proved a stressful combination and she became a chain smoker, with a cigarette perpetually clamped between thumb and first finger.

❦ ❦ ❦

Early in 1932, while Ernestine was working on a story in Perth, she interviewed a member of the Karrakatta Club and heard for the first time about Mrs Daisy Bates, a widowed gentlewoman of the Irish ascendancy who had lived for a decade and a half with the Aborigines camped beside the Trans-Australian railway, spending all her money on feeding and looking after them. Ernestine decided she must interview the elderly Mrs Bates, whose story would surely be a scoop. There was no way to contact her by phone, so Ernestine took the train, bound for Ooldea.

Ernestine needed this scoop: the previous year, her career had suffered a serious setback. After she wrote a glowing article about a gold strike in The Granites, northwest of Alice Springs along the Tanami Track, there had been a rush of prospectors to the area and a stockmarket boom. Hundreds of Ernestine's readers bought shares. When the fabled gold turned to dross the prospectors were stranded. Some of them lost almost everything they owned and threatened legal action against the newspaper. Ernestine badly needed to redeem her reputation. A front-page story in the *Sunday Sun* about a saintly lady who nursed dying Aborigines seemed an excellent idea.

Ernestine descended from the train hefting a heavy suitcase, a bulky camera and her portable typewriter, and inquired where she could find Mrs Daisy Bates. A fettler's wife, warning her that Mrs Bates could be cantankerous, told Ernestine that her camp was a brisk walk from the train siding, near the natural amphitheatre that housed the soak.

It was Daisy's custom to walk from her camp to the siding after the train departed, to check if there was any mail for her, and just at that moment she arrived on the scene. Ernestine took careful note of her unusual appearance. Daisy was wearing a battered straw hat with a veil thin as a spider's web, beneath which a pair of shrewd blue eyes peered out. Her flared coat of pale tussore silk must once have been a couture garment. Beneath it she wore a long dark skirt, a neat shirt with a stiff white collar, and a narrow, pale blue ribbon tie. Around her waist, a small billycan and two pannikins jingled and jangled, hanging from a silver chain. Black stockings, court shoes with coquettish bows and a pair of white cotton gloves completed the ensemble, together with a black umbrella tucked under Daisy's right arm. Soon Ernestine would learn the story of how it had been touched by the regal hand of the Duke of York during that Federation ceremony in Perth.

Daisy Bates appeared delighted to see a fellow writer. Cautiously Ernestine suggested she might stay with one of the fettlers' wives and interview Mrs Bates the following day. Daisy would not hear of such a thing. Of course Mrs Hill must come to her camp and stay in her spare tent.

The rapport between the two women was immediate; indeed, they were about to strike up a friendship that would last for the rest of Daisy's life. Seen together, they looked strangely incongruous, an odd couple — Daisy prim and neat in her wasp-waisted Edwardian coat and skirt, and chain-smoking Ernestine with her slim, boyish figure and bare bronzed legs, wearing a short-skirted dress and open-toed sandals.

In spite of what had happened to her, Ernestine was still a romantic at heart. Single motherhood had robbed her of a chance to make that great Australian rite of passage, the overseas trip to Europe. To Ernestine, Daisy's tales of upper-class life in the stately homes of Ireland and England and her 'association' with the Outrams were truly romantic; she swallowed them all hook, line and sinker. Another journalist might have asked Daisy some searching questions and checked with the secretariat at Buckingham Palace as to when Daisy was presented at court — or contacted the Outram family in Dorset. That would have meant the end of Daisy's tall tales. But Ernestine believed every word Daisy said. This was the Real Life Story of an upper-class lady who had renounced civilisation to live beside the Aborigines. Perhaps it would become the lead story for the *Sunday Sun*!

Chasing this story, which Ernestine envisaged as a serialisation, she lived in Daisy's work tent, surviving on a diet of porridge, damper, boiled eggs and the odd piece of rabbit supplied by friendly

Aborigines. Ernestine knew that Daisy had a huge amount of information stashed away in her tin hat-boxes, with many more papers in her bough shed. But there was no index system and Daisy wasn't able to lay her hands on specific items of information when she wanted them. Daisy talked of turning her material into a book, but Ernestine realised that she was no longer capable of doing so. Suddenly she had an exciting thought. Why shouldn't she, Ernestine Hill, a popular journalist, ghostwrite the story — assuming that Daisy would trust her sufficiently for this to happen? Daisy had told her how badly she had been treated by Radcliffe-Brown, how he had used her work without acknowledgement and vilified her reputation, with the result that her academic manuscript remained unpublished. Now Ernestine planted a new idea in Daisy's mind. As Daisy had been unable to obtain publication for *The Native Tribes of Western Australia*, her academic work, why not try a 'popular' book about an Irish gentlewoman who devoted her life to helping the Aboriginal people? It might prove a great success and earn good money.

After spending five weeks at Ooldea, Ernestine departed by train, bearing the photographs she had taken of Daisy and leaving her to think about this notion.

Ernestine claimed that she sent Daisy a proof copy of the initial article she wrote, but Daisy never mentioned receiving it. All we know is that Ernestine's article, along with photos she took of the 'little Irish aristocrat' ministering to ailing Aborigines and playing with Aboriginal children, was chosen as the front-page story for the 19 June 1932 issue of the *Sunday Sun*. Ernestine's story brought Daisy out of obscurity. It tried to persuade Australians that they had their very own Florence Nightingale toiling away in the desert. The story was slanted to make Kabbarli appear as a nursing aide rather than an aspiring ethnographer.

When Daisy read the story she realised there could be repercussions — about certain inaccuracies — from her family in Ireland if they were ever to read it. However, she was happy simply to be noticed. She did not mind that Ernestine had described her as a cross between Florence Nightingale and a nursing aide. Ernestine had singlehandedly created the legend of Kabbarli, grandmother of the Aboriginal people, and Daisy, smarting from her rejection by the academic fraternity, liked the legend better than the truth.

Ernestine kept in touch with Daisy by letter. Mrs Bates was far too good a story to let go. Besides, she had grown fond of the older woman, who was clearly lonely. For her part, alone in the desert, Daisy began to rely on those amusing letters from 'my darling Ernestine', as she called her new friend. Both women hoarded anecdotes and information for use in the forthcoming book. Ernestine's shorthand notes were clear and neat; Daisy's were scrawled on scraps of paper and sometimes illegible.

༄ ༄ ༄

Nearly two years were to elapse before the two women met again, by which time Daisy had attended her investiture and received her CBE. In Adelaide, Lloyd Dumas, director of the newspaper group that included *The Advertiser*, told Ernestine that he might be interested in sponsoring a book about Daisy Bates, CBE, but first he wanted her to write a series of articles about 'the little lady', as he called Daisy, which would be syndicated to Perth's *Western Mail* and other papers. After that the articles could be amalgamated into a continuous narrative and book rights sold in Britain and possibly in the United States. Ernestine promised Dumas she would ghostwrite the book so carefully that Daisy, Queen of the Desert, would think she had written it herself. Ernestine's promise reassured him — he had seen articles Daisy Bates had previously submitted to *The Advertiser*, which had been rejected because they were so rambling and confused. This scheme would benefit all three of them and bring kudos to his newspaper group. Dumas, an ambitious man, had his eye on a knighthood.

At this point Ernestine was alarmed to hear from Daisy that bushfires were starting to break out around her, and that railway men had saved her camp by cutting firebreaks. There was a possibility that her mulga fence might catch fire. In addition, there was a shortage of drinking water at Ooldea Soak. Ernestine told Lloyd Dumas that Daisy should be brought to Adelaide as a matter of urgency. She read him extracts from Daisy's latest letter, claiming that the temperature had reached 110°F (43°C) in the shade. Dumas gave in.

So the 'Kabbarli' project took off, thanks to Ernestine's desire to protect Daisy and also to make enough money on her own account to pay Bob's school fees. It was agreed that Dumas would aim to sell the book rights in London, the centre of publishing, rather than in Australia. They might even sell film rights. Ernestine was to take down Daisy's rambling accounts in shorthand, type them out and edit them. She would provide finished copy that would require very little final editing. But she would need a capable secretary to provide help. She assured Dumas there was money in this project.

Dumas, still dreaming of a knightly accolade, made it quite clear to Ernestine that her articles should include the things city dwellers wanted to know about Aborigines, including stories of cannibalism, blood-letting and initiation ceremonies. This was the stuff that would make both his newspapers and the book sell. He loved the 'angle' of an aristocratic Florence Nightingale in the desert, spending her personal fortune on the Aborigines, and didn't seem overly concerned whether the story was one hundred per cent accurate. What was vital was to get it down before Daisy finally lost her memory. The memoirs of the Queen of the Desert in her prim Edwardian clothes living among naked cannibals might even outdo the bestselling memoirs of the explorer Mary Kingsley, which Dumas knew had made a fortune for her publishers. Miss Kingsley was another prim English lady in a long skirt and high-button boots, who had braved cannibals and crocodiles in West Africa.

This is how Daisy Bates's unreliable memoir started off. Not exactly a literary hoax, it was nevertheless filled with misleading information, sheer fantasy and self-promotion on Daisy's part, as well as racist slurs against part-Aborigines. Above all, however, it introduced the legend of Kabbarli to the general public.

Subsequent correspondence between Lloyd Dumas and Ernestine Hill refers to his 'sponsoring' of Ernestine for the projected book. She was well paid for her syndicated articles about Daisy, who was given only her travelling and accommodation expenses until such time as the book rights were sold to a publisher, when she would receive an advance against royalties. The contract between Hill and Dumas did not specify whose name should appear on the cover of the book.

Somehow these two quite difficult women managed to remain friends throughout the whole process of writing the newspaper articles and later preparing them for publication as a book.

❦ ❦ ❦

Once the contract with Lloyd Dumas was signed, Ernestine wrote to Daisy advising her to come to Adelaide at once. An excited Daisy (she had, it seems — true to form — been exaggerating the risks of bushfire) caught the next train to the South Australian capital. She brought with her a battered tin trunk and hat-boxes containing documents and printed articles she had written years ago, all jumbled together willy-nilly. Wearing her outdated clothes, she was taken to a hotel and then went on to the offices of *The Advertiser* group of newspapers to meet Lloyd Dumas. He had arranged for Daisy and Ernestine to share an office, together with a mature, very competent secretary, Miss Elizabeth Watt, who had a university degree in English. Daisy took to Miss Watt from the first and enjoyed working with her.

Ernestine needed to bridge substantial gaps in Daisy's memory. She realised that while Daisy was suffering short-term memory loss, she was able to recall events farther back in time. 'We decided she would talk and I would write and she would read for additions and amendments,' Ernestine recorded.

Coming to Adelaide gave Daisy a new interest in life. Ernestine reported that she would bound up the stairs each morning, refusing to take the lift, eager to start work. All three women worked hard on producing Ernestine's series of articles, scheduled to appear daily in *The Advertiser* and in Perth's *Western Mail* from 4 January to 20 February 1936. Extracts would appear later in other papers.

Daisy began by relating rambling, disjointed stories from her childhood. Ernestine opened her first article in Ireland, with Daisy's birth in her grandmother's farmhouse at Ballychrine. She included the grim tale of the death of Daisy's mother when her little daughter was only four, and told how the banshee had wailed, foretelling her passing. Daisy left out a few of her siblings and omitted to mention that her father was an alcoholic bootmaker. Instead, she produced the old fabrications, including being the daughter of a gentleman farmer, the owner of Ashberry House.

Ernestine did not inquire too deeply into Daisy's private life, and Daisy kept quiet about a good deal of it. Ernestine, at heart an aspiring romantic novelist rather than a trained historian — her bestselling novelised biography of the explorer Matthew Flinders, *My Love Must Wait*, would be published in 1941 — did no checking at all.

She described Daisy's work among the Aborigines in glowing terms. Both Ernestine and Daisy ignored the fact that, although Aboriginal numbers had declined rapidly during the measles epidemic of 1904, they were now building up again. The articles emphasised the 'doomed race' theory and maintained that Daisy was 'smoothing the pillow' of a dying race.

Ernestine's daily articles, which appeared under the title 'My Natives and I: The Life Story of Daisy M. Bates', were widely read. Kabbarli became a living legend. It was the middle of the Great Depression of the 1930s. Thousands of Australians were out of work and homeless. The Anglo-Irish orphaned gentlewoman who came to Australia because she had a spot on her lung, married a cattle baron and after his death dedicated her life to nursing naked cannibals had a fairytale quality that Lloyd Dumas knew would sell. And for ghoulish interest in the tabloids there was the bloodthirsty story of Dowie, the 'Aboriginal monster' who supposedly killed and ate his baby sisters and later his wives, which further helped to sell Dumas's newspapers like the proverbial hot cakes.

Once the work at Adelaide was completed, Daisy returned to Ooldea, ordering a copy of each issue of *The Advertiser* to be sent to her by train. She enjoyed reading her alleged 'life story'. She must have been aware that the tales of her sighting of Queen Victoria as a child, her travels with the Outrams and her careful avoidance of anything to do with Roscrea and the bootery on Main Street could, if discovered, destroy her credibility, but her pride was soothed by Ernestine's flowing prose.[1]

※ ※ ※

Dumas's plan to sell Kabbarli's story overseas took another two years to put into effect. The book was handled through the Curtis Brown Literary Agency in London, which sold the manuscript and the rights to use the photographs taken by Daisy and Ernestine to Sir John Murray, one of London's leading publishers, whose long-established company had published the works of Lord Byron. Once the book contract was signed, the plan was that Daisy would return to Adelaide so that Ernestine's articles could be welded together to make a smoother narrative, with a few discrepancies sorted out.

Daisy would then receive her advance against royalties, followed by more royalty cheques every six months based on continuing sales of the book. To a woman with almost nothing in the bank, who had for years been denied an income by the government, this financial prospect was exciting.

Asked for clarification on certain points regarding her alleged English childhood with the aristocracy, Daisy refused to answer so cuts were suggested in the manuscript held by the publisher.

Since Ernestine was about to start writing *The Great Australian Loneliness*, a nonfiction work describing her outback travels, which would be her own first published book, Lloyd Dumas appointed another editor, a former journalist named Max Lamshed, to help Daisy shorten her story. So Daisy returned to Adelaide to work with Lamshed. The fantasies of the little Irish heiress living with Sir Francis Outram and his family in Dorset and travelling with them through Europe were deleted. The book to be published by John Murray would now begin with Daisy, a married woman, returning to Western Australia from London at the turn of the nineteenth century, with a commission from *The Times* to investigate the treatment of Aborigines there. Perhaps she was secretly relieved. The missing sections from Daisy's account of her childhood were decades later published by Hesperion Press of Western Australia in the book *My Natives and I*, edited by Peter Bridge, and with an

Introduction by Professor Bob Reece describing the story behind the publication of *The Passing of the Aborigines*.

Finally, the advance on royalties came through. After having spent so many years living on almost nothing in the desert, Daisy proved extremely generous to old and new friends. Declaring she was a 'giver' rather than a 'taker', she bought books for her acquaintance Lady Hayward and toys for friends' children, and sent off parcels of tinned corned beef, jam, fruit and boiled sweets to 'her' natives — Cooroomagum, Yalli-Yalli, Dhambilnga and others.

In addition, Daisy spent money on having her clothes smartened up. She told Ernestine that her hand-tailored suits, which had been made by an Italian tailor in Perth, were exact copies of the model suits she had brought back with her from London. 'The famous little figure, proudly erect, never changed,' Ernestine wrote, 'but her wardrobe was refreshed.'

> Collars and cuffs, toques (smart brimless hats), ties, veils, gloves, shoes . . . were replaced by new ones. Dyers and invisible-menders tinted and trimmed the frayed and faded suits and coatees, resurrected the neat little jockey jackets and nine-gored skirts, while millinery magic redeemed the perished ribbons and flowers of the turn-of-the-century hats . . . [Mrs Bates] loved to be the pivot of attention.

This last remark is an important observation: a desire for attention motivated Daisy's actions for the major part of her life.

Ernestine, who was slightly in awe of Daisy, realised her friend was not good at finding her way around Adelaide on her own; in 1936, while they were working on the manuscript, Ernestine tried to accompany her most of the time and make sure she did not get run over in the city traffic. It was obvious that Daisy was totally unused to motor vehicles; she simply strode out into the road expecting them to halt for her.

At times Ernestine's descriptions make Daisy sound like an over-excited child — taking intense pleasure in being recognised in the street and enjoying introducing herself to the people she encountered. Physically she was incredibly fit for her age and walked everywhere. Unable to cope with money, she would hand her purse to startled waiters and shopkeepers, saying: 'Here, take whatever you need.' She insisted on tipping everyone — 'noblesse oblige, don't you know,' she would say in explanation, playing the role of Anglo-Irish gentlewoman to the hilt.

Daisy acknowledged that Ernestine was responsible for the publication of her memoirs in book form, even though the name Ernestine Hill would not appear on the title page. Ernestine's papers are blank about this omission, but it must surely have been hurtful for her contribution to be ignored in this way. Yet the friendship between the two women survived, although at the end of her life Ernestine admitted there had been turbulent moments.

The fact that Daisy had not written her memoirs herself would only be publicly revealed long after her death, when Ernestine Hill's book *Kabbarli*, written as a tribute to Daisy, was published in 1973 — by which time Ernestine herself had died. Unfortunately, *Kabbarli* was written by an author who never realised she hadn't been told the full truth and who repeated Daisy's fantasies of a privileged childhood — as, two years later, did Elizabeth Salter in her biography, *Daisy Bates*.

※ ※ ※

Daisy was now suffering badly from conjunctivitis, the ailment for which she had treated so many Aborigines at Ooldea. As a result of years of sandstorms and blinding glare, her eyes were giving her a great deal of discomfort. She could not afford an expensive operation and feared that she would not be able to cope by herself in the desert. By this time she had exhausted the advance from the publishers; the bank failed to honour some of her cheques and would not grant her a loan. She was not due to receive another royalty cheque for six months.

Horrified at her situation, Daisy fled northeast to Pyap on the River Murray, where she pitched her tent on the bank, surrounded by gum trees. There she was visited by Lady Hayward, who brought with her in her Rolls-Royce, Daisy's old friend from her days in the hostel for upper-class girls in London, Hester Cayley, who was on a visit to Australia. No doubt worried about what sort of food Daisy might provide, Lady Hayward's cook had prepared tempting delicacies and for Daisy there was a present of a brightly striped jacket — 'a coat of many colours', which Daisy loved. She wore it as she posed for a photo sitting in a deckchair outside her tent.

Daisy wrote to Sir John Murray in London, saying there had been so much 'confusion, postponement, alteration and worry that I have had to run away from it all'. Her next letter to Sir John seems to indicate that she had descended one more step in the staircase-like progression of her vascular dementia. She told him that she was worried about the possibility of Germany declaring war and what would happen to the fruit growers of German descent around Pyap should Adolph Hitler invade Australia. She added that she had written to Hitler to intercede on their behalf. 'I wrote a friendly letter to Herr Hitler, telling him of my arrival here for rest and quiet.' It's hard to believe that Daisy could imagine the Nazi Fuhrer reading her letter; it reveals how out of touch with reality she had become.

Daisy's book, *The Passing of the Aborigines*, was published in London in March 1938. It was to prove a great success.

Daisy Bates in her eighties

CHAPTER 19

DAISY BATES, A LEGENDARY FIGURE

Mrs Bates is a nomadic Florence Nightingale . . . almost unique in her devotion to principle and humanity.

GLASGOW MORNING HERALD REVIEW OF
THE PASSING OF THE ABORIGINES

Late in 1938, the year of the publication of her book, Daisy went into hospital for a second eye operation, performed in Adelaide.

It was Ernestine who made this possible. She wrote to various government departments in Canberra, explaining that the operation was vital for a woman about to become internationally famous — the 'Florence Nightingale of Australia'.

Perhaps there were worries in Canberra that, as an investigative journalist, Ernestine Hill might expose the fact that the elderly Mrs Daisy Bates, CBE, had been ignored by a government that had refused to recompense her for her aid work with the Aborigines. A scandal might arise if the book really did become a bestseller. Daisy was informed that her eye operation would be paid for by the Commonwealth government.

She soon began to receive congratulatory letters from friends who had already seen copies of her book, as well as from State governors, pastoralists and some academics. At last the bootmaker's daughter from Roscrea had achieved success. In December she wrote to Sir John Murray: 'There is one universal opinion in every letter — how fortunate and happy I must be to have my book published by such a distinguished firm and how beautifully they have turned it out.'

She herself did not see a copy until mid-January 1939, when she wrote to her publisher again:

> I am writing to you with my new eyes and my new
> glasses and new strength. I have just gone through your
> beautiful book . . . and I see in every page of it the kindly
> work of John Murray in making it what it is . . . There is
> to me such a delicacy in the whole book that I can use
> only that word. It is what I have striven for and you have
> accomplished.[1]

The jacket of the first edition bore a photograph supplied by Daisy, showing the torso of a naked Aborigine, his chest bearing ceremonial scars. On publication day in London, John Murray's window in fashionable Albemarle Street was filled with copies, and it was also on display at Hatchards bookshop in Piccadilly, Harrods in Knightsbridge and other shops all over Britain. The British reviews were outstanding. 'One of the most thrilling adventure stories ever written', proclaimed the *Daily Herald*. The hype continued. In the book's Introduction, written by the elderly Arthur Mee, who had accepted many articles from Daisy in past years for his newspaper and encyclopaedia produced for young readers, she was compared to both Florence Nightingale and Father Damien, a saintly figure who lived and worked with lepers in the South Pacific.

The book sold and sold — it would eventually go into six editions. Copies were exported to America for sale, and advance orders from Australia were excellent.

To Australians, *The Passing of the Aborigines* revealed Aboriginal lore, art and ceremonies in a way that fascinated the general reader. Most Australians had until now ignored the extraordinary ancient culture that existed in their midst. However, while it was clear that Daisy Bates had carried out a great deal of self-sacrificing work among the Aborigines, the book also aroused fierce criticism from anthropologists, who regarded it as over-sentimentalised and highly offensive to part–Aboriginal people. Its very title (chosen by the publisher and initially approved by Daisy) was controversial,[2] as

The front cover of the first edition

were Daisy's claims of widespread cannibalism and her assertion that she had special magical powers acquired through a *bamburu* given to her by a sorcerer. These things caused her to be viewed as a highly problematic figure in anthropological circles and among Aboriginal activists and others trying to help the Indigenous people to find a place in Australian society.

Daisy Bates has been accused of manufacturing the idea that Aboriginal people were dying out, principally from leprosy, tuberculosis, venereal disease and measles epidemics. In fact, she inherited this theory as the received wisdom of her era from a series of public servants and politicians. In South Australia the theory of Aboriginal demise dated back to 1860. An examination of the minutes of the South Australian Legislative Council's Select Committee on Aborigines concluded that Aboriginal people in that State were doomed to extinction, so that any relief measures would only be temporary. Faced with such bleak prognoses, along with huge numbers of deaths from the causes listed above and the point-blank refusal of the government to provide drought relief at Ooldea, Daisy can hardly be blamed for believing in the 'passing away' theory.

In *Kabbarli*, Ernestine Hill recorded how Daisy was feted after her book went on sale in Australia. Once again living in her tent at Pyap, she was invited back to Adelaide for an official book launch and stayed at the Queen Adelaide Club, the equivalent of Perth's Karrakatta Club. In the city she was recognised everywhere she went and her autograph was frequently requested. She loved all this attention, but flatly refused to answer telephone calls. A secretary was supplied to accompany her everywhere; like royalty, she never needed to carry money.

No doubt embarrassed that after all Ernestine's hard work on the book her name did not appear in it, Daisy insisted on buying some expensive jewellery for her collaborator — and for Miss Watt, who had helped prepare the manuscript.

Daisy was in her element, being taken for drives in the Adelaide Hills and invited by Lady Hayward to stay at her beautiful house, Carrick Hill. Its oak-panelled walls were imported from an English manor house, its walls were hung with Australian and English paintings and its magnificent gardens were widely admired.

❦ ❦ ❦

World War II broke out in the first week of September 1939, with the fate of the Pyap fruit growers of German descent still unresolved. Daisy eventually returned to Ooldea, but didn't stay there long. She found that the Aborigines she knew had gone, so she returned to Adelaide. In 1941 she moved her tent and her few possessions to Wynbring Siding, east of Ooldea. From there she continued to correspond with Ernestine Hill at least once a month. Bob Hill, Ernestine's son, was now sixteen or so. He had declared himself a pacifist and travelled with his mother as her assistant on outback trips, where she obtained her material for the freelance articles that funded her books. Like Daisy, Ernestine was fearless: she sailed around the Gulf of Carpentaria on a lugger, braved a thousand kilometres of crocodile-infested rivers, and dared to venture into Arnhem Land, with its rich treasuries of Aboriginal art. This was an area in which so many Europeans had been murdered that it had been decided to discourage settlement and gazette the land as a vast Aboriginal reserve.

In 1941, too, Daisy stopped writing for newspapers and magazines, just as Ernestine was becoming a successful book author. At the end of that year Daisy's old friend and patron Arthur Mee died suddenly. His death depressed her considerably, bringing to a close an era. No one else wanted articles from her any more. Finally Daisy let down her guard and admitted to Ernestine that she was 'poor as wood'. Even worse for her was the knowledge that her old way of life at Ooldea had vanished without trace. All the syphilitics she had tended with such care had died. The remaining Aborigines capable of surviving a move had gone to live on missions or in compounds. The war changed everything: most of the young girls had been taken away to government homes. The fittest of the young men had enlisted in the army or been employed in allied works, building military installations, roads and bridges from the Arafura Sea to the south of Australia.

At this point Daisy acted on an earlier proposal that she should donate her research notebooks to the Parliamentary Library in Canberra, which was about to be re-formed as the National Library of Australia. Ninety-nine boxes of papers were donated by Daisy to the National Library.

Among Ernestine Hill's records is a note from Daisy (dated only 1941) claiming that Sir William Mitchell, then Vice-Chancellor of the University of Adelaide, was so worried by news of her poor health that, realising the value of her research, he had arranged for a Commonwealth Literary Fund grant of 800 pounds to be paid to Mrs Bates. The sole condition was that she must work at the University of Adelaide with two secretaries paid by the university, which would own the copyright of her works after her death.

Daisy agreed to this proposition. So that the mounds of notebooks and scraps of paper on which she had written her notes could be sorted and catalogued, she again spent some months in Adelaide, staying at the Queen Adelaide Club or in hotels. She was not very satisfied with the secretaries provided by the university. Nor did Mrs Bates receive the promised hand-over ceremony at the National Library with her adored Governor-General Lord Gowrie, and was bitterly disappointed she was unable to stay at Yarralumla with the governor and his wife.

Daisy hoped that, by making her donation through the auspices of the University of Adelaide, she might receive an honorary degree, which would stand as a vindication of the quality of the research she had carried out initially on Western Australia's Aborigines and their languages and culture. She expressed this hope to Professor John Cleland, a distinguished pathologist and amateur anthropologist with an interest in disease in the Aboriginal population, and a member of the University of Adelaide's governing body. Daisy and Cleland had corresponded for years over various Aboriginal topics, including cannibalism.

In an attempt to support her allegations of cannibalism, in 1920 and again in 1932 Daisy had sent Cleland two boxes of charred bones she claimed to be the remains of cannibal victims. The first box turned out to contain the bones of a cat; the second lot were identified by Cleland, albeit reluctantly, as human remains. But he did not wish this to be publicised, fearing it could be used to cut welfare payments to Aborigines. Many years later, in 1969, Cleland told the author Elizabeth Salter that Daisy could have been purposely misled over such evidence by her Aboriginal informants, perhaps as a joke — as has since been alleged in the case of Samoan contacts of Margaret Mead over information she was given on sexual matters. Or else one group of Aborigines may have wanted to implicate a rival linguistic group in scandal.

Although Daisy hoped that Cleland would recommend her for an honorary degree, he told her regretfully that he could not do so. Her hopes of academic recognition for her work were dashed once again.

Daisy's money dwindled until finally the bank refused to honour a cheque she had written. She had little option but to retreat to her tent at Pyap, where she finally finished sorting her papers. It was there, in an effort to obliterate her sad childhood and failed marriages, that Daisy decided to burn all her private records. One can imagine the determined, white-haired old lady in her long skirt building a bonfire and throwing onto it her diaries, her marriage certificates, letters from three husbands, letters from her sisters; photos of Marian in her nun's habit, of Kathleen wearing a fashionable Edwardian gown, of curly-haired Jim outside the Main Street house, taken on Daisy's final trip to Roscrea — all the evidence she did not want anyone to find, knowing it would spoil the image of Kabbarli that she and Ernestine had created.

Daisy must have lit a match and watched the flames curl round the photographs and brown the edges of all those letters, finally bursting into a devouring fire. One can only speculate on her feelings as she watched her mementos vanish for ever.

Soon the news leaked out that Daisy Bates's bequest to the National Library would contain none of her personal papers, even though she had agreed to donate everything. Asked to explain her action, Daisy climbed onto her high horse. She said that she 'did not want her relationships with important people vulgarised by exposure to the common gaze'.[3]

Then, having divested herself of her secret past, she sat outside her tent at Pyap and tapped away at her typewriter amid the peace of the riverside. She sent complimentary copies of *The Passing of the Aborigines* to all those she wished to impress, together with copies of Ernestine's successful new book, *The Great Australian Loneliness*.

कः कः कः

By now Daisy Bates was famous. An envelope addressed to 'Mrs Daisy Bates, The Little White Tent on the Murray' was successfully delivered to her. This gave her considerable pleasure; she kept the envelope, which was later found among her papers at the National Library.

Despite her fame, lacking money, a home and any family around her, Daisy lived virtually alone during most of World War II. She and Ernestine both made unsuccessful attempts to contact Arnold through the Salvation Army and the Minister of the Interior. Finally, Daisy discovered that he was working in New Zealand; he had married a Lola Davidson, a young Australian music teacher, and had a family — and so she learned that she had a grandson and a granddaughter. However, Arnold insisted he did not wish his mother to know his address. Daisy must have been shocked and hurt; doubtless Ernestine provided some comfort when she found out about this.

Daisy used a lined writing pad for her letters to Ernestine; her handwriting, bold and flowing, gradually became wilder as her dementia increased. The final letters are very sad and often indecipherable. They reveal that at times Daisy seems to understand that her memory is going; at other times she ignores this fact but seems puzzled by certain events.

By 1944 Daisy was still living at Wynbring Siding, east of Ooldea. From there she could visit Adelaide whenever she could afford the fare. The South Australian government, displaying great insensitivity, had turned down her request for a free rail pass based on the service she had given to the Aborigines in that State for so many years.

Towards the end of that year there was concern in high places after Daisy sent a series of bizarre telegrams to the premier of South Australia, Sir Thomas Playford, and to Prime Minister John Curtin, claiming that she was being 'threatened by dangerous people' who had got off the train at Wynbring to attack her and that she had been forced to defend herself with her revolver. She requested that the government should move her to Adelaide. An official investigation revealed that no such incident had occurred. It was whispered that Mrs Bates was having trouble distinguishing truth from fiction.

It did indeed seem that the redoubtable Daisy Bates, Protector of Aborigines, was in need of protection and care herself. After she wrote another long, rambling letter about mobs of hostile people, kind acquaintances in Adelaide alerted the Port Augusta Inspector of Police, suggesting that, for her own good, Daisy should be removed from the desert, by force if she refused to leave voluntarily.

The inspector ordered Policewoman Alvis Brooks and Police Constable A.W. Grovermann to escort Mrs Bates to a private nursing home at Port Augusta selected by the Prime Minister's Office, which had agreed that the government would meet the cost of her rest and treatment. In January 1945 Brooks and Grovermann drove to Daisy's camp in a small ambulance to take her to the Port Augusta train.[4]

Policewoman Brooks found Daisy 'very difficult'. Like many elderly people, Daisy hated the idea of leaving her home and relinquishing her independence. In fact, she was furious. She refused to travel by train and demanded a government car. Although her eyes were now so bad again that she could scarcely see, she stoutly maintained that she could carry on living at Wynbring Siding. Yet Alvis Brooks found only some tea, a tin of powdered milk, red with rust, one tomato and some eggs in a meat safe hung from a nail on a tree beside Daisy's tent. She and Constable Grovermann insisted that Mrs Bates should go with them. Brooks told Daisy very politely that they had received instructions that she could no longer live in the desert alone.

As always, Daisy was polite and dignified, but once more refused to go, whereupon the two officers left.

The next morning they returned. This time, believing that Alvis Brooks was a nurse, Daisy invited her into her tent for 'a cuppa'. The policewoman noted that Daisy ate nothing, but drank a cup of black tea with a raw egg in it. She offered the rusty tin of powdered milk to Brooks, who described its contents as unusable. Still believing Brooks to be a nurse, Daisy sat quietly, allowing her to pack. But then she refused to leave and was distraught when the police bundled her into the ambulance, kicking and screaming. During the struggle, the watching Aborigines allegedly later said that Kabbarli fell out of the ambulance and had to be helped back inside again. Years later Daisy maintained in a letter to Ernestine that the fall had injured her back muscles and she had been in pain ever since.

> I was compelled into a vile car, bundled in just as if I had
> been caught up by a huge beast and thrust into a corner
> . . . I was doubled up and carried in that way the eighty
> miles to Tarcoola. When I fell out of a car . . . the back
> muscles and tendons were overstretched by the position I
> was lying in.[5]

At Tarcoola Daisy, still utterly mortified, refused to get into the train with Alvis Brooks. The policewoman knew how much Daisy loved her treasured black umbrella, so she picked it up, saying firmly, 'This umbrella's coming with me to Port Augusta', and climbed onto the train without a backward glance. Daisy knew when she was beaten and followed her. By now she realised that the young woman was not a nurse but a police officer, and she behaved towards her with hostility.

At the nursing home Daisy demanded to see the press. Stories were leaked to the newspapers, causing a public outcry. The public was told that Mrs Bates was suffering from malnutrition and would spend several weeks there. With professional nursing and good food, and surrounded by caring people, Daisy slowly grew stronger. She enjoyed the luxury of hot baths and bossing the nurses around. She was then moved to a nursing home in Adelaide, once again paid for by the government. Newspapers headlined the fact that the heroic and saintly Kabbarli was in Adelaide convalescing but had no proper home. (The fact that she was increasingly demented, had not been eating properly and was unable to care for herself was covered up.) Offers of accommodation in private homes came from Daisy's many admirers, but she still insisted she could return to the desert. Her possessions, however, had been sent to Adelaide by the police, and it was hoped that she would stay there.

CHAPTER 20

LONELY, THOUGH NOT ALONE

I am one of two people . . . one I like and the other I do not know . . .

DAISY BATES, NOTEBOOK, MANUSCRIPTS DEPARTMENT,
NATIONAL LIBRARY OF AUSTRALIA

In the nursing home at Adelaide, unable to read with her failing eyesight, Daisy felt lonely and unhappy. She was right when she claimed she was two people: she could be rude and uncooperative with the staff on 'bad' days and pleasant and courteous on 'good' days.

Perhaps feeling guilty that no acknowledgement of Ernestine Hill had been made in *The Passing of the Aborigines*, Daisy sent her an emotional letter, saying: 'I have been unworthy of your friendship in many ways, dear friend, and ask your pardon.' She would repeat this statement in several later letters.

After bitter conflicts in the nursing home with an officious and bossy matron, Daisy discharged herself, choosing to ignore doctors' orders that she must get plenty of bed rest. She had by now received money from a royalty cheque for the Australian edition of her book, which appeared in 1946, and took a taxi to a boarding house in the beachside suburb of Henley. But it seems that another bounced cheque, conflicts with the boarding-house staff and increasing frailty forced her to return to the nursing home.

The next time she and the nursing-home matron had a clash of wills, Daisy discharged herself again. Somehow or other she managed to find a bus that took her to Streaky Bay, a former whaling station that had originally been given its name by Matthew Flinders because the water there was streaked green with seaweed. To begin with she stayed at the bayside Flinders Hotel, but her money soon ran out (she told Ernestine that she had miscalculated how much she would receive from the royalties) and she had to move to cheaper accommodation.

Early in 1947 Daisy rented a room in a private house twenty kilometres beyond Streaky Bay, the home of Mrs Thompson, a kindly farmer's wife. Here she ate meals in her room and existed on a simple diet: tea, biscuits and jam, and baked or mashed potatoes. Initially her landlady described her as 'a nice harmless old lady', but later she would complain to Ernestine Hill that Mrs Bates could be extremely difficult.

Daisy's correspondence with Ernestine shows that she moved frequently between three farmhouses near Streaky Bay, including the one owned by the Thompsons and another belonging to Mr and Mrs Matthews. Whenever she needed to go to Adelaide, she stayed in a modest boarding house in Norwood.

Daisy seems to have had some insight into her condition. She now realised that she was no longer capable of editing her vast collection of Aboriginal myths and legends into a book. Accordingly she proposed giving the manila folders containing her detailed notes to Ernestine and asking her to edit them. In a letter to Ernestine early in 1948, she said she needed her help to complete the project. Ernestine agreed that if she came to Streaky Bay she would take the folders back with her to Western Australia, but that meanwhile she must finish her forthcoming book for Angus & Robertson (*The Territory*, published in 1951).

In another letter to Ernestine, Daisy said that she regretted giving her papers to the National Library and would like to have the library send back 'those lovely ninety [sic] folios so I can sit in my chair and hold each and every one of them'.[1] It seems the National Library heard about this, for they did make copies of some of the documents and sent them to her.

Once again there was very little money in Daisy's bank account, but she refused any help she felt smacked of 'charity'. It has been said that she seemed to expect people to care for her for nothing. Her gums hurt — possibly the onset of scurvy that went unrecognised — and her diet now consisted mainly of cups of tea and slices of bread-and-butter with the crusts cut off. Her difficulty in eating solid food was endangering her health, but stubborn as always, she refused to admit this and re-enter a nursing home.

In various letters Daisy kept repeating that she wished to come to Western Australia, buy a caravan and live beside Ernestine. She promised she would be no trouble at all. Ernestine's replies to Daisy have not been saved, but it seems she pleaded pressure of work as the reason why it would not be possible for Daisy to live with her. To give Ernestine her due, she never stopped writing to Daisy. Using royalties from her bestselling novel *My Love Must Wait*, the romanticised biography of explorer Matthew Flinders which Angus & Robertson had published in 1941, Ernestine sent Daisy gifts of money and a comfortable upholstered armchair. Daisy's latest landlord, a Mr Williams, wrote to Ernestine complaining how difficult Mrs Bates had become and how she refused to sit in the chair, complaining, as back sufferers do, that a soft chair wasn't nearly as comfortable as a hard one. Mr Williams was clearly worried: there seemed to be no one who wished to accept responsibility for Mrs Bates, now a legendary Australian figure — thanks to Ernestine's work on the articles that made up 'My Natives and I' and *The Passing of the Aborigines*.

In fact, Ernestine Hill now seemed to be the only long-standing friend who cared about Daisy.

☙ ☙ ☙

The story of Daisy's ninetieth birthday, spent with no one to celebrate it with her, can be pieced together from a despairing letter written by Mrs Matthews to Ernestine Hill and dated 19 October 1949, three days after Daisy turned ninety. She said that from mid-October Mrs Bates had been moody and difficult. It seems Daisy must have been hoping against hope that Arnold would finally make contact with her on such an important anniversary. When there was no word from him, she must have become angry that her son had abandoned her. She tore the page out of her birthday book that recorded his birthday, symbolically erasing him from her life.

That afternoon she went out for a walk. By tea-time she had not returned and the local people became worried. Mrs Thompson contacted the police, telling them that Mrs Bates had set off for a walk through the barley fields at two o'clock. By bedtime there was still no sign of her. Search parties went out with torches. Eventually they found her at two the next morning. She had walked through the fields and either fallen or thrown herself over a low cliff onto some granite rocks, hitting her head and blacking out. She had regained consciousness but was unable to move. The search party carried her back to the Thompson farmhouse, where she was given brandy and put to bed.

The police treated the event as an accident. However, it seems significant that it happened at this time, and that she had removed from her birthday book her son's date of birth. Could it have been her despairing wish to end it all?

'Why didn't Mrs Bates's son get in touch with his mother on her ninetieth birthday?' the Thompsons were asked over and over again, once it was realised that no one had taken the trouble to celebrate the day with her.

'A son should take responsibility for his widowed mother,' the Thompsons replied. But try as they might, they were unable to contact Arnold Bates.

Eventually the half-blind Daisy became so difficult to handle that the responsibility borne by the long-suffering Thompsons became almost too much. Mrs Thompson reported that sometimes Mrs Bates shut herself in her room and cried for an absent son, calling for William rather than Arnold.[2] In the end, Daisy packed her belongings and said she was returning to stay with Mr and Mrs Matthews.

At first she seemed grateful for everything the Matthews did for her. Then, according to Mr Matthews, she had one of her bad turns. She became paranoid, claiming that some of her possessions were missing and accusing Mr and Mrs Matthews of stealing her letters and parcels. Mrs Matthews wrote to Ernestine Hill again, telling her that she was the only person who could help. She was 'Mrs Bates's only friend'.

So Ernestine made the long journey from Western Australia, accompanied by Bob. She talked at length with Daisy and suggested she should move back to Adelaide, where the medical care was better. Ernestine cooked potatoes in their jackets in the oven the way Daisy liked them, then they talked of the old days at Ooldea. Daisy was still very slim. Ernestine took colour photographs of her wearing the suit in which she had met the Prince of Wales almost thirty years before, and also of her wearing a faded silk evening gown with tiny satin dancing shoes on her feet. The photographs were intended for another book Ernestine thought she might write about Daisy, bringing her story up to date, but unfortunately the film was lost by the firm that developed it.

At night Ernestine sat on the edge of Daisy's bed in the darkness while Daisy relived the past, her voice low and dreamy as though she were reading from a book. Ernestine, romantic as ever, described Daisy telling stories about her life with the Outrams in their Dorset mansion, making the Grand Tour, her presentation at Buckingham Palace, and the rollicking life of outback New South Wales in the days of blade shearers and handsome drovers.

One night Daisy set her bed alight. She had heated up a house brick to warm the bed and wrapped it in a blanket, a normal practice from her Irish childhood. Although she only narrowly escaped being burned, Daisy remained cool as a cucumber.

However, aware of her own mortality, Daisy gave Ernestine her two most precious possessions: her *bamburu*, the finely carved message stick given to her by an Aboriginal *kadaicha*, or medicine man; and the brown manila folders containing her notes on Aboriginal myths and legends. For years Daisy had been hoping to turn them into a book, originally intending to dedicate it to the young English princesses, Elizabeth and Margaret Rose. Ernestine agreed to take on the task and produce a book for children, but in the end the project came to naught. Daisy's notes finally ended up in the Barr Smith Library in Adelaide, where they would be rediscovered by Elizabeth Salter when she arrived to carry out research for her biography *Daisy Bates* in the 1970s. Salter mentioned them to Barbara Ker Wilson, who was then in charge of the Angus & Robertson children's book department, working from Adelaide. Ker Wilson, a specialist in folklore, had already published several collections of myths and legends from around the world. She was fascinated by the legend of Daisy Bates and eagerly delved into the tin trunk, its interior still scattered with sand from the desert. She unearthed Daisy's notes on a large number of legends in rough form, exactly as they had been taken down from the tribespeople who fled across the desert to Ooldea Soak in the terrible time of drought. Several of Daisy Bates's Aboriginal vocabulary notebooks were also in the trunk. In 1972 under the title *Tales Told to Kabbarli*, Ker Wilson published thirty-four of the myths and legends which were illustrated by Harold Thomas, an Aboriginal artist on the staff of the South Australian Museum.

At this point Daisy accepted an invitation from her old friend Beatrice Raine, whom she had escorted years ago to her brother's Nullarbor Station, beyond Eucla, to occupy the granny flat under Beatrice's house on the outskirts of Adelaide as a paying guest. There, too, she had days when she retired to her room and cried her heart out — again strangely for a missing son called William — but also more spirited days.[3] When Douglas Glass, a well-known British photographer, visited the house, he was able to take a photograph of Daisy skipping like a child in the garden, to demonstrate how 'young' she was at ninety — in spite of the spasmodic pain she suffered from her lower back.

At last the time came when Daisy entered another nursing home in an Adelaide bayside suburb. She rallied a little, had treatment for her gums and started to eat solid food again. She would go out for a morning walk holding a bag of pennies, intent on giving them to children she met, some of whom were in awe of her, while others mocked the quaint-looking old lady. She

Daisy Bates in old age

carried another bag containing crumbs for sparrows in the park; they, it seemed, had replaced Aborigines as recipients of her benevolence. Giving had become her way of life. She did not know how to live without it.

Sometimes she would lose her way and have to be brought back by strangers whom she might direct to Government House. The governor, Sir Willoughby Norrie, always declined to see her and issued orders that she was to be driven home by the duty police officer. On two occasions Daisy's former nemesis, Policewoman Alvis Brooks, on duty outside the front gates of Government House, recognised Mrs Bates and took her home in the police car. Brooks was very tactful; to salvage Mrs Bates's pride, she told Mrs Bates the governor had supplied his own car.

Daisy was often lonely in the nursing home but was cared for by kindly staff, one of whom sent bulletins about Mrs Bates's health to Ernestine Hill, who was travelling around the goldfields of Western Australia at this point. Ernestine mistakenly believed that friends in Adelaide were visiting Daisy. She received only one letter from her at this time, an illegible scrawl.

❧ ❧ ❧

By now Daisy had given in to the pains of old age and had taken to wearing a faded green dressing-gown with woolly slippers. A group of women visiting the nursing home in which Daisy now lived noticed the threadbare state of her dressing-gown and clubbed together to buy a new one, rose-pink in colour. But how to persuade Mrs Bates to accept the gift without taking offence at such charity?

A young Irish nurse to whom Daisy had taken a liking solved the problem. 'I'll tell her the dressing-gown's a present from the governor,' she said, and carried it into Daisy's room. Daisy put it on at once, exclaiming how beautiful it was. She wore it every day.

Finally, thin as a winter leaf, Daisy Bates waited for the mystery of death the Aborigines call *nalba*. On 19 April 1951, aged ninety-one, she died in her sleep, released from the twilight world of dementia by another small stroke, a common form of death for sufferers of vascular dementia. Ernestine received a letter from the Irish nurse who had looked after Daisy, saying that she had felt no pain — she had simply gone to sleep and not woken up.

Kabbarli was not buried among Aboriginal friends, together with her digging stick, which she had told Ernestine was her wish. Nor did she, although she was the government-appointed Protector of Aborigines, receive a government funeral, as Beatrice Raine and Ernestine Hill had hoped. She was buried in the North Road Anglican cemetery in the lee of the Adelaide Hills. An inscription on the granite slab above Daisy's grave states:

> *Erected by the Commonwealth Government as a tribute to her*
> *life-long work in the interests of the Australian Aborigines.*

Arnold Bates, still residing in New Zealand, did not attend his mother's funeral but sent his son to honour her passing. A photograph taken by the Australian artist Hal Missingham shows a lone Aboriginal woman among a sea of white faces.

Ernestine sent a wreath of scarlet and black Sturt's desert pea, an apt choice for Kabbarli.

Daisy bequeathed Aboriginal weapons and sacred objects to the Museum of South Australia and left the sacred *bamburu*, which both Daisy and Ernestine had always regarded as a lucky talisman, to her

Daisy's grandson attends her funeral at Adelaide's North Cemetery in April 1951.

Two memorials to Daisy Bates: the first in Adeliade, the second at Ooldea.

loyal friend. After Ernestine's death, Bob Hill donated it to the Western Australian State Museum. As it is a sacred object, the museum is unable to put it on display.

୫ ୫ ୫

Ernestine Hill's later life was as sad as that of Daisy Bates. Although she made copious notes for future novels, plays and filmscripts, all were doomed to become abandoned projects. Ernestine's life, like Daisy's, was plagued by financial worries and health troubles. Like Daisy, she was badly affected by a poor diet on her outback travels, and the Craven A cigarettes she smoked ceaselessly gave her the hoarse, racking cough of emphysema.

In 1959 Ernestine Hill received a Commonwealth Literary Fund Fellowship, but her condition worsened and she couldn't put the grant to best use. She attempted to settle in North Queensland, then abandoned that idea and once more set off on her travels. Like Daisy, too, she refused to admit that her mind was failing. She dragged swags of notes and future book ideas around, always restless and unhappy over the way her life had turned out.

Her portrait was painted by Sam Fullbrook, who was undergoing treatment for alcoholism. He later revealed that he and Ernestine had been drinking heavily when he painted his 'impression' of her in old age, with bright lipstick slashed across her face. The portrait, now in the Queensland Art Gallery, is not as good as the psychological study of the much younger Ernestine by Elizabeth Durack, which hangs in the Fryer Library at the University of Queensland.

In August 1972, made up with spots of rouge on each cheek and fighting for breath, Ernestine was wheeled out of her bedroom by her son to be interviewed by Margriet Bonnin, a young student seeking material for a thesis. Ailing and unhappy, Ernestine begged the young woman to act as her amanuensis — just as she herself had for Daisy Bates — so that her manuscript about a heroic Aborigine called Johnnie Whitecap, which Angus & Robertson had been waiting for for years, could finally be finished. Margriet Bonnin told Ernestine that unfortunately it was impossible, as she was about to leave for Melbourne.

'I'll die if you go,' Ernestine said. Three days later, she kept her promise.

❦ ❦ ❦

Daisy Bates's will was written in 1941 and probated ten years later. Her executors, the University of Adelaide, carried out her wishes that her estate and all future royalties be distributed 'for the improvement of the conditions of life among Australian Aborigines residing in or resorting to the district of Ooldea and in Western Australia'. This phrase is important as it contradicts the cynical viewpoint that Daisy Bates sought only to exploit Aboriginal people rather than help them.

EPILOGUE: A PERSONAL NOTE

Virgina Woolf claimed that writing the perfect biography was impossible, as everyone has secrets to conceal. Woolf's statement certainly applies to Daisy Bates, a difficult subject for any biographer to tackle. But in Ireland I was dealing with two complex stories riddled with secrets and lies: my own story and that of Daisy Dwyer, later Daisy Bates. My quest to find the truth about her past became entangled with my personal desire to find my own Irish birth parents, for I was an adopted child. When I was growing up in England, adopted children did not possess the right to know the identities of their biological parents. I was fortunate to be adopted by a kind and loving couple, and had no desire to hurt them by admitting my yearning to discover who my birth parents were and why they had given me away. And later in life, tired of doctors asking me if heart trouble or diabetes ran in my family, I wanted to learn their medical histories.

To obtain both Daisy's story and my own, I made two trips to Ireland, having last visited that romantic (but at the time rather sad) country with my adoptive parents when I was twelve. My adoptive father's cousin, Sir Tyrone Guthrie, and his wife, Judith, had at one time thought of adopting me, but then they passed on my details to his cousin James Guthrie Adamson. I was taken to visit Lady Guthrie of Annaghmakerrig, the Guthries' former home near Newbliss, and the town of Monaghan, where my birth mother had taught at the National School. But no one mentioned her name or told me that she was living nearby.

My biological mother had done what Daisy Bates may have done with her purported son by Breaker Morant. My birth mother was a deserted wife on the tiny salary paid to teachers before World War I. She gave away her child in order to keep her job and her respectability, and support herself and my half-sister. I cannot blame her for giving away a love child, born out of wedlock to a married man, a charismatic author from an Irish 'big house', with a reputation as a charmer of women. He had three more marriages so it seems she did the right thing.

In 2001 I spent part of the summer at Tyrone Guthrie's former home, now an Arts Centre, on a writer's fellowship from the Literature Board. By this time I had begun my research on Daisy Bates, using my newly acquired knowledge of how to search for my own Irish forebears, as I tried to solve the puzzle of her background. Was Daisy really a member of the Anglo-Irish gentry, as she claimed in her memoirs, or did she come from modest Catholic stock? What was she covering up with so many false tales and tangled webs? The story nagged at my brain, gave me no peace.

Three years later I was happy to be back in Ireland, determined to solve the enigma of Daisy's childhood and her sometimes strange behaviour.

In the magnificent domed building of the National Library of Ireland I worked at Desk No. 1, thrilled by the thought that great Irish writers like Yeats, Shaw and Synge might have sat at the same leather-topped desk, with its brass reading lamp. I saw Daisy's name inscribed in the baptismal register of St Cronan's ancient Catholic Church. Then I went to Roscrea, viewed the graveyard where Daisy's mother is buried, and was shown the Dwyers' former shop and living quarters on Main Street, where Daisy's mother had wasted away from tuberculosis. But there were so many fantasies and dead ends. Daisy's story was proving so troubling and troublesome that I thought of abandoning the project. Then a strange coincidence persuaded me to think again. In London, on my way home to Brisbane, I stayed with a former schoolfriend whose husband, the Rt Hon Michael Alison, a former Member of Parliament and a Queen's Privy Councillor, was descended from the Burdekin pastoral dynasty. (Old Burdekin House once stood in Sydney's Macquarie Street.) Michael had recently inherited a Sidney Nolan portrait of a woman who meant nothing to him, and he wanted to know who the sitter was.

I received a shock. She was Daisy Bates, wearing her straw hat, long black skirt and white gloves, standing amid the red desert sand of the Nullarbor Plain. The work was a smaller version of the Nolan painting owned by the National Gallery of Australia. I knew that Nolan had gone by train to inspect what remained of Daisy's old camp at Ooldea a few years after her death. He regarded Daisy Bates as a gallant survivor of the desert, unlike Burke and Wills, whose ill-fated expedition was the subject of a series of other Nolan paintings. The artist saw the two explorers as failures, unable to cope as Daisy had succeeded in doing.

I looked long and hard at the portrait hanging there in Michael's Chelsea house. Was Daisy urging me to explain why she had behaved as she did, urging me to understand the fierce prejudice against penniless Irish migrants in the Australia she came to in 1883? I could imagine her agony as a motherless child. I too had cried for a mother I would never know. I thought that perhaps I should try to tell Daisy's story and attempt to explain how an abusive stepmother might have warped the personality of a clever little girl, who compensated by becoming an arch-fantasist incapable of maintaining deep relationships — and who finally, like that other peripatetic woman, Hester Stanhope, sought refuge in the freedom and space of the desert.

At this time the Alisons were attempting to trace my various siblings from the four marriages of my birth father. They understood the difficult time I was going through but urged me to continue with the Daisy Bates story. And in the end I did.

In death Daisy Bates has become a controversial figure, featured in stained glass windows, in an opera and a ballet, in scores of portraits and at least three plaques — two in the Australian outback and another in her birthplace of Roscrea — and in those previous books that recount a mistaken version of her life.

The story about Daisy I like most was found among Ernestine Hill's papers. Well over eighty and with a wicked twinkle in her eye, Daisy told Roderick Cameron, a handsome young British writer who had come to interview her: 'Be good. But if you're *always good* you'll be dull!'

Not even Daisy Bates's harshest critics could claim that she was dull.

AFTERWORD BY BARBARA KER WILSON

Over several decades I have been aware that I had unfinished business where the enigmatic Daisy Bates was concerned. I first 'met' Daisy in 1964, when I came from England to South Australia and subsequently spent twelve years living in Adelaide. There I encountered many people who recalled the elderly Mrs Bates, CBE, including her loyal friends and supporters Sir Edward and Lady (Ursula) Hayward of Carrick Hill and the writer Geoffrey Dutton, who remembered seeing her when he was a schoolboy visiting the city with his mother. Attired as always in her Edwardian costume, the formidable Mrs Bates would thread her way through the traffic to the other side of North Terrace in dire peril of her life, while Geoff's mother shook her head in disapproval.

When I was appointed managing editor of Angus & Robertson's children's books in 1965, I set up offices in Adelaide and paid frequent visits to A&R's Sydney headquarters as well as their London offices. As a newcomer to Australia I became intensely interested in Aboriginal culture, especially the myths and legends of the Dreamtime.

My real involvement with Daisy Bates began in 1970, when Angus & Robertson were preparing to publish Elizabeth Salter's

272 | DESERT QUEEN

biography *Daisy Bates.* In common with a number of other writers, Salter failed to discover the facts about Daisy's childhood and adolescence in nineteenth-century Ireland, and how she became a governess then later sailed from Cork to Townsville, in North Queensland. Nor was she aware of Daisy O'Dwyer's marriage to Breaker Morant at Charters Towers. Relying on Daisy's own unreliable memoirs, Salter regurgitated the high-falutin' fantasies that Daisy made up as a lifetime escape from her traumatic childhood: like a number of other women of the Edwardian era, Daisy boldly reinvented herself. Salter was hoping that a film based on Daisy's life, starring Katherine Hepburn, would be produced by Robert Helpmann. (Like Helpmann, Elizabeth Salter was born in Adelaide.) She worked on a film script, but in the event the film was never made.

Elizabeth Salter lived in England for many years and was a personal assistant to the poet Edith Sitwell. When Salter came to South Australia in 1969 to carry out extra research for her biography of Daisy and to confer with Helpmann about the proposed film, she made an exciting discovery in the Barr-Smith Library at the University of Adelaide. One of Daisy's tin trunks, a battered relic of her desert camp at Ooldea and elsewhere, was stored there. Inside was a collection of papers that Salter, who was aware of my interest in Aboriginal folklore, thought I should examine. She told me about the collection as we lunched at the Queen Adelaide Club. (The club, with its series of portraits — from eager girlhood to sad old age — of Queen Adelaide, consort of William IV, and the Waterford jugs of homemade barley water provided at luncheon, had been a favourite haunt of Daisy Bates.) I took a genteel sip of barley water and waited to hear more about Elizabeth's discovery.

I knew that Daisy, as part of her work in what was then the recently established field of social anthropology, had over a period of some forty years gathered a valuable collection of Aboriginal myths and legends, some in languages now extinct, told to her by the tribespeople as she sat down with them at their various campsites in Western Australia and the Nullarbor Plain. Over this period, as Kabbarli, a grandmotherly figure, she offered the Aborigines food and medical help as they fled their desert lands during years of drought. I was also aware that she had asked the journalist and novelist Ernestine Hill, author of the bestselling historical novel *My Love Must Wait* (1941), to sort out the collection and retell some of the stories for young readers. Ernestine had previously helped to prepare Daisy's account of her desert years — 'My Natives and I' — for serialisation by the Adelaide *Advertiser* and syndication throughout Australia in 1936. Two years later the London publisher John Murray published Daisy's autobiographical work *The Passing of the Aborigines*, which incorporated much of the material in 'My Natives and I'. Towards the beginning of World War II, Ernestine selected fifteen legends from Daisy's collection and retold them in a manner redolent of the 1930s, when children were often 'written down to' in a somewhat cosy style. Her manuscript was sent to London, but John Murray decided not to publish the legends.

'Come with me and I'll show you what's there!' Elizabeth Salter said now. So we abandoned the Queen Adelaide Club and crossed North Terrace, which Daisy herself had braved so often, and entered the Barr-Smith Library, where Elizabeth flung up the lid of the battered black tin trunk.

Inside lay untidy scraps of paper of all shapes and sizes containing notes that Daisy had made over several decades. They were the original notes she made immediately after listening to the legends told to her by the desert Aborigines. Some of the tales lacked beginnings, middles and endings: I would discover that sometimes those missing parts appeared in other notes recorded at different times.

Daisy wrote: 'These tales and myths are told by the grandfathers and fathers to their children, and in this way only have been transmitted from father to son throughout the ages of their being; no written record and, in many tribes, no symbol of any kind helps to keep alive the memory of these traditions. All is oral, and because in many tribes the custodians of these oral traditions have faulty memories themselves, or were careless listeners in their young days, I have had to listen to hundreds of unfinished tales, so disconnected and scattered that it has been impossible to bring coherence to them . . .'

These were far more than stories told for pure enjoyment. They represent the oral culture of a people, the beliefs and traditions of the Aboriginal race. Daisy told how in the Aboriginal camps, 'sitting by their fires at the hour of storytelling', she would listen to the old men as they related the legends and lore. 'It is impossible to convey the dramatic gesture, the significant "flick" of fingers or features which accompanied the narration . . . the flash of eye as the spear is driven home, the tracks made of the hand or footprint of the bird or animal of the story . . . only those who have watched the storyteller can fully appreciate the dramatic recital.'

There were myths and legends of contrasting genres: many sought to explain the creation of outstanding features of the landscape; there were different versions of the story of how fire was discovered, so that raw food could be cooked and the tribespeople could warm themselves in the long-ago cold or *Nyitting* time. One legend told how death first came to the tribes — for in the beginning they had possessed everlasting life. Others sought to explain the characteristics of the tribal totem creatures. There were 'instructive' tales that described hunting skills and the everyday practices of Aboriginal lore. Above all there were the wonderfully imaginative stellar legends that transported the deeds of earthbound folk to the stars and constellations of the clear night sky above the desert that Daisy loved to explore through her telescope.

Carefully I removed this treasure trove, and as I gently shook out those pieces of paper, grains of desert sand scattered to the bottom of the old tin trunk. Besides the papers, there were several vocabulary notebooks compiled by Daisy as she recorded the different tribal languages, listing Aboriginal words with their English translations: these proved very helpful when I came to rewrite some of the legends, for I was able to incorporate many Aboriginal words and their English equivalents within the narrative. I spent days working in the library, transcribing Daisy's notes and vocabularies on my portable typewriter (the day of the universal computer had not yet dawned). Then I attempted to piece together those stories that were incomplete. In the end I chose thirty-four legends and commissioned Harold Thomas, an Aboriginal artist who worked at the South Australian Museum, to illustrate them. I kept my narrative style simple and direct, introducing Aboriginal words to help convey a sense of another world, the Dreamtime.

The collection, published by Angus & Robertson in Sydney and London as *Tales Told to Kabbarli — Aboriginal Legends Collected by Daisy Bates*, appeared in 1972 and went through several reprintings. An American edition was published by Crown Publishers in New York. I felt satisfied that Daisy's careful collection of this unique material could finally be shared by readers young and old alike — for folklore surely belongs to people of all ages.

Daisy entered my life again in 1985, when Hodder & Stoughton, who were producing an educational series for young readers featuring famous Australians, commissioned me to write a brief, illustrated account of Daisy Bates. The truth about Daisy's life had still not emerged. Today, now that so much more has been revealed about Daisy, I consider her personality far too complex to present to young readers.

To bring my association with Daisy Bates up to date, in 2005 Susanna de Vries asked me to edit her biography of Daisy, to be published by HarperCollins. I was fascinated by Susanna's meticulous research in Ireland, England and Australia, the contacts she had established, and her historical overview, as well as her heartfelt empathy with Daisy. As Susanna writes in her Epilogue, Daisy Bates is a difficult subject for a writer who tackles her life story. The author is left with no option but to speculate about certain passages in her long lifetime. The fact that shortly before Daisy's death she burned her intimate letters and diaries, as well as many legal documents, makes it impossible to tie up every detail of her existence. In many ways it would be much easier to write a novel based on the life of Daisy Bates, inventing motives and events in fictional form as in the 'faction'-style narrative adopted by Julia Blackburn for her novel *Daisy Bates in the Desert*, 1994. During the editing of this new biography, Susanna and I engaged in many speculative discussions concerning possible motives for Daisy's behaviour and actions at different stages of her life.

As a result of my contribution to this latest account of Daisy Bates's extraordinary life, I feel I have at last been able to complete the 'unfinished business' of my own sporadic involvement with this most unusual woman.

ENDNOTES

Prologue

1   Daisy Bates, 'Three Thousand Miles in a Side Saddle', *The Australasian*, 16 February 1924.

2   Parts of 'My Natives and I' were edited and republished in 1938 by John Murray, London, as *The Passing of the Aborigines: A Lifetime Spent Among the Natives of Australia*. In 2004, Hesperian Press published *My Natives and I*, a version of *The Passing of the Aborigines* with the passages that had been deleted during its initial editing restored, and an Introduction by Professor Bob Reece (ed. Peter J. Bridge). Later quotations in the text from *My Natives and I* refer to this later publication.

Chapter 1: Irish Orphans

1   Information provided by historical researcher Jim McJannett of Bamaga, and from a file on the shipboard journey of Daisy Bates in the Historical Section of Townsville Public Library, and *Almora*.

2   See Queensland Immigration Records p. 451, IMM /117 451, Folio M 1698 Special Collections, State Library of Queensland, showing arrival 13 January 1883 (assisted passage).

3   The names of the *Almora*'s matron, captain and surgeon are cited in two *Almora* diaries, one owned by Jim McJannett, the other in the

State Library of Queensland, Box 9220 of its Heritage Collections. Also cited in an article published by Townsville College of Further Education, August 1989, in the History Section of Townsville Public Library. Matron Chase's diary of her voyages to Australia are held in a private collection in Bexhill, Kent.

4   From *Almora* diary held by Jim McJannett. The anonymous writer of the *Almora* shipboard diary in the State Library of Queensland also called Matron Chase 'the old girl' and recorded her making one of the ailing girls cry by saying she did not have long to live, so she should behave herself better. The diarist is indignant at the inhumane way the girls in steerage were treated by the matron and the captain.

5   In the incident cited in the State Library of Queensland *Almora* diary (ref OM 90-78) confusingly the diarist refers to Daisy borrowing an evening dress as a 'nightgown' to attend the concert held on top deck, and mentions a Mrs Diggins as being involved in the incident. It cites a confrontation with Matron Chase who vented her spite by refusing to let the ship's surgeon visit Daisy when she was sick.

6   *The Hayes Indexes to the Manuscript Collection of the History of Irish Civilisation*, Boston, Mass., 1965, cites the Brownriggs of Dublin (Kathleen Dwyer's in-laws), as wealthy Dublin lawyers and landowners, subject of a lawsuit regarding one of their investment properties which took place in the 1890s.

7   Records show Ashberry (now spelt Ashbury) as a large stone house, built in a plain Georgian style. Timothy Bridge was a lawyer, a churchwarden at St Cronan's Protestant Church and a Justice of the Peace.

8   Kathleen Moloughney, *Roscrea, My Heart's Home*, Roscrea People, 1992, National Library of Ireland, call number 92m466a.

9   Many Irish census records and Church of Ireland parochial records were destroyed when the Public Record Office of Ireland went up in flames during the 'Troubles'. I consulted several Griffith's Valuations (Richard Griffith, *Primary Valuation of Ireland*). This lists

land occupiers, household tenants and householders in each county from 1858 to 1864. Eineclann, the professional researchers of Trinity College, provided firm evidence that Daisy's father, James Edward Dwyer, boot- and shoemaker, held the lease of Lot 17 (later No. 2) Main Street, a 'four-room tenement — house, office and yard' on a lease that varied between two and three pounds per annum, then a fairly large sum, from 1858 to his death in 1864.

10 Ledger in the care of the priest at St Cronan's Catholic Church, Roscrea. The original ledger, now too fragile to handle, is recorded on microfiche at the National Library of Ireland. Elizabeth Salter mistakenly believed Daisy had a birth certificate which had been burned when the Public Record Office caught fire during the 1918 Troubles (when the wills of both Daisy's grandfathers were destroyed). Ireland was then a British Colony: birth certificates were only issued after 1863 for Catholic Irish children. Daisy was born in 1859, so she did not have a certificate. Daisy also claimed that she was born at Ballychrine, in the North Riding of Tipperary, at a property not far from Roscrea which belonged to her mother's family, the Hunts, 'for many generations'. As it was not at all unusual for a young woman to return to her mother's home to give birth, Daisy's statement seems reasonable.

11 Daisy Dwyer's baptism entry from the register of Killaloe and Roscrea Baptisms, August 1832–1863. The old St Cronan's Catholic Cathedral where Daisy was baptised was replaced by a new church, the records archived, and a microfiche copy stored in the National Library of Ireland, Dublin with another at Roscrea's Heritage Centre.

12 Information from the North Tipperary Family Research History Society, Nenagh, from Griffith's Valuations, and from the reports in the *Tipperary Star*, quoted in a talk by Kathleen Molonghney at the Roscrea Heritage Centre in 1988 on Daisy Bates.

13 Daisy's mother's burial certificate specifically mentions consumption of the lungs for two years' duration as the cause of death. Church of Ireland records for Ballychrine are missing so it was not possible to search these at Roscrea, but Daisy's mother is

buried in the Protestant side of the cemetery of St Cronan's Church, Roscrea.

14 At one time James was reputed to have died at sea. By law, all deaths at sea had to be made known to the port of departure and passed to the Public Record Office. Elizabeth Salter muddied the waters when she found a death certificate for the wrong James Dwyer returning from America rather than going there, and included it as fact in her biography of Daisy Bates. My search of Mormon websites finally produced evidence that James Edward Dwyer of Tipperary, 'labourer as well as bootmaker', died in Virginia in 1865 and was buried there in a pauper's grave so never returned to Ireland. See Mormon listing of www.myancestors.com/.

15 Information from Tipperary North Family History Society. Research into those houses and shops or offices leased by members of the Dwyer family on Main Street researched by Dr Robert Somerville-Woodward for Eineclann, Dublin.

16 Griffith's Valuations show Mary Dillon Dwyer returning to take over the remainder of the lease on Lot 17 (up to 1874) on what is now No. 2 Main Street, Roscrea renting house, offices and yard, from Elizabeth Fowcett, who in turn rented the premises from the head landlord, John Sydney Smythe, who had purchased the property from the Earl of Portarlington. These records have been transferred by the author to the Fryer Library of Australian Literature, University of Queensland, and arrangements are being made to place a plaque on No. 2 Main Street, the house where Daisy lived as a child and in adolescence.

17 *Tipperary Star*, quoted by Kathleen Moloughney, 6 August 1988.

18 Information from Griffith's Valuations, provided by the Tipperary North Family History Research Centre.

19 *Ibid.*

20 In her talk at the Roscrea Heritage Centre, Kathleen Moloughney mentioned the ill-feeling between the Dwyer girls and their stepmother.

21 In his book on children who become compulsive liars and how to spot them, Dr Charles Ford postulates that neglected or traumatised children often exhibit a compulsive need to impress others, and in adult life express this by claiming associations with prestigious figures. They are unable to sustain long-term relationships, feel normal rules do not apply to them and are prone to contracting multiple marriages. Ford calls this syndrome *pseudologica fantastica*. This could explain Daisy's fantasies of an aristocratic childhood in England, her fictitious engagement to the nephew of the Governor of New South Wales, her disastrous relationships with three husbands and her son, and two bigamous marriages with no attempt at divorce. See Ford, *Lies! Lies! Lies! The Psychology of Deceit*, American Psychiatric Association, Washington, 1998, the standard textbook on *pseudologica fantastica*.

22 *My Natives and I*, ed. P. J. Bridge, Hesperian Press 2004. Descendants of Sir Francis Outram have ruled out any possibility that Daisy told the truth about her association with the Outrams. Several members of the Outram family, including Sir Allan Outram, denied that Daisy lived with them or had known the family.

23 Elizabeth Salter's *Daisy Bates: The Great White Queen of the Never Never* was published in 1971 and several scripts were produced for a movie to star Katherine Hepburn, and produced by Robert Helpmann. According to researcher Eleanor Witcombe, Helpmann travelled to Ireland to scout for locations, but the project was abandoned after Hepburn contracted Parkinsons disease and Helpmann also fell ill. Telephone interview, Eleanor Witcombe, October 2007.

24 Richard Hayes, Manuscript Sources for the Study of Irish Civilization, R.G. Hall, Boston, 1990.

25 Information from the North Tipperary Family Research History Society via Nancy Murphy and backed by consultation of Griffith's Valuations.

CHAPTER 2: IN SEARCH OF DAISY DWYER

1 The growth of motor traffic would cause the Market House to be removed.

2 Information from Brendan Carmody of Roscrea's Heritage and Tidy Towns Committees.

3 Ernestine Hill's memoir of Daisy Bates, *Kabbarli*, was published by Angus & Robertson in 1973, the year following Hill's own death.

4 This legend is related by the Rev. M. Kenny, vicar of Borrisoleigh, a neighbouring town to Roscrea, in his book published in Daisy's lifetime titled *Glenkeen of Borrisoleigh*. A copy of the Rev. Kenny's collection of the rich legends and folklore of this part of North Tipperary is held in the National Library of Ireland.

5 Daisy Bates, *My Natives and I* (ed. P. J. Bridge), Hesperion Press, Carlisle, WA, 2004, p. 2.

6 *Ibid.*, p. 2.

7 *Ibid.*, pp. 1 and 2.

CHAPTER 3: THE GETTING OF WISDOM

1 Details from Slater's Guide to Roscrea for the 1850s and 1860s.

2 Records of Daisy attending Roscrea's National School are held by the Archivist of the Order of the Sacred Heart of Jesus in Dublin.

3 See Moloughney, *Roscrea, My Heart's Desire, op. cit.* National Schools aimed to give their pupils a good standard of education. Teachers were required to have high moral values and were forbidden to attend cattle fairs or political meetings or to lodge in public houses. The pupil-teacher system from Ireland's National Schools was later adopted in New South Wales.

4 Tom Prior and George Cunningham (eds), *The Convent of the Sacred Heart in the Nineteenth Century*, Roscrea, 1992.

5 Mrs Betty Donegan's memories of her schooldays at Roscrea and other reminiscences from Tom Prior and George Cunningham, *op. cit.*

6 Interestingly, Daisy claimed to have stayed with a Mrs Goode, widow of the Dean of Ripon, as an eight-year-old child; see Ernestine Hill, *Kabbarli*, Angus & Robertson, Sydney, 1973, p. 18. Nick Bleszynski in *Shoot Straight, You Bastards*, Random House,

Sydney, 2002, suggests that Daisy spent time in an orphanage. National School registers for Roscrea held in the archives of the Order of the Sacred Heart in Dublin and their Archivist suggest that this religious Order never operated any orphanages.

7   Griffith's Valuations record that one of Daisy's aunts lived close to Main Street.

8   The 1881 London census records Ernest as living with his parents and one unmarried sister. Information about the Bagleholes also comes from Ted Robl, who researched a book about the poetry of Breaker Morant; and from the papers of the late Miss Elizabeth Rose of Kilravock, Nairnshire, Scotland.

CHAPTER 4: MEETING AND PARTING

1   This misleading passage from a newspaper article printed in 1936, now held in the Fryer Library, University of Queensland, was later deleted from Daisy's memoir, *The Passing of the Aborigines*. See *My Natives and I*, Hesperian Press, Carlisle, WA, 2004. Mount Krakatoa erupted in August 1883. The resulting tsunami caused great destruction to the surrounding area. Had Daisy sailed through the South Seas some four to five months after the eruption, as she stated, experts claim volcanic dust in the atmosphere would have abated. Other ships in the South Seas in the early months of 1884 did not describe witnessing specially 'magnificent sunsets'.

2   Cited in *Famous Australians*, London, 1952.

3   Names cited in the *Almora* diary owned by Jim McJannett. Their ages ranged from twenty to twenty-eight and they are described as having gone to families including the Turners, Allens, Bennetts and McNamaras.

4   Townsville's Immigration Barracks have been demolished and all records of the inmates lost.

5   Hill, *Kabbarli*, *op. cit.*, p. 20.

6   Bates, *My Natives and I*, *ibid.*, p. 5. Professor Bob Reece, in *Daisy Bates: Grand Dame of the Outback*, National Library of Australia,

Canberra, 2007, p. 19, suggests that Daisy stayed with the Hanns and denies her assertions that she stayed with Bishop Stanton, a view also held by Jim McJannett. Reece also claims Daisy met James Hann, son of the station owner, William Hann, aboard the *Almora*. William Hann did not have a son James, and the passenger list shows a Henry Hann of Ipswich aboard.

7   National Library of Australia, Daisy Bates papers. Letters 11/11/40; 30/12/40; 4/2/41. References kindly supplied by Ted Robl.

8   Ernestine Hill, *Kabbarli, op. cit.*, pp. 20–21.

9   Elizabeth Salter, *Daisy Bates: The Great White Queen of the Never Never*, Angus & Robertson, Sydney, 1971, pp. 12–18 describes 'an affair' at this time between Daisy and Philip Gipps, cousin of Daisy's 'friend' Hester Layley, an aristocratic Englishwoman, and nephew of the Governor of New South Wales. However, according to Jim McJannett who has sighted Hester Cayley's birth certificate, Cayley was not in Australia at the time and could scarcely have noticed very much as she was only three years old. She visited Australia as a mature woman and met Daisy at Pyap but never knew her in Tasmania or in Queensland as Daisy stated. Philip Gipps died in a riding accident shortly after Daisy arrived in Australia.

10   The Jim McJannett papers contain an account of Arnold Colquhoun's career in Charters Towers, his suicide note to John O'Kane, and material on the inquest.

11   Inquest report, Queensland State Archives, JUS/N97, on microfilm Z3554. Information courtesy Jim McJannett.

12   Deposition, *ibid.*, from Dr Graham Browne makes this case even more interesting. Clearly, Daisy was wise not to get involved with such a man.

13   Inquest report, *ibid.*

CHAPTER 5: A MARRIAGE OF SORTS

1   Information on Frederick Hamilton from 1883 and 1884 editions of Cox and Cummings magazine, in the papers of Jim McJannett.

Copies also held in John Oxley Library, State Library of Queensland.

2   Index to Assisted Immigrant Arrivals in Queensland 1880–1899, Vol. 3. See also Nick Bleszynski, *op. cit.*

3   Some authorities have disputed the identification of Edwin Murrant with Harry 'Breaker' Morant. The *Australian Dictionary of Biography*, Vol. 10, links Edwin Murrant of Bridgewater, Somerset with 'Breaker' Morant, shot for treason by the British during the Boer War. Authors Margaret Carnegie and Frank Shields (*In Search of Breaker Morant: Balladist and Bushveldt Carbineer*, H.H. Stephenson, Armadale, Vic, 1979) both believed Murrant/Morant to be the same person and noted striking similarities between their signatures. Similarly, *The Bulletin* for whom Breaker Morant wrote bush ballads, traced a likeness between the signatures of Edwin Murrant, son of the workhouse keeper, and Henry Morant who is linked with the horsebreaker on Manooroo Station. Jim McJannett discovered Muttaburra Hospital records which show a horsebreaker named Morant admitted as a patient in May 1887, giving his birthplace as Devon, and his mother's name as Catherine Morant née Hunt (Hunt being the name of Daisy's mother) and his father's name as Edwin and occupation as a clergyman (see Queensland State Archives, Hospital Admissions, A 58401: microfilm Z/281). Nick Bleszynski, whose book *Shoot Straight, You Bastards!: The Truth Behind the Killing of 'Breaker' Morant* has Morant marrying Daisy Bates, contains a chart showing Breaker Morant's journey south which passed through Longreach where there is evidence he worked on Manooroo Station in 1887 and was admitted to Muttaburra Hospital. No record of any arrival for a Harry Harbord Morant into Queensland has been found.

4   Jim McJannett believes Daisy was pregnant and has referred to a child's riding crop owned by Morant, engraved with the name William Harry Morant.

5   This was the same date given by Harry Morant when jailed in South Africa. Morant again listed his parents' names as Edwin and Catherine.

6   Bleszynski, *op cit.*, pp. 70–71.

7   *Ibid.*, pp. 67–71.

8   Carnegie & Shields, *op. cit.*

9   *Ibid.*, p. 68.

10 For details of the difficulty of divorce for women in this era see Marilyn Yalom, *The History of the Wife*, Pandora Press, London, 2001.

CHAPTER 6: DAISY, THE DROVER'S WIFE

1   The Hon. Harold Finch-Hatton, *Advance Australia!: An Account of Eight Years' Work, Wandering and Amusement, in Queensland, New South Wales and Victoria*, W.H. Allen, London, 1886.

2   Ernestine Hill, *Kabbarli, op. cit.*, pp. 23–24.

3   *Ibid.*, p. 25.

4   *Ibid.*, p. 75.

5   See NSW Registry of Births, Deaths and Marriages, Registration number 7148/1885. *The Australian Dictionary of Biography*'s entry for Daisy Bates says that she and Jack married at Nowra and records this as Daisy's sole marriage, failing to mention her earlier or later weddings. Curiously, Ernestine Hill records in *Kabbarli*, p. 26 that Daisy and Jack Bates were married at Bathurst.

6   The late Dr Isobel White and the late amateur historian Arthur Queale searched for evidence of a divorce or annulment of the Dwyer–Murrant marriage but without success; see Dr Isobel White, *The Native Tribes of Western Australia*, National Library of Australia, 1975, p. 4.

7   Information from Ted Robl, roblt@bigpond.com.

8   Death certificate for Major Robert Brownrigg DYA 552295, registered 18 April 1884.

9   Eleanor Witcome was the first person to bring to light Daisy's third marriage to Ernest Baglehole, and Nick Bleszynski in his biography of 'Breaker' Morant, *Shoot Straight, You Bastards*, the first to publish the fact. Neither of them have been more successful than I have in tracing details of Baglehole's death.

Chapter 7: The Mystery of the Third Husband

1   Copy of certificate No. 02853 from Ted Robl via Jim McJannett; searched for by Joy Murrin, Transcription Agent, New South Wales.

2   International Genealogical Index, Batch C006302, source no. 0384871 (Film Printout Call No. 0883639); information via Ted Robl.

3   Information from London census records via Jim McJannett.

4   Records of all deaths at sea were meant to be lodged by ships' captains in the Public Record Office in London but there are none for Ernest Baglehole. His father William Baglehole's will was obtained from the Public Record Office but contained no mention of the time and place of Ernest's death. William Baglehole's son-in-law (daughter Maude was deceased) was the sole heir and executor. There was no mention of Jessie Rose Baglehole, Daisy or Arnold.

5   The story about Daisy and the doctor was related by Elizabeth Salter, who was unaware of Daisy's bigamous marriage to Ernest Baglehole.

6   Ernestine Hill, *Kabbarli*, *op. cit.*, p. 28 describes Daisy as being listed as 'stewardess' on a peppercorn or token wage, and says that Daisy 'kept a diary of an exciting story she never had time to write in after life'. It seems this was another diary that she burned just before her death.

Chapter 8: A visit to Ireland and a Training Job in London

1   Information from Jim McJannett, October 2004.

2   Marian Dwyer died in 1917.

3   The changes in ownership of various houses in Main Street, Roscrea, are recorded in the alterations to Griffith's Valuations, extracted by Eineclann of Dublin at the request of the author.

4   Elizabeth Salter *op. cit.*, refers to the death of this aunt, sister of Daisy's late mother, p. 105. Julia Blackburn, *op. cit.*, mentions a deceased aunt but not the grandfather, p. 41.

4a In 1912 he was a passenger on the ill-fated *Titanic*; he was described as helping women and children into the lifeboats before the ship went down and he perished. The fact Stead was aboard the *Titanic* was a mystery. Several leading spiritualists had predicted he would die at sea. Stead, who published *Borderland*, the spiritual magazine on which Daisy worked, ignored their warnings.

5 Daisy Bates, *My Natives and I, op. cit.*, p. 7.

6 Salter, *op. cit.*, p. 47.

7 *Ibid.*, p. 56.

8 Sydney writer and journalist Louise Mack would later work for Stead, and in her book *An Australian Girl in London* relate how Stead praised Daisy Bates for her hard work and aptitude as a journalist.

9 *Ibid.*

10 Reece, *op. cit.*, pp. 26–28.

11 See Blackburn, *op. cit.*; Salter, *ibid.*, pp. 51 and 58; Jim McJannett, personal communication.

12 Blackburn, *op. cit.* From Daisy's article 'My First Job'.

13 Salter, *op. cit.*, p. 59.

14 See *My Natives and I* and Salter, *ibid.*

15 Salter, *ibid.*, p. 59.

16 *Ibid.*

17 *Ibid.* p. 61. See also Reece, *op. cit.*, p. 30.

18 From information supplied by the late Miss Elizabeth Rose of Kilravock, Nairnshire and Rose family papers. The papers also suggest a rupture between William Baglehole and Jessie Rose over her inability to produce a son, and suggest William Baglehole gave money away to an alleged 'wife' of Ernest. Very little money remained in his estate after his death. Information provided by Jim McJannett.

CHAPTER 9: TO THE NORTHWEST AND ON TO BEAGLE BAY

1 See entry on Daisy Bates in *The Australian Dictionary of Biography.*

2   The original MS of Daisy's paper, with amendments by Dr Jull, is in the Manuscripts Department of the National Library in Canberra.

3   Manuscripts Department, the National Library of Australia, contains receipts for Daisy's annual subscriptions to the early work of the Fairbridge Society and letters from Kingsley Fairbridge thanking Daisy for her contribution.

4   Matthew Condon, 'Vice-Chancellor John Hay: Class Act', *Courier-Mail*, Weekend Magazine, 14–15 January 2005.

5   Letters from Daisy Bates to Kingsley Fairbridge. After the death of Daisy's friend Kingsley Fairbridge, former Rhodes Scholar, the Fairbridge Farm Schools were too numerous to be run solely by his wife and family so managers were employed. Paedophiles and sadists entered the system and abuses took place which would have horrified Fairbridge himself and Daisy who had genuinely believed she was helping orphaned children to lead a better life.

6   Bates, *My Natives and I, op. cit.*, pp. 15–16; Bates, *The Passing of the Aborigines, op. cit.*, p. 3; and private journals of Meares and Withnell families. See also Susanna de Vries, *Great Pioneer Women of the Outback*, HarperCollins Publishers, Sydney, 2005, Ch. 2.

6a   In an article published in Perth in 1901 and titled 'From Port Hedland to the Carnarvon River by Buggy'.

7   See Daisy Bates, 'From Port Headland to the Carnarvon River', *Journal of the Department of Agriculture, Western Australia*, Vol. 4, 1901; and *My Natives and I*, for passages edited out of Daisy's description of the journey by John Murray, the publishers of *The Passing of the Aborigines*.

8   Daisy Bates, *The Passing of the Aborigines, op. cit.*, p. 34.

9   *Ibid.*, p. 34.

10   *Ibid.*

11   Bishop Matthew Gibney to Daisy Bates, 1900. Daisy Bates papers, National Library of Australia. The Library holds Daisy's watch as well.

CHAPTER 10: AT GOVERNMENT HOUSE AND OFF THE BEATEN
TRACK

1   Bates, *My Natives and I, op. cit.*, p. 46.

2   This account is taken from pp. 105–6 of Salter's *Daisy Bates, op. cit.*
     Another account, written by Daisy in the *Adelaide Observer*,
     describes the cattle as being lost on a beach after stampeding at the
     sight of the sea.

3   See Isobel White in her Introduction to Daisy Bates, *The Native Tribes
     of Western Australia, op. cit.* Daisy was living in an era when women were
     rarely accepted as scientific researchers. Gertrude Bell, that intrepid
     traveller in the Middle East, was initially rejected for membership of
     the Royal Geographical Society. Margaret Mead, famed in the annals
     of social anthropology, was disparaged by male academics. However,
     like Gertrude Bell, Daisy would gain a coveted Fellowship of the
     Royal Anthropological Society of Australia and become a
     correspondent of the Royal Anthropological Institute of Great Britain
     and Ireland, achieving nearly as many honours as Bell and Mead did.

4   R.D. Joynt, Ten Years' Work at the Roper River Mission Station,
     Northern Territory, Australia, Melbourne, C.M.S., 1918, viewed at
     http://www.anglican.org.au/archive/document/143.pdf 9 August
     2007. See also Carl Lumholtz, Among Cannibals: An Account of
     Four Years Travel in Australia and Camp Life with the Aborigines of
     Queensland, trs Rasmus B. Anderson, Scribner's Sons, New York,
     1918, in which he asserts cannibalism took place in Australia and
     various Pacific islands.

5   See Salter, *op. cit.*, p. 62.

6   A listing of Daisy Bates's published materials can be found on the
     Australian Institute of Aboriginal and Torres Strait Islander Studies
     website: www.aiatsis.gov.au

CHAPTER 11: CONTRADICTIONS, COMPLEXITIES AND RESEARCH

1   Ernestine Hill, *Kabbarli, op. cit.*, p. 70. See also Bates, *My Natives and
     I, op. cit.*, pp. 64, 66–7 and iii.

2   Bates, radio interview with Russell Henderson, ABC, Sydney, 18 February 1941, National Library of Australia, oral TRC 160.

3   The Karrakatta Club has had several different locations.

4   *Revue d'Ethnolographie*, Vol. 41, 1924.

5   *The Euahlayi Tribe*, Archibald Constable and Company, London, 1905. Langloh Parker's story is related in de Vries, *op. cit.*

6   Introduction to Bates, *The Native Tribes of Western Australia*, ed. I. White, National Library of Australia, Canberra, 1985.

CHAPTER 12: TO THE ISLES OF THE DEAD

1   E.L. Grant Watson (1885–1970) would become an anthropologist, biologist and a novelist. His papers are held in the National Library of Australia and include his manuscript and correspondence with Havelock Ellis and Carl Jung.

2   Bates, *The Passing of the Aborigines, op. cit.*, p. 98.

3   *Ibid.*, p. 99.

4   *Ibid.*, pp. 99–100.

5   *Ibid.*, p. 100.

6   *Ibid.*

7   Rodney Needham, *Remarks and Inventions; Skeptical Essays about Kinship*, Tavistock, London, c1974, examines the relationship between Daisy and Radcliffe-Brown and revived the charges that Radcliffe-Brown plagiarised Daisy's work.

CHAPTER 14: CAMPING AT JERGALA CREEK

1   Bates, *My Natives and I, op. cit.*, p. 124, article titled 'The Freedom of the Totem'.

2   Bates, *The Passing of the Aborigines, op. cit.*, pp. 121–22. Daisy also refers to group sex taking place at corroborees. In a remark made by her in a radio interview with Russell Henderson on 18 February 1941, about initiation ceremonies she said, 'Aboriginal customs are sexual to a high degree . . . especially at girls' initiation ceremonies.

The elderly men take the women —'. Daisy is about to elaborate on this but Henderson hastily changes the subject.

3   *Ibid.*, p. 123.

Chapter 15: Joining the High and Mighty

1   Bates, *My Natives and I, op. cit.*, p. 131.

2   *Ibid.*, p. 34.

3   See Needham, *op. cit.*, who examines the relationship between Daisy and Radcliffe-Brown and believes the young professor did plagiarise Daisy's work. Isobel White is less certain of this than Needham. See her Introduction to *The Native Tribes of Western Australia, op. cit.*

4   Ernestine Hill papers, Fryer Library, University of Queensland.

5   *Ibid.*

6   For detailed descriptions of Ooldea see Anthony Bolam, *The Trans-Australian Wonderland*, Modern Printing Company, Melbourne, 1930, pp. 71–72.

7   *Ibid.*, pp. 12–15.

8   Bates, *My Natives and I, op. cit.*, p. 63.

9   *Ibid.*, p. 162.

10   *Ibid., op. cit.*, pp. 67, 158.

11   Bolam, *op. cit.*, p. 60.

12   *Ibid.*, p. 161.

13   *Ibid.*, p. 159.

14   *Ibid.*, p. 59.

15   Julie Marcus, 'Daisy Bates, Legend and Reality', from *First in Their Field, Women and Australian Anthropology*, Melbourne University Press, 1993, p. 57.

16   An article from *Women's World*, 1920, pp. 99–100, by Francis Taylor, cited by Ernestine Hill. See Ernestine Hill papers, *op. cit.*

CHAPTER 16: 'GREAT WHITE QUEEN OF THE NEVER-NEVER'

1   Bates, *My Natives and I, op. cit.*, p. 190.

2   Roderick Cameron's typed manuscript is among the Ernestine Hill papers, *op. cit.*

3   See Peter Beaucleerk-Dewar and Roger Powell, *Right Royal Bastards: The Fruits of Passion*, Burke's Peerage, London, 2006; and Susanna de Vries, *Royal Lovers and Mistresses* forthcoming.

CHAPTER 17: MRS DAISY BATES, CBE, AT CANBERRA AND OOLDEA

1   Letter in West Australian Archives.

2   Bates, *My Natives and I*, p. 206.

3   *Ibid.*

CHAPTER 18: BIRDS OF A FEATHER

1   A full set of the articles may be found in the papers of Ernestine Hill at the Fryer Library, Brisbane. In 2004 they were reprinted in book form by Hesperion Press, with an introduction by Professor Bob Reece of Murdoch University, Western Australia. This publication includes material relating to Daisy's early life which was cut by her publisher John Murray.

CHAPTER 19: DAISY BATES, A LEGENDARY FIGURE

1   Daisy Bates to Sir John Murray, 16 January 1939. From Sir John Murray's files, courtesy Virginia Murray. The Murray Archive is held by the National Library of Scotland. Daisy's letters to Sir John Murray are still at Murray's premises, 44 Albemarle Street, Mayfair.

2   The title *The Passing of the Aborigines* was based on the words of Lorimer Fison and William Howitt, whose work *Kamilaroi and Kurnai*, published in 1880, stated: 'Australian tribes are melting away before the touch of civilisation even more rapidly than American

aborigines . . . *rapidly passing away* through the destructive influence of superior races.' Many Australians still believed this statement, but it was to prove highly offensive to Aborigines and to the activists working on their behalf.

3   Daisy Bates to William Hurst, January 1941, Hurst papers, National Library of Australia.

4   An ABC radio interview with Policewoman Alvis Brooks by Marian Hinchcliffe, c. 1983 mentions PC Grovermann helping her 'remove' Daisy Bates to Adelaide and a subsequent meeting with Daisy outside the gates of Government House, Adelaide. ABC Library, Sydney/National Library of Canberra, Oral History Dept.

5   Daisy Bates to Ernestine Hill, 1945, Ernestine Hill papers, Fryer Library, University of Queensland.

CHAPTER 20: LONELY, THOUGH NOT ALONE

1   Daisy Bates to Ernestine Hill, 1948, Ernestine Hill papers, *op. cit.*

2   Beatrice Raine, as well as several nurses in the nursing home where Daisy eventually died, remarked how she often cried for someone she called 'William'. Possible candidates are William Hurst, the editor of *The Australasian*, with whom she kept up a long and chatty correspondence but only met on one occasion; her first mentor in journalism, William Stead; the son she may have given away for adoption; or maybe it was merely a muddled brain forgetting Arnold's proper name.

3   Letter from Beatrice Raine to Ernestine Hill, Ernestine Hill papers, *op. cit.*

PICTURE CREDITS

Pages 27, 28 (left and right) and 42: photographs by Susanna de Vries. Pages 36 and 39: photographs by Brian Redmond. Pages 62, 66, 73 and 112: photographs courtesy of Jim McJannett. Pages 147, 174, 186–7, 188, 221, 241 and 245: photographs from Daisy Bates, *The Passing of the Aborigines*, John Murray, London. Page 203: photograph by station master A.G. Bolam. Page 214: the front cover of *The Sphere*, London, November 1934. Page 263: photograph from the collection of the National Library of Australia, Canberra.

FACING HARDSHIP, DANGER AND DEPRIVATION

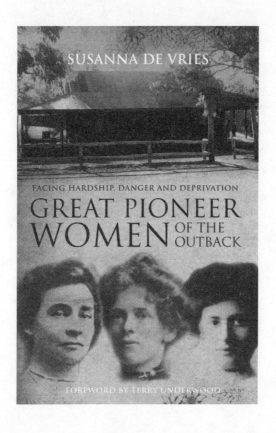

Ten female pioneers and their brave stuggles

FROM FEDERATION TO FREEDOM

Twenty courageous women who broke down the barriers of
prejudice to enter the professions and the arts

FROM PIONEERING DAYS TO THE PRESENT

More Australian women are celebrated for their hard work,
intelligence, talent, dedication and compassion

ASTONISHING TALES OF BRAVERY, FROM GALLIPOLI TO KOKODA

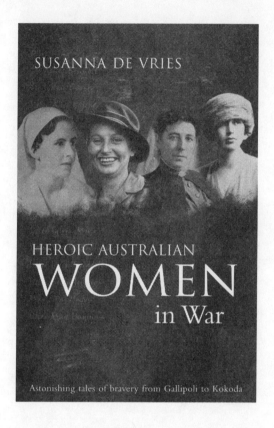

The love, dedication and selflessness of eleven Australian women